French politics today

MANCHESTER
UNIVERSITY PRESS

Politics Today

Series editor: Bill Jones

French politics today

today

New edition

David S. Bell

Manchester University Press
Manchester and New York

distributed exclusively in the USA by Palgrave

This edition published 2002 by
Manchester University Press
Oxford Road, Manchester M13 9NR, UK
and Room 400, 175 Fifth Avenue, New York, NY 10010, USA
www.manchesteruniversitypress.co.uk

Distributed exclusively in the USA by
Palgrave, 175 Fifth Avenue, New York,
NY 10010, USA

Distributed exclusively in Canada by
UBC Press, University of British Columbia, 2029 West Mall,
Vancouver, BC, Canada V6T 1Z2

British Library Cataloguing-in-Publication Data
A catalogue record for this book is available from the British Library

Library of Congress Cataloging-in-Publication Data applied for

ISBN 0 7190 5875 9 *hardback*
    0 7190 5876 7 *paperback*

This edition first published 2002

10 09 08 07 06 05 04 03 02   10 9 8 7 6 5 4 3 2 1

Typeset in Photina
by Servis Filmsetting Ltd, Manchester
Printed in Great Britain
by Biddles Ltd, Guildford and King's Lynn

In memory of
Peter Morris

Contents

Preface

The Fifth Republic is not uncontested but is now the second of French Republics in longevity – only the Third Republic survived for longer. This book looks at the structure of power in contemporary France, focusing particularly on the strong presidency. The presidency has to gain and maintain political support in order to exercise its authority. Presidential power has no constitutional base and very little traditional backing and is thus an exercise in political self-levitation. Where that presidential politics fails, authority passes to the Prime Minister, who then exercises executive power. Furthermore, if the President does not have a supporting majority in the National Assembly, there ensues a period of 'cohabitation' with a Prime Minister from one political camp and a President from another. Hence Fifth Republic politics, although 'normally' presidential, can become prime ministerial overnight. The main part of the book is therefore an examination of the forces of opposition and government in their wider context. This means, principally, political parties, which are the main vector for the mobilisation of political support, but also local government, pressure groups and social developments. The focus is the struggle of the contending forces around the presidency to maintain their authority.

I would like to thank my colleagues and friends who helped me by commenting on this book or on drafts of it. I owe particular thanks to John Gaffney, Erwin Hargrove and to Bruce Graham.

D. S. Bell
University of Leeds

Abbreviations

AREV	Alternative rouge et vert
CAP	Common Agricultural Policy
CD	Centre démocrate (centrists 1966–74)
CDP	Centre démocrate et progrès (centrists 1969–76)
CDS	Centre des démocrates sociaux (centrists 1974–95)
CERES	Centre d'études, de recherches et d'éducation socialistes
CFDT	Confédération française démocratique du travail (union confederation)
CFTC	Confédération française des travailleurs chrétiens
CGC	Confédération générale des cadres
CGT	Confédération générale du travail (Communist-run unions)
CNIP	Centre national des indépendants et paysans
CNPF	Conseil national du patronat français
CNSTP	Confédération nationale syndicale des travailleurs-paysans
CPNT	Chasse, pêche, nature et traditions
DL	Démocratie libérale
DOM–TOM	Départements et territoires d'outre-mer
ECSC	European Coal and Steel Community
EEC	European Economic Community
EMS	European Monetary System
ENA	Ecole nationale d'administration
EU	European Union
FD	Force démocrate
FEN	Fédération de l'education nationale
FFA	Fédération française de l'agriculture
FLN	Front de libération nationale (Algerian nationalists)
FN	Front national (Le Pen's party 1972–)
FNRI	Fédération nationale des républicains indépendants
FNSEA	Fédération nationale des syndicats d'exploitants agricoles
FNSP	Fondation nationale des sciences politiques

FO	Force ouvrière (unions)
GATT	General Agreement on Tariffs and Trade
GDP	Gross Domestic Product
GE	Génération écologie
GNP	Gross National Product
LCR	Ligue communiste révolutionnaire
LDI	La droite indépendante
LO	Lutte ouvrière
MDC	Mouvement des citoyens
MEDEF	Mouvement des entreprises de France
MEP	Member of the European Parliament
MODEF	Mouvement de défence des exploitants familaux
MPF	Mouvement pour la France (de Villiers)
MRG	Mouvement des radicaux de gauche
MRP	Mouvement républicain populaire (Christian democrats 1944–66)
NATO	North Atlantic Treaty Organisation
PCF	Parti communiste français
PLO	Palestinian Liberation Organisation
PR	Parti républicain
PRG	Parti radical de gauche
PRS	Parti radical-socialiste
PS	Parti socialiste
PSU	Parti socialiste unifié
RPF	Rassemblement du peuple français (gaullist party 1947–55 and the 1999 breakaway from the RPR)
RPR	Rassemblement pour la République ('neo-gaullist' party 1976–)
SFIO	Section française de l'internationale ouvrière
SGG	Secrétariat général du gouvernement
SNCF	Société nationale des chemins de fer français
TGV	Train à grande vitesse
TUC	Trades Union Congress (UK)
UDCA	Union de défence des commerçants et artisans (Poujade's party)
UDF	Union pour la démocratie française (centre parties' alliance 1978–)
UDR	Union pour la défense de la République (gaullist party in June 1968)
UDR	Union des démocrats pour la République (gaullist party 1971–76)
UDVe	Union des démocrates pour la Ve République (gaullist party after January 1968)
UN	United Nations

| UNR | Union pour la nouvelle République (gaullist party created in October 1958) |
| WEU | Western European Union |

Part I

Political forces

1

French political culture

The French political system is one of the great, rich and intricate political cultures of the western world. France, along with the other societies of Western Europe and North America, has for many years been working out the principles of liberal democracy and putting them into practice. This position in the heart of western political life means that many of the issues, conflicts and institutions in French politics are similar to those in the English-speaking world. There are conflicts over socialism, free market policies, Europe, international involvement as well as the issues of human rights and the rule of law. Hence France has been one of the societies usually studied by students of politics in Britain and America and it stands as an obvious comparator.

However, many key political features familiar to these students are lacking in the French case and there are novel formations as well as different ways of looking at things. This has come to be known as 'French exceptionalism'. The end of that 'exceptionalism' has been confidently pronounced on many occasions in the past, but France remains both similar and different. There have been cleavages in French politics that express familiar issues with an unfamiliar intensity, but there are also social forces, movements and problems which are without parallel. For the student of politics there are striking political developments and unusual continuities to consider. A brief review of the factors in the history of French politics will help explain why France is different and also why the Fifth Republic departs from French norms.

The Revolution and the Third Republic (1870–1940)

The Great Revolution of 1789 is the starting point for contemporary French political society. Many of the cleavages of French politics can be traced back to the lack of an enduring settlement after the Revolution. The Revolution divided French society and introduced many ideas with a long half-life and some of these ideas remained contentious until well into the Fifth Republic. Where

3

people stood, relative to the Revolution, was a political factor of deep significance and was for over a century the fault line between left and right.

This meant that all French political regimes were internally contested from
the time of the Revolution onwards. Many forms of regime were tried
(Bonapartist dictatorship, royalist and Republican) without finding a set of
institutions that were accepted by society as a whole. When one regime fell its
partisans remained in the successor but looked for an opportunity to exploit the
new regime's weaknesses. Opponents were sometimes merely a destabilising
factor, sometimes a real threat to the future of the regime. One result was the
repeating cycle of regimes throughout the nineteenth century and up to the
Vichy regime of 1940–44 as Republics were replaced by monarchies or by dictatorships.

Emerging, as it did, from the collapse of monarchism, the Third Republic,
which lasted from 1870 to 1940, may have been the Republic which divided
France least, but it was nevertheless frequently challenged. Members of the
Third Republic's political class were deeply suspicious of those social groups
that they believed would try to overthrow the Republic. This can be distinguished from the British case where there was little opposition to the parliamentary system itself and the issue was rather one of who could participate in
it (the extension of the franchise).

In these French disputes there were the partisans of the Revolution who
favoured a Republican regime and who promoted the ideals of liberty, equality,
justice and universal suffrage. This tradition (mainly Radical in the Third
Republic) looked to a form of parliamentary sovereignty which was similar to
the doctrine developed in the United Kingdom. In this Republican view, the
people were sovereign, of course, but the people could not all meet to decide the
great questions of the day. Hence the people's representatives in the National
Assembly exercised this sovereignty on behalf of the nation in between elections. Parliament was conceived as the people meeting in conclave and as such
could decide on the direction of affairs in any area where its scrutiny fell. That,
at any rate, was the justification for parliamentary (sometimes capricious)
interference in matters.

But there was also a reaction against the Revolution, and parts of the French
political nation advocated an emphasis rather on authority and hierarchy. To
them the symbols of the Republic were anathema. Republican symbolism,
which appears innocuous to the outsider, was inflammatory to the Republic's
opponents. In the Vendée region where the anti-Revolutionary insurrection
cost about a million lives, some town halls refused to display the bust of the
Republic (Marianne). These opponents of the Republic included the extreme
right royalists and the Bonapartists.

Royalist reaction to the Revolution took extreme forms and it was with late
nineteenth-century royalism that the ideas of the modern extreme right took
shape. Amongst those opposed to the Republic some began to challenge the
notion of political equality and developed pseudo-scientific notions of racial

hierarchy: in other words human beings were not equal. By the same reasoning some people had a right to rule and other orders had to be kept from the levers of power. When royalism faded as a political force it remained a factor of instability because these ideas endured and were taken up by new forms of extreme protest.

An important formative issue for the right was the head-on challenge that the Revolution presented to the Catholic Church. For many Republicans the Church and the monarchy worked for the same cause and so anti-clericalism became a feature of Republican politics. By the same token strongly Catholic areas tended to support the right and were the heirs to the counter-revolution. Hence people's religious outlook was politically highly relevant and religion became a better indicator of political position than did class: the more people identified themselves as Catholic, the more likely they were to vote for the right. This association of politics and religion, although it no longer has the emotional force it once had, remains broadly true today. However, after 1892, when Pope Leo XIII's Encyclical declared that Catholics 'should accept the civil power in the form in which it exists', the link with the extreme right was broken. Extreme right-wing movements still drew their support from Catholic milieu but the bulk of the Church supported the Republic.

However, it took time for the quarrel to subside and even so disaffection remained. Bitterness was increased in the wake of the Dreyfus Affair when the Republic broke off diplomatic relations with the Vatican, and in 1905 the Separation Act severed all the state's connections with the Church and abrogated the Napoleonic Concordat of 1802. Henceforth relations between Church organisations and the Republic were to be conducted as with any other association and the state (like unions, for example). But the state did not interfere in Church affairs or religious activities and had no hand in the appointment of bishops (Rome's affair from that time onwards). With the disestablishment of the Church came the establishment of the neutrality of the secular state; although the Vatican at first refused to accept the new laws, they were in practice applied.

In the Third Republic the main anti-clerical battleground was education and the Church's role in it. Republican politicians determined to create a state education service which would provide free compulsory education for French citizens and which would be secular. The secular (*laïque*) concept has no equivalent in the English-speaking world. It did not mean a militant atheism (although in the heat of the battles in the 1900s it often sounded like that), but the impartiality of the state on religious matters. Religious instruction was not provided in school and religion was kept for the home and family. It meant, however, the Republic competing with the high standard of teaching provided by the Church and also removing religious moral instruction from the schools. It was a long battle eventually decided in the state's favour. But in the process the Republic had confronted powerful social strata and challenged their basic assumptions.

There was also another aspect in which the Revolution caused century-long problems: the agricultural question. At the Revolution Church land and some noble estates were divided up (and many feudal dues were eliminated). France emerged from the Great Revolution with a huge peasantry of perhaps three million small and medium landholders (nobody knows how many). Many plots were too small to provide adequate subsistence and many large estates were divided up for sharecropping. This subdivision of land at a stroke made the agriculture of France inefficient and only fitfully integrated into a market economy. Markets remained mostly local and small-scale until the development of the rail network during the Second Empire (1852–70).

French farms in the nineteenth century were not the equivalent of the yeoman farmers or small farmers of northern Europe. Parcellisation created peasants who were in the main subsistence farmers producing for their own needs and then selling the surplus (if there was one). French agricultural backwardness should not be exaggerated, and there was steady improvement in the nineteenth century, but there was no 'agricultural revolution' of the sort England experienced. Moreover, this peasantry was not only inefficient, it was a block to the development of a modern agriculture in what is a naturally fertile country. From the peasantry there also came from time to time mass support for extreme anti-Republican movements and also for the more extreme leftists.

The other side of the agricultural coin is that France was, until the Second World War, under-industrialised. During the nineteenth century France began to develop as an industrial power but this, like agricultural improvement, was a slow process. French industry was, in comparison with its European neighbours, uncompetitive (and protected behind tariff barriers) and lagged behind the United Kingdom and Germany (and Belgium). French industry was located in the Nord-Pas-de-Calais, Lyons and St Etienne, the Paris region and Alsace-Lorraine. There were textiles and iron and steel factories of substance and there was the development of transport (particularly railways) but there was no industrial revolution in France at this time. The population growth of France stagnated in the nineteenth century (when other countries were 'exporting' immigrants) and this inhibited the dynamism of an expanding internal market. In business culture there was also a preference for the small and medium enterprise, which tended to be unadventurous.

From the slow progress of industrialisation stemmed the precarious position of the working class in French society. Workers were organised by the burgeoning socialist movement but they were not integrated into the regimes before the Third Republic. In 1871 the brutal repression of the Paris Commune (by the army under the command of the royalist majority) left a legacy of bitterness which was slow to dissipate. The revolutionary rhetoric of the left and the rise of the Communist Party (Parti communiste français, PCF) did not help. The distrust of the revolutionary impulse of the French workers by the political elite (leading to the abolishing of the Paris mayor) meant that they were kept at arms length. This distrust was reciprocated, notably in the union movement but also in the parties. These representatives of French workers doubted whether they could participate in 'bourgeois' institutions. French socialists participated in the defence of France in the First World War but the undertow of suspicion remained and was picked up by the Communist Party in 1920. Unions, for their part, developed a quasi-revolutionary stance backed up by the doctrine of 'syndicalism' and they kept the parties out of their world. Hence the close socialist–union symbiosis did not develop as it did in other European countries.

Colonies were not divisive to the same extent in the Third Republic. Some Republicans tended to be anti-colonial and to regard the expansion of the Empire as an unnecessary squandering of energies. Clemenceau, for example, expressed this view frequently. Monarchies had used colonial expansion to divert attention from problems at home and had conquered and subdued Algeria for France only after much expense. French colonies also enabled the Catholic Church to extend its missionary activity and had some Catholic support. Yet, when it came to it, in the late nineteenth century, Republican governments were not averse to expanding the French Empire, and the idea of the world mission of a France with the world's second empire had some success. Great power rivalry led Republican France to extend its dominions much like other European powers of the time.

In addition, France faced the German problem. Bismarck demonstrated a unified Germany's arrival on the stage as the principal European power by quickly over-running France in the Franco-Prussian War of 1870. This war, which the Second Empire of Louis Napoleon blundered into, deprived France of its two most advanced provinces, Alsace and Lorraine. What to do about the lost provinces remained a continual problem in the late nineteenth century and as a result the Third Republic was prone to patriotic spasms leading to instability and demands for 'revenge'. These demands could not be satisfied and the problem remained. It did not disappear after the First World War and after the Second it reappeared in a new form as the problem of German rearmament and as the European question. Three major wars with Germany in the space of one lifetime were devastating for French society. The effects of the First World War, with the massive loss of lives and the destruction of France's northern areas, were also slow to dissipate.

One further factor marks French 'exceptionalism' and that is the role of the state. The Great Revolution brought the state into central focus and gave it a dominant role in French political life. This Republican state was built on the pre-Revolutionary foundations of a monarchy that had forged France out of separate lands and through numerous wars. For most political groups the state provides the continuity of French public life and is the active creator of the French nation. But the deep-rooted state tradition meant that the outlook of French liberalism has been different from that in the UK and the USA. The idea of the separation of powers and the autonomy of the individual has not been strong in a society that has been more concerned with the dynamic role of the state than with freedom from interference. Judges have come under the authority of the Ministry of Justice and political control has been exercised over careers in the judiciary. People look to the state for support and leadership in a way they do not in the UK or the USA. This has applied to both right and left, as the liberalism of J. S. Mill or Adam Smith has been a distinctly minority current in French political life (though a distinguished one).

It was the state, as de Gaulle believed, which brought together the French people and created unity from diversity. Moreover, in the process of industrial and agricultural development the state played a more active role than it did in the UK or USA. This so-called 'developmental state' is a continental phenomenon (and France is not the only example of it). In the French case state intervention built on a long tradition of state power and state industrial action going back to Louis XIV's Chief Minister Jean-Baptiste Colbert in the late seventeenth century. In the eighteenth century the royal state had built industries and had run them, and the Second Empire of Napoleon III also directly ran and promoted industry. The idea of *dirigisme* or state intervention in industry is an old one.

French governments, whatever the regime, have tried to channel the forces of the market, shifting resources into more productive sectors and promoting the conditions that would enable industry to grow and modernise. After the Second World War, assisted by the prevailing Keynesian consensus, the French state was a force behind the reconstruction and the modernisation of France and the determination to open the country out as an exporting economy. French governments protected fledgling industries and restructured French industry using a variety of instruments ranging from tax incentives to direct subsidies and large-scale projects like the high-speed train (Train à grand vitesse, TGV), nuclear power and the Ariane rocket. Some of these projects have been immensely prestigious and the state has not fallen into discredit in the way it did in (for example) Mrs Thatcher's Britain. '*Dirigisme*' had support from most parts of the French political spectrum and the creation of a 'minimal state' (reduced to essential functions of law and order and foreign relations) was not a popular cause in French politics.

The Fourth Republic (1946–58)

The Fourth Republic is remembered as a regime with little to commend it. The main reproach is of the 'revolving door' of governments: between de Gaulle's government of the Liberation in 1944–45 and his return in 1958, there were 25 governments. But there was nothing inherently wrong with the Fourth Republic. Its instability resulted from the lack of stable majorities and the nature of the issues that fragmented the political elite. Fourth Republic majorities were put together by intricate negotiation. The opponents of the regime on the right and the left together amounted to a substantial force and governments had to find their support from within the remaining groups. These were principally the Socialist Party (or Section française de l'internationale ouvrière, SFIO) and the Christian democrats (or Mouvement républican populaire, MRP) but there were also fragmented groups of conservatives and centrists (like the Radicals and the Centre national des indépendants et paysans, CNIP). However, they agreed on very little other than that the Republic should be kept in being against its enemies. This led to a paralysis known as 'immobilism' in which majorities to prevent action could be mobilised but majorities for determined courses of action were rare: this dilemma was solved by not doing anything.

On the left it was the large Communist Party which was the main problem. About a quarter of the vote went to the Communists during the Fourth Republic's time. After the onset of the Cold War the Communists became determined opponents of the regime. They failed to bring it down in 1947 when the Komintern ordered the Communist Party into offensive action against the 'bourgeois' institutions, but the Republic was badly shaken. The Communist Party looked to the Kremlin in Moscow, and not to Paris, for its 'line', and the USSR's policy was one of hostility to the west. Hence the Communists were unavailable for political support and for coalition building. In 1945 the party had polled 28 per cent of the vote and had 183 seats and in 1951 it polled 26 per cent and had 101 seats. This isolated Communist Party removed a substantial ballast from the Republic.

On the right there was General de Gaulle. This most substantial figure in France was opposed to the Fourth Republic and repudiated it. In 1947 there was a gaullist tidal wave of support in local elections and in the general elections of 1951 over a fifth of the vote went to the gaullist party (Rassemblement du peuple français, RPF). De Gaulle's rhetorical stance threatened the Republic although it was not insurrectionary. De Gaulle's supporters in the Assembly and outside made no secret of their desire to overthrow the regime (by legal means) to build another more in keeping with France's needs – as they saw it. De Gaulle was no mere bystander, no Cassandra. His supporters were waiting for the final crisis which would bring the General back to power and many were actively engaged in bringing the crisis about. The existence of the General on the sidelines (whose supporters won 40 per cent of the vote in 1947) criticising the Republic for its decolonisation policy, its foreign policy and its 'spinelessness' was debilitating and undermined the legitimacy of the Republic's governments.

That left just over half of the Fourth Republic's Assembly from which to find government majorities. Moreover, the gaullists and Communists had sympathy beyond their formal party ranks and cut into the electorates of the mainstream parties. Unsurprisingly the Fourth Republic governmental majorities were unstable and the parties of the centre and centre right struggled to find common ground. Few were successful and only the (conservative) government of Antoine Pinay and the (Radical) government of Pierre Mendès France are much remembered, although the continuity of ministers was greater than the turn-over of governments might suggest and substantial policy measures were implemented (in European integration, for example).

During the Fourth Republic there were also issues of extreme complexity

Gaullist parties

There have been many incarnations of the gaullist party. René Capitant founded the Union gaulliste pour la IVe République in 1946. It was the only party to use the General's name but was dissolved when de Gaulle started the Rassemblement du peuple français (RPF) in April 1947. This was in turn wound down slowly over the years after it failed to win a majority in the general elections of 1951 but its networks formed the basis for the Fifth Republic party. De Gaulle supporters in the Assembly were briefly grouped together as the Centre national des Républicains sociaux in March 1954 but it was mainly a small parliamentary group and had little impact.

In October 1958 the gaullist Union pour la nouvelle République (UNR) was formed with Roger Frey as its secretary general. It was in coalition with the tiny left-wing gaullist movement of the Union démocratique du travail. In 1967 the gaullists were reformed as the Union des démocrates pour la Ve République (UDVe) and then in June 1968 renamed as the Union pour la défense de la République (UDR).

The contemporary neo-gaullist party dates from the reorganisation of gaullism by Jacques Chirac and the creation in December 1976 of the Rassemblement pour la République (RPR). This reamins the biggest neo-gaullist party; the former Interior Minister Charles Pasqua founded the new Rassemblement pour la France in 1999 after a successful European election but it had split by June 2000.

which cut across party lines and which the Republic had to wrestle with even as it rebuilt after the devastation of the Occupation and the Second World War. These issues included the problem of what to do about the Empire. In the French view the colonies would eventually (after a long time) form part of the Republic but had, unlike the British Empire, no tradition of self-government. Decolonisation proved traumatic and was a major factor in discrediting the Fourth Republic, which appeared to drift rather than to take the initiative. Interest groups, in particular settlers, had the feeling that the Republic could be pushed into their way of thinking. In 1954 the French Army was surrounded and defeated at Dien Bien Phu in Indochina by the Vietminh. This, one of the great military disasters, was the first time a European army had been defeated by insurgents and was taken as a humiliation.

Defeat in Indochina brought the decisive Mendès France government to power and reform in the colonies then began in earnest. However, although the Fourth Republic set the framework for independence in the rest of the Empire in 1956 (the Defferre outline laws), there were still those who determined not to cede an inch of territory in the future. Colonial lobbies linked with politicians and army officers in efforts to sway the Fourth Republic's policy.

In addition there was the reappearance of the German problem. There was, at the end of the Second World War, a debate about what the future of Germany should be, but since this was being decided in Washington, there was not a great deal that the Fourth Republic could do directly. In 1950 centrist politicians involved with the European Coal and Steel Community worked out a new co-operative relationship between France and Germany. The Communists and the gaullists (and others) opposed this institutional arrangement and, although it was implemented, European policy became a stick with which to beat the Republic.

But the Fourth Republic was the beginning of the *'trente glorieuses'* years of economic expansion. France made a determined effort at economic modernisation and investment. French agriculture was transformed, but industry also began to respond to the wider European market, and to the change in policy, which promoted rebuilding. There was encouragement to buy agricultural machinery, to create co-operatives and to amalgamate small plots. As a result the old intimate and village-based peasant society rapidly dissolved but the productivity of the land increased and the output rose – much going to the new and larger European market. Only small pockets of the old peasantry remained in the Fifth Republic and the commercial agriculture style of northern Europe predominated. Over the years industry changed from being inward-looking and protectionist to a new exporting sector with a strong performance in the developing fields of avionics, electronics and so on.

The Algerian crisis

The Fourth Republic received a series of hammer blows over its short life and the last of these, the Algerian crisis, was fatal. Algeria had been acquired in 1830 and was administered as three departments of metropolitan France from 1848. Although considered to be a part of France, Algeria's situation was anomalous: both the settlers and the Muslims had 'equal' representation in the National Assembly. In effect the settler lobby was predominant in Paris and in Algeria some one million European settlers (so-called *pied noirs*) dominated ten million Muslims. Thus the settlers were able to prevent any progressive solution of the inequalities in Algerian society and to impose their view on Paris. This was not unprecedented in French colonies where governors would often ignore orders from Paris. Fourth Republic governments could not, after about 1956, make their will prevail against the local authorities.

Serious internal disturbances had started in Algeria in 1954. The Fourth Republic's response was to twin track: to press forward reforms to benefit the Muslim majority (the 'progressive' ideal of the time) but to crack down on nationalist insurgents (the Front de libération nationale, FLN). On the one hand, the reforms intended to reconcile the indigenous population to the Republic were generally too little too late and were often thwarted by the settlers and the colonial administration. On the other hand the imposition of law and order was brutal and undermined the 'hearts and minds' intentions of the reformers. The fight against the FLN was progressively devolved on to the military. Fourth Republic politicians relied increasingly on the military to find a way of re-establishing order

---

Algeria

Algeria was occupied by France in 1830 and pacified by 1847. It was administered as three departments of France. A *pied noir* settler population of about one million loyal to France in effect operated a system which excluded the nine million or so Muslims from political rights. In 1954 the FLN started a guerrilla war for independence which became increasingly bitter. In 1958 army officers and settlers feared that the Republic was about to negotiate with the insurgents and staged a coup in Algiers. De Gaulle returned to power but a peace treaty was signed with the FLN at the Swiss spa town of Evian in March 1962 and most of the settlers fled to France when Algeria became independent later that year. The numbers killed in the course of the war are difficult to verify. Over 17,000 French soldiers died and over 140,000 Muslims were killed in the fighting. However, the insurgent Organisation de l'armée secrète also killed about 10,000 and the estimates of the numbers of Muslims killed varies from 300,000 to one million. France did not end relations with Algeria and Algerian workers continued to flood into France to take jobs in the expanding industries of the 1960s. French trade with Algeria declined but it remains the country's most important supplier. In the 1990s the rise of islamic fundamentalism in Algeria contesting the authority of the FLN government drew France into internal problems and although it tried to distance itself it was alleged to be propping up the Algerian régime.

---

in Algeria. By 1956 the generals were making policy in Algeria without Paris's permission. The principal indication that the government had lost control was probably the kidnap of the FLN leader Ben Bella in October 1956. The government was presented with a *fait accompli* by the army and chose to go along with it. After that time Paris was being led and not leading.

But the war intensified in Algeria and the 'methods' became increasingly unscrupulous. The army, still mindful of the defeat at Dien Bien Phu, was determined not to lose again to insurgents and the settlers had substantial support in the Assembly (not just on the right). The crisis came to a head in mid-May 1958 when the investiture of Pierre Pflimlin as Premier prompted a seizure of power in Algiers by the army, which called for the return of de Gaulle to power. Settlers and officers believed (wrongly) that Pflimlin wanted to negotiate with the FLN. Fourth Republic politicians desperately tried to regain control of the situation but were unable to do so. It began to appear that the choice was between the return of de Gaulle to power or an army take-over.

De Gaulle had no intention of being granted power by the grace of army generals or coming to power through a *putsch*. Senior politicians trekked out to meet de Gaulle at his home in Colombey-les-deux-Eglises (a distance which symbolised de Gaulle's independence) and he kept in touch with all sections of opinion. Everybody thought they knew de Gaulle's intentions, but these were kept ambiguous except that there would be a 'solution' to the crisis. At the end of May President Coty called on de Gaulle to form a government and he was invested by the Assembly on 1 June and voted full powers on 2 June. The Fourth Republic had fallen. It had been broken by a military uprising but had thrust power on to de Gaulle. A committee was given the authority to write a new constitution, which was completed in a very short time. It inaugurated the Fifth Republic. The new institutions were quickly set up and de Gaulle's supporters (now renamed the Union pour la nouvelle République, UNR) won 199 seats (the left took 86, the centre 57 and Independents 133).

The Fifth Republic Constitution

The Fifth Republic Constitution was overwhelmingly endorsed by a 79 per cent 'yes' vote in the referendum of September 1958 and became law on 9 October 1958. The Constitution is the document that defines political practice. France is a country of written laws and neither custom nor traditions are recognised as sources of constitutional law. In addition the Constitution, having been voted by the people, is the text to which lawyers must refer and not the current practice.

The Fifth Republic (1958–)

French political fault lines run deep. It might be asked what happened to these problems in the Fifth Republic. They diminished in intensity and, although they still underlie many contemporary problems, they no longer structure French politics:

1 De Gaulle entered the Fourth Republic as its Prime Minister and then dismantled it. With de Gaulle inside the tent the Republic had the bulk of conservative support and the backing of all sectors of opinion except the extreme right.
2 The Revolution was no longer the same issue in the Fifth Republic. The form of regime was not contested. People still talked about reform of the Constitution and of adapting the presidential system, but the main political forces accepted the institutions of the Republic and resolved to work within them. Anti-Republican rhetoric took other forms, notably the National Front (Front national, FN). All the same, a Revolutionary tradition remains on the extreme left. It was used at various times by the Communists and is currently used by the Trotskyists.
3 The old anti-parliamentary right disappeared, although the extreme right re-emerged as a mass movement led by J.-M. Le Pen in the 1980s.
4 Church/state relations had settled into a *modus vivendi* by the 1930s and this was confirmed at the Liberation. The education issue was the subject of a settlement that enabled Church schools to continue outside of the secular

state system. After the Second World War the Vatican withdrew from political involvement to concentrate on its mission and the Christian democratic party steadfastly supported the Republic. Secular education was accepted and Church schools continued to provide private education. Attempts by the left (in 1984) and by the conservative right (in 1995) to call this settlement into question were met with huge opposition and ultimately were abandoned.

5 The peasantry as a class began to disappear very rapidly in the 1950s with the industrial development of France. At the Liberation there were over four million working in agriculture but by the 1980s there were only just over 400,000. Agriculture nevertheless remained a formidable force in French politics and one prone to direct action.

6 French industry expanded exponentially and modernised at an unprecedented rate after the Second World War. By the 1960s France was a world rank industrial power and by the 1970s it had surpassed the United Kingdom.

7 As a result the French social structure was changed, with more women entering the labour force and the managerial middle class growing very rapidly.

8 With Khrushchev's arrival and consolidation of power in the Soviet Union the policy of *détente* was instituted and the Communist line changed. Local Communist parties (including the French) were told to take the 'parliamentary road' to power. The French Communist Party became available for parliamentary politics, although the invasion of Hungary in 1956 and the Algerian war prevented its reintegration in the last years of the Fourth Republic. In the Fifth Republic the working class was brought into the political system and the Communist Party was incorporated into the coalition of the left (victorious in 1981).

9 There was a brief attempt to create a French Union with the remaining colonies but decolonisation in sub-Saharan Africa was quickly put into effect. When Algeria had been disposed of there was no outstanding problem of Empire left. There were Imperial nostalgics, but they belonged to the past and they had no influence on policy.

10 De Gaulle inherited a rapidly expanding economy and provided the political stability to continue that expansion during his years as President. In the Fifth Republic, as in the Fourth Republic, rapid economic growth was regarded as highly desirable and an impressive achievement. However, growth also caused problems for a society that had changed slowly over the century. It was rapidly transformed and wrenched out of its familiar patterns.

De Gaulle's return to power dramatically altered the political landscape. The divisions that ran through French politics were simplified and immediately became a question of for or against de Gaulle. Then the situation changed to one of left/right competition around the presidency itself. This did not eliminate the old cleavages but it meant that the new coalition politics of the Fifth Republic took on a more novel (for France) aspect and became more like other European societies. French politics is still traversed by the older faults but there are now more active fissures, which will be examined in the next chapter.

The emphasis in Part I of this book will be on the political forces at work in France. The starting point is an overview of the social and economic background to the Fifth Republic and this is followed by a discussion of the building of coalitions in the Fifth Republic from the party material available. Behind the coalitions lie the political parties – the Fifth Republic, despite de Gaulle's stated intention, is party government (as indeed is representative government in the rest of Europe). These parties, and other interest groups, are examined in the rest of Part I. Part II focuses on the structures through which these political forces work, particularly the distinctive presidency of the Fifth Republic. The relations of President and Prime Minister will be examined, as well as the workings of Parliament and foreign policy.

Summary

- Historically, political divisions in France have been about what kind of regime the country should have and these have only recently subsided. There remain questions about the role of Parliament and the President but these are small in comparison with past conflicts.
- The main institutional problem remains that of the executive presidency and the continuation of the presidency as an active force rather than a passive 'dignified' part of the Constitution.
- France has been bitterly divided by disputes about the status of its colonies, decolonisation, German policy, war and the nature of society itself (the socialist/capitalist debate).
- Although these divisions have also waned in the Fifth Republic, there remain the problems of redistribution and social justice (as in all western countries), and there remains a radical presence in politics. Thus while Europe is a foreground issue in French politics as in most European Union (EU) members, the National Front's challenge is unusual.
- In the past, because of divisions, it was difficult to bring together coalitions for positive and determined action. Fifth Republic politics has not been immune to division but has had more cohesive majorities.
- The French state plays a much larger part in civil society (in both economics and social life) than in some other countries. The state has provided a continuity in the life of the nation and that has not been seriously challenged in the past.
- The *dirigiste* outlook currently goes against the grain of 'globalisation' and free market fashions elsewhere in the western world. There has, as with other western societies, been a withdrawal of the state since the 1980s but not to the same extent as elsewhere.

Further reading

Beriss, D., 'Scarves, schools and segregation: the *foulard* affair' *French Politics and Society* 8: 1, 1990, pp. 1–3

Donegani, J.-M., 'The political cultures of French Catholicism' *West European Politics* 5: 2, 1982, pp. 55–71

Gildea, R., *The Past in French History* (Yale University Press, 1994)

Hargreaves, A. G., *Immigration, 'Race' and Ethnicity in Contemporary France* (Routledge, 1996)

Hazareesingh, S., *Political Traditions in Modern France* (Oxford University Press, 1994)

Hoffmann, S., 'Heroic leadership: the case of modern France' in L. J. Edinger (ed.), *Political Leadership in Industrialised Societies* (John Wylie, 1967).

Horne, A., *A Savage War of Peace: Algeria* (Macmillan, 1977)

Larkin, M., *France since the Popular Front* (Second Edition, Oxford University Press, 1997)

Maclean, M., *The Mitterrand Years* (Macmillan, 1998)

Maclean, M., 'Privatisation, dirigisme and the market economy: an end to French exceptionalism?' *Modern and Contemporary France* 5: 2, 1997, pp. 215–28.

Macmillan, J., *Dreyfus to de Gaulle: Politics and Society in France 1889–1969* (Arnold, 1985)

Marquand, D., *The Unprincipled Society: New Demands and Old Politics* (Cape, 1988)

Williams, P. M., *Crisis and Compromise: Politics in the Fourth Republic* (Longman, 1964)

Questions

1 In what ways can the distinctiveness of French political culture be traced back to the Great Revolution?
2 What is the 'Republican tradition' in France?
3 What are the factors making for political stability and instability in France?

2

The social and economic context

For most of the nineteenth century France had a population of some 40 million people and this hardly increased over the first half of the twentieth century. However, in common with most western societies, the country's demography was transformed by the post-war 'baby boom' with its high point in 1949 and a second peak in 1964. After the war there was also an increase in life expectation and an influx of foreign workers. According to the 1999 census France had a population of 60.4 million (and was second only to Germany in the EU). However, with a surface area of 543,945 sq km, 1990s metropolitan France had the lowest population density in the EU – 107.7 persons per sq km. Although the birth rate (at 1.77 per female) was second behind Ireland in the EU, France has an ageing population below the critical renewal rate of 2.1 per cent. It is a population which is not being renewed, and higher living standards and medical advances mean that life expectancy for women, at 83 years, is the highest in the EU (for men it is 75 years).

France is a modern society. It has put behind it both the years of stagnation of the nineteenth century and the traumas of the wars, and after 1945 both industry and agriculture were modernised. These 'thirty glorious years', as they have become known, changed France from being an inward-looking and closed (mainly agricultural) economy into a European and export-oriented industrial economic force. This was effected through the impetus of the state in a process of stimulation and incentive which would have been familiar to the French of the previous century but which went further under the Fifth Republic than even Emperor Napoleon III would have anticipated.

It has to be kept in mind just how spectacular the transformation was. During the nineteenth century France struggled to keep up with the industrial nations and protected its own fledgling industries behind tariff high barriers, later reinforced by the experience of the depression in the 1930s. Despite the endeavours of the state, nineteenth-century France remained a sluggish economy and industrial production lagged behind the major European powers.

It was the post-war expansion and the loss of the protected empire market which forced changes. There was an industrial working class and a middle class but the social fractures ran deep. Over the same period the industrial working class increased and the service sector expanded to form over half of the active population. Some of these trends were intensified by the onset of crisis signified by the 'oil shocks' of the mid-1970s and have increased the service sector as well as the number of women in the workforce (which increased by three million in 1970–2000). In 1954 34.2 per cent of the workforce were women but by 1990 this had reached 46.4 per cent.

In the post-war years international trade increased and so did competition. France adapted to the international market and developed an export trade of world status. Hence it entered the twenty-first century as the fourth largest economy with 5.3 per cent of the world market – ahead of Italy and the United Kingdom – and also as the fourth exporter in the world. France is also the world's third largest arms seller. Foods and agricultural produce (of which France was the second exporter in the world after the USA), high technology, railway rolling stock and cars made up its healthy balance-of-payments surplus at the turn of the century. France's banking and insurance sector developed rapidly after the war to make the country an international investor and, although it is a destination for foreign capital, its invisible exports also contribute sizeably to the surplus. Europe has played a big part in this expansion: about 62 per cent of French exports go to the EU and 63 per cent of imports are from that region. In 1998 France's gross national product (GNP) per inhabitant ($21,150) was the tenth highest in the world: behind Germany (sixth) but ahead of Italy (seventeenth) and the UK (nineteenth).

Agriculture

France before the Second World War was principally rural and the main component of gross domestic product (GDP) came from agriculture (only in 1934 did the number of urban dwellers surpass the rural, although this had happened in the UK in 1851). In the post-war boom the old peasantry was virtually eliminated and those left holding the land became modern farmers producing for the market. Since the Liberation the numbers of those working on the land has diminished to fewer than 4 per cent. This was not just a numerical change but the integration of farming into the market and, ultimately, the global system with a change in outlook and the disappearance of the peasant of rural France. It was a revolution in techniques, land management and consumer tastes which was promoted in the Fourth Republic and continued in the Fifth. Many smallholdings have been eliminated, the numbers working on the land have fallen, and the size of holdings has increased, as has productivity. Agriculture contributes substantially to the trade surplus.

Modernisation was promoted by the state with the support of farmers – and sometimes under farmers' impetus. Many measures were used to rejuvenate

---

Farming

Over the Fifth Republic the percentage of those working in agriculture has steadily fallen and by the mid-1990s it stood at just over 4 per cent. This figure was lower than the European average, below Spain and Italy, though above Germany, the UK and Sweden. There were only about 700,000 farms in the mid-1990s and only about half were full-time; small farms usually ran other enterprises like bed-and-breakfast or farm-produced foods. Small farms have managed to subsist although the numbers have diminished and there is a big sector of large farms (over 125 acres). France is still the biggest food producer in Europe with the richest lands, and accounts for over one-fifth of European production. Europe is still key to the situation of French farmers as EU subsidies (of about $13 billion) make up half their income. About 80 per cent of this goes to the big cereal farmers.

José Bové

The emergence of the farmworkers' union leader José Bové as a hero touches on one of the anxieties of rural France and the cultural uncertainty of France as a whole. He set up the small leftist Confédération paysanne in 1987 and has a long history of protest actions, but is essentially a sheep farmer from the Causse du Larzac where he produces milk (mainly for cheese like Roquefort). Protests started when the European Union refused to allow American hormone-treated beef from entering Europe and the USA retaliated with sanctions on European foods (including Roquefort). This US action, although endorsed by the World Trade Organisation (which oversees free trade), was widely resented and McDonald's became the target for protests. Bové was one of those arrested in August 1999 for destroying the foundations of a McDonald's in Millau (Pyrenées). He was put in jail and then bailed but had become an overnight star. Farm workers around Bové had managed to capture in their protest fears about 'Americanisation', junk food and the destruction of French traditions. Bové's book (with François Dufour) is published in English as *The World is not for Sale* (Verso, 2001).

French farming, educate farmers and promote research, and these included the 'Pisani laws' of 1960–62 through which the state intervened actively and developed rural life. Of course, the European Common Agricultural Policy (CAP) assisted this change through tariffs, price support and the creation of a larger market. France is in the world premier league of wine production (second), poultry (sixth), beef (fifth), and cereals (fifth), and produces 23 per cent of European agricultural output. In addition a large food industry has grown to an export value of 40 billion francs per year.

Political problems, however, remain with French agriculture. France, traditionally protectionist, currently produces high value products and is now beginning (though with reservations – see, for example, the case of José Bové) to look on access to world markets as more important than keeping out imports. There is the tendency of farmers to protest against decisions and institutions they dislike and to demand a special status. Success, and the CAP, have led to overproduction in certain products, and methods to deal with this (like quotas and set-aside) have been only partially successful. The cost of the CAP has also become controversial. There is also a remnant of the old small farms sector that has persisted but is steadily being eroded.

Industrial growth

There have been two phases of French industrial development: the extraordinary transformation of the post-war years; then the slow-down after the oil shock and the restructuring of the last two decades. State action has been crucial in both these phases and France has generally tried to preserve a national interest (and French presence) in industry across all sectors. French industry is above all concentrated in the Paris region (the Seine basin) or the upper valley of the Rhône, although the older regions of the Nord-Pas-de-Calais and Alsace remain important. Throughout the post-war period industry was the motor of French economic growth. These were the years of the *trente glorieuses* miracle during which the French economy was one of the fastest growing in the world, averaging 5 per cent growth per year. France became a major industrial power and by 1965 industry made up 47 per cent of GNP. Industry expanded rapidly, provided employment and drew the rest of the economy along with it.

However, the onset of the second phase after the oil crisis in 1973 led to a recession in 1974 and to a slow-down (3.1 per cent growth 1973–79). This led to a mutation in the old 'smoke stack' industries of steel and textiles, which contracted, and new investment began in firms that adapted to the rise of foreign competition by moving ahead in the product cycle and developing 'high-tech' products. But many firms were shut and unemployment began its inexorable rise at this time. It was also revealed by the oil price rises that France, lacking oil, coal or gas reserves, was highly dependent on imported oil. The government in 1976 set up a crash programme of nuclear energy production and in 2000 about 75 per cent of French electricity was nuclear. Even so, France in 2000 remained dependent to about 49 per cent on overseas energy.

At the end of the 1970s industry had ceased to expand and employment in industry began to fall. From 1979 to 1985 the rate of growth was 1.4 per cent per year and although there was a brief rally in the late 1980s it was back to 1.5 per cent from 1990 to 1997. During this time the contraction of the heavy industries in the Nord-Pas-de-Calais, Lorraine, Creusot and Saint-Etienne meant that they lost jobs and production while the south and Mediterranean littoral have gained. Restructuring of weak industries through the state's nationalisation programme of 1981 (nine industrial groups were taken over) and then adaptation to the market then went ahead. After 1986 privatisation began in earnest and continued even under the Socialist government of 1997. Europeanisation has meant that foreign firms have penetrated French industry and foreign investment (UK, German and US) is now important. A third of industry was foreign-owned in 2000. France, like other western countries, has undergone deindustrialisation but it still has a handsome trade surplus in cosmetics, railway equipment and stock, aeronautics, automobiles and electronics.

Privatisation 1993–97

BNP	Rhône-Poulenc
Renault	Bull
ELF	UAP
Usinor-Sacilor	AGF
Péchiney	SEITA

Privatisation 1997–2000

April 1998	Thompson CSF (state share 42.94 per cent)
July 1998	Groupement des assurances nationales (87.1 per cent bought from the state by Grouparama)
	Aérospatiale fused with Matra: half to the Lagadère group, quarter sold and 5 per cent to the company workers
	Thomson Multimédia – 30 per cent sold to Alcatel and others.
August 1998	New president of the privatisation committee (F. Lagrange) nominated
February 1999	Matra-Aérospatiale (state kept 49 per cent)
June 1999	2.7 million buy Matra shares (8.7 per cent)
July 1999	7.4 million buy Crédit Lyonnais shares (state keeps 10 per cent)

French industry is currently composed of a myriad of small firms (under 500 employees) and a few major companies. Family firms predominate and even many big firms (like Michelin) are family concerns. These small companies are often specialist producers and are linked to larger enterprises – often multinational. Thus the motor industry and aerospace are served by a host of companies making particular products and dependent on the success of the larger firms in the sector. By the same token French firms are not, with one or two exceptions, amongst the biggest of the world multinationals. Governments in the 1990s have encouraged mergers and these have proceeded rapidly and are changing the pattern of ownership.

Services

The service sector is the principal employer in France and this has been so for some time. In 1975 51 per cent of jobs were in the service sector and in 2000 this figure had grown to 69 per cent. People working in services are employed by the state, in transport, banking, insurance and the professions, and in marketing, trade and sales. Tourism is of particular importance to France as it is the world's main tourist destination and earns a big surplus (the French travel abroad in big numbers as well). France receives some 70 million visitors per year and these are not (as in the UK) short-term visitors passing through. There are about a million jobs involved with tourism and it accounts for 10 per cent or so of GNP. There has been a post-war boom in tourism as affluence has spread through the western world. France developed ski resorts for mass tourism, and the Mediterranean coast and Paris have remained big attractions. In the 1980s has taken the American model of Disneyland was taken to Paris and was applied to other theme parks (Astérix, for example).

One of the paradoxes of the last two decades was that they started with the nationalisation of the banking sector and ended with an internationally viable finance system. In 1982–86 the state took over almost all of the banking system but this proved a prelude to liberalisation. From 1986 a privatisation programme began, accompanied by deregulation and market reform. This process continued in the 1990s and under the Socialist government of 1997. As a result of the new policies the banking sector was opened to international competition and the Paris Stock Exchange became an important institution (though not in the same league as New York or London). As elsewhere in industry, mergers and acquisitions have been encouraged and sometimes supported by the French state to give a bigger French presence in Europe and on the international stage. Measures have also been taken to lessen the threat of international take-overs in what is still (by global standards) a fledgling industrial sector.

Social class

According to the sociologist Henri Mendras, the make-up of French society has become more fragmented but less hierarchical than it was after the war (see Figure 1). There are two main groups – the popular classes and the central middle classes – but there is also a small elite and a small underclass of poor people. About 25 per cent belong to the central group, which is composed of professional people and middle management, and the specialists in information. Education, in particular, has expanded at secondary and tertiary levels providing the skilled 'managerial class' that has grown the fastest of all groups in post-war France. The new occupations of the second 'industrial (information technology) revolution' have swelled this group. This new group has been

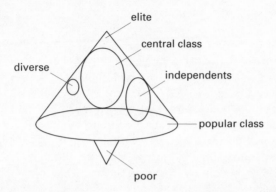

Figure 1   Social class in France

Source: H. Mendras, *La Seconde Révolution Française* (Gallimard, 1994).

behind many cultural and social changes: it is meritocratic (depending on skill and knowledge) and it is educated. There is a small elite at the head of society (3 per cent) of owners of businesses, upper civil servants and intellectuals, which is the nearest equivalent to an aristocracy in contemporary France.

Popular classes of workers and employees make up about 50 per cent of the population and are less well educated than the central group. Within this working class the presence of industrial workers had decreased from the 38 per cent of the 1968 census to around 27 per cent in the 1990s and the differentiation within the strata has decreased. These workers have faced the stress of readjustment to the new economy and class solidarity has decreased. Then there are the poorest classes at the base that make up some 7 per cent. This division has been described as the 'social fracture' and the underclass includes not just the highly visible problem of the homeless (whose numbers are difficult to estimate accurately) but also, in the 1980s and 1990s, it included a disproportionate number of women, young people and children. Unemployment has cut some people off from society and the institutions that once integrated people into society – such as trade unions, political parties, churches – have ceased to be effective for many.

France in the 1990s had a workforce of some 23.3 million people. Women have increased rapidly as a proportion of this workforce (by three million in the

---

France's poor

The poverty line in France in 1999 was defined as 3,800 francs per month for a single person and 7,900 francs per month for a couple, putting about 5.5 million people below the standard. In addition 3 million were jobless and 3 million workers earned less than 5,000 per month.

Unemployment

Unemployment had started to rise during the 1960s but from a very low point so that it became a political issue only after the turbulence in the world economy of 1973 and the oil price rises which caused the rate to rise to 700,000. It continued to rise during the 1970s despite political concern and by 1980 it stood at 6.7 per cent of the labour force; the length of time spent on the hunt for a job also extended over that period. The French Socialist government of 1981 had hoped to bring down the rate of unemployment. However, it proved stubbornly resistant to traditional methods of government spending and after 1983 the government switched to policies dealing with the supply side and social measures such as training and job creation through tax incentives and helping people leave the workforce and so free jobs for the young. The young unemployed were a particular concern (youth unemployment is twice as high as the average) and government measures have tended to concentrate on them and on the long-term unemployed. In the mid-1980s the rate reached a plateau of over 10 per cent of the workforce (2,500,000) and vigorous growth under the Rocard government of 1988–91 did not succeed in bringing unemployment down. In the 1990s it began to edge upwards again and by June 1997 it was, at about 12.6 per cent, one of the highest in the industrial nations, although it had fallen to 8.5 per cent by May 2001.

Social class structure

	1983 (%)	1997 (%)
Professionals	19.3	19.7
Farmers and associated	7.2	2.8
Artisans, shopkeepers, small business	8.2	6.6
Managers, professions	9.0	12.1
Employees	25.5	29.2
Workers	30.7	27.2
Total workforce	21,379,000	25,582,000

Source: Institut national de statistiques et d'études économiques 1998

previous 30 years compared to 900,000 men) and constitute 43.7 per cent of it. Farmers and workers have declined in the total but the numbers of managers and professional occupations as well as salaried workers have expanded. These mutations are a reflection of the increased service sector and the drift from the land (and mechanisation of farming). Economic change has given advantages to the educated and the skilled over the manual workers in the old economy.

Recent changes

If the French economy has changed rapidly over the post-war years, the 1990s were no exception. France seized the new global and information revolution on the bound and emerged the stronger. There were those who argued that the same force that had made France modern, that is the state, would prevent it embracing the 'post-modern' global world and that it would lose out. France has stood out amongst the major industrial powers (the G7) as an opponent of the vogue for free market 'liberalism' sweeping the world. France's opposition, from both left and right, to 'Anglo-Saxon' capitalism's deregulation, individualism and Thatcherite minimal state has been marked. French tradition has looked to the state to prod, inveigle and goad industry into modernising and moving in new directions but also, at times, to run them. Republics from the Revolution to de Gaulle have stood for strong government, centralism, equality and welfare. In France the state's interference in the economy (its *dirigiste* tendencies) remain greater than in the UK or USA. (Something like half of French national income is spent by the state.)

In the early 1990s the French economy grew by only 1.3 per cent but it picked up to reach 3 per cent in 1998 and by 2000 it was growing at 3.7 per cent per annum. Yet France became (and remains) the fourth or fifth biggest economy in the world and is a leader in high-tech areas such as high-speed trains, aerospace, telecommunications (of which the multinational Vivendi is an example) and civil engineering. France developed its successful 'Minitel' computer network in the 1980s but this slowed its move to the internet; there are 29 personal computers per 100 population in France, well below Sweden (63) and slightly below the UK (36) but above Italy (16). France has subsequently moved strongly in the e-commerce sector, which accounted for 20 per cent of French production in 2000. High-tech start-ups have grown and an entrepreneurial sprit has spread amongst the young (applications for the civil service college have fallen by a third and applications for information technology courses have exploded). France's high-speed TGV rail network is a monument to the country's engineering tradition and its capacity to see imaginative projects on a big scale.

Economic recovery started under the government of Alain Juppé in 1996 but a series of mistakes (leading to strikes and stoppages) meant that there was a pessimistic mood about the economy. Jospin's government managed to revive confidence by lowering interest rates, reducing the deficit in government finances and cutting taxes. Employment also improved and job creation was promoted through deals between both sides of industry. Morale steadily improved from 1997 and in 2000 was at its highest since 1987 (when the polling of how people felt about their future and living standards started). In addition all the sectors of the economy (except beef cattle hit by the BSE problem) and all regions were the beneficiaries of the growth.

'Privatisation' is not a concept that has found much favour on the left but the

Privatisation

Of the major industrial countries, France was the one in which nationalisation had been carried furthest and this reached its apogee under the Socialist government's measures of 1982. After then the nationalised industries produced some 30 per cent of GNP but the pendulum began to swing back. Denationalisation started in France under the centre right 1986–88 'cohabitation' government and, although it had aimed to privatise substantially, it was scaled down after the 1987 stock market crash and the return of the Socialists to power in 1988 (they did not rationalise). In the first tranche the glass factory Saint-Gobain, the Paribas bank and the Assurances générales were sold to the public and during the programme some five million new shareholders were created. It was not, however, overwhelmingly popular because, unlike in the United Kingdom, public enterprise was not in universally low esteem, state industry was ideologically acceptable and the conditions of sale raised questions. The conservative parties continued the programme when they returned to power in 1993 and so did the Socialist government of 1997.

The 35-hour week

This measure, promoted in the 1997 election by the left as a way of increasing employment, was implemented on 1 January 2000 to change the working week from 39 to 35 hours in firms of over 20 employees (by 2003 it will apply fully to all firms). Doctors, executives, lawyers, journalists and the army are exempted. It was accomplished against a certain amount of objection from both employers and employees. It was made possible by introducing flexible working (which is what the employees disliked and went on strike about) so that productivity could be maintained. Employers calculated the hours on the basis of the total number of hours worked in a year and divided the number by 52, instead of introducing a standard week. This enabled businesses to vary working quite considerably to suit demand and thus increase productivity. The assertion that the measure would create jobs by forcing businesses to hire extra help to make up for the shorter working week is unproved.

Average hours in France in 1999 were 1,656 per year as compared with 1,574 in Germany, 1,731 in the UK and 1,966 in the USA (International Labour Organisation).

Jospin government has been more pragmatic than rhetoric would lead outsiders to expect. Jospin's government of 1997–2000 has seen through more sales of shares in state-owned companies (over $24 billion) than did the previous conservative government of 1995–97. State giants like Thomson Multimedia, Air France and France Télécom have all been opened to private capital. The government also encouraged the flexibility of labour through the promotion of the 35-hour week and has loosened the corset in which work rules were bound with pro-business measures (which angered some unions). Most big companies used the opportunity to renegotiate contracts and held wage costs down so that productivity did not decline. Jospin's 1997 government also introduced a 'negative income tax' (a proposal normally associated with the extreme *laissez-faire* right) to help eliminate the poverty trap.

Welfare

France is proud of its generous health and welfare system. Its foundations were laid at the Liberation by the combined forces of the Socialists, the Christian democrats and Resistance gaullists (with the Communists at that time supporting their efforts) and it has been progressively extended so that virtually everybody is covered by it. On that basis it became part of the post-war consensus until the 1970s when it began to come under attack, but it remains widely popular with the French public. It is a comprehensive system that covers illness, pensions, maternity and invalidity, to which unemployment insurance was

---

Social security

De Gaulle's government set up the French social security system in legislation in 1945–46. French welfare provision is generous. It is intricate but the main part is in three branches: one deals with family benefits, one with accidents at work and with illness, and a third deals with social insurance for maternity, invalidity and so on. Welfare was intended to cover all citizens and provide uniform benefits and the branches are administered by joint boards of employers and employees. Welfare is bigger than the rest of the state budget: spending has reached 2 trillion francs per year and the accumulated debt has reached 230 billion francs (4 per cent of GDP). Much of it is funded by a tax on payrolls, which makes the burden on business heavy, but a special income tax devoted to social security was introduced in 1991 (the *cotisation sociale généralisée*) and that eased the situation. France has the fourth highest level of health spending in the world, costing about one-tenth of GDP; by World Health Organisation figures it ranks first in terms of efficiency and sixth in quality (the UK ranks eighteenth in efficiency and ninth in quality). It spends comparatively less than Belgium, the Netherlands and Denmark, about the same as Germany, much more than the UK and above the European average. Social security is run by boards of elected representatives of the unions and the employers and spends around $265 billion a year on old age, health and unemployment benefits. It was the attempts of the 1995–97 Juppé government (heavy-handed it must be said) to reform the system by cutting costs and limiting expenditure that brought about crippling strikes in December 1995. Social insurance amounts to 45.5 per cent of salary costs in France (14.5 per cent in the UK).

Pensions

Almost all pension provision in France is made by the state and the retirement age of 60 for men and women is one of the lowest in the western world (for men it is 65 in the UK and 62 in Italy). Some French public workers can retire on a full pension at 55. However, it takes 9.7 per cent of French GDP to pay for the pensions and as the numbers of old rise in proportion to the working population and as people live longer the burden is likely to grow (though these actuarial projections are notoriously unreliable for population growth).

---

added in 1958. It is financed mainly through contributions from workers and employers and it is run jointly by unions' and employers' representatives. Social security was intended to be self-financing but the state has had to step in to finance deficits (for example, when unemployment rose) and the gap between income and expenditure (*trou de la sécu*) became politicised. With the increasing problems of unemployment and social breakdown the cost has risen and there have been complaints about the burden on business and about inefficiency. These reservations were given added weight by the rise of neo-liberal ideology critical of state action and in the 1990s the questions of high taxes and the large 'deficit' became regular features of political debate.

There is a tension in French economic policy between its large public sector and its welfare state, which is extensive and requires government funding through tax, and economic competitiveness, which requires low tax. Some 27 per cent of the French workforce are in the public sector (which is higher than Sweden) and public sector workers have good conditions. At 45.3 per cent of GDP in 1998 the French tax burden is relatively high but it is also skewed. Only 50 per cent of households pay taxes (in the UK it is 90 per cent) and the state prefers to collect indirect taxes and taxes on employers which are politically easier to manage.

Health expenditure in 1998 was around 9.8 per cent of GDP. It is a system funded from a tax on wages and by employers and the government. Health expenditure has usually been responsible for the budget problems of social security and it has grown faster than other costs. Patients pay for treatment and are reimbursed, but there are also private (mutual) insurance funds to which many people also contribute. In 1994 the total costs of the various allowances (health, old age, family and unemployment) came to over a quarter of GDP. However, in 1995, the Juppé government's attempts to limit health spending and control the budget more tightly led to strikes and to a government backdown.

According to the World Health Organisation, which has 191 members, French public health ranks sixth (ahead of the UK, Germany and the United States). France spends 9.8 per cent of its GDP on health as compared with 5.8 per cent in the UK, 13.7 per cent in the USA and 10.5 per cent in Germany, but its expenditure is efficiently used (France ranks first on that particular measure). Health expenditure has grown continuously and, as elsewhere, medical expenditure has tended to increase faster than the overall economy, although this has slowed in the 1990s. Patients can choose their doctors and hospitals and waiting lists are short. The problems are sometimes over-capacity rather than lack of availability. Moreover the costs of drugs are high and attempts to restrict prescriptions (which are at the doctors' discretion and can be very expensive) have not been a success. The French health system is not completely free at the point of use because patients pay a proportion of some treatment or hospital stays. However, the state or department can reimburse this and the repayment is means-tested. It is generous and results in a deficit in the social security budget in most years (though usually not during economic booms).

Public health spending 1999–2000 (% of GDP)

Country	Public %	Rank
United States	44.2	1
Germany	75.3	2
Switzerland	73.4	3
FRANCE	76.4	4
Norway	82.8	5
Belgium	89.7	6
Netherlands	70.4	7
Italy	68.0	8
Sweden	83.8	9
Denmark	81.6	10
Greece	56.8	11
Japan	78.3	12
Spain	76.9	13
United Kingdom	84.2	14
Hungary	76.5	15
Poland	72.2	16

Source: Organisation of Economic Co-operation and Development

Unemployment pay is relatively generous and attempts were made in the 1990s to reduce the cost on employers (especially for unskilled workers). Unemployment was one of the principal political problems afflicting society at the turn of the century. For the '*trente glorieuses*' unemployment was (at 3 per cent) at a minimum consistent with people changing jobs or relocating, and immigrants entered France to make up a shortfall of demand. After the Middle East oil crisis of 1973 unemployment began to rise and few companies were unaffected, which led to a pervasive insecurity (increased by the generalisation of short-term contracts for new workers). Of particular concern were the problems of youth unemployment and the linked difficulty of the long-term unemployed (over twelve months) who were unlikely to find work. In the 1990s

French unemployment rose above the European average and was particularly bad amongst the young (reaching 25 per cent of that age group in 1995) but there were also significant numbers of long-term unemployed. Despite the tendency of growth in the economy to create (relative to the USA) few new jobs, France's unemployment figures fell in the late 1990s from the disturbing 12.6 per cent to under 10 per cent, aided by the 350,000 state-subsidised jobs offered to young people by the 1997 government. Governments in the 1990s also acted to increase the flexibility of the labour market. That is, they encouraged workers to retrain with new skills, promoted new working hours and tried to lighten the taxes on businesses. By 2000 there were two significant if small changes: youth unemployment was falling (it had reached 24.5 per cent in 1998), as was the length of time people spent unemployed.

Pensions are another problem area of the French welfare state. They are generous (and early retirement has been used to reduce unemployment) but the anticipated difficulty is that France, unlike the UK, faces the prospect of a diminishing workforce and an increased pensions bill for the 'baby boom' generation retiring and living longer. At the 1990 census the average age was 35.5 and at the 1998 census it was 38.3. This is expected to become a problem when the 'baby boomers' begin to reach retirement age between 2005 and 2015. These figures have been received with predictions of gloom and questions about whether France will be able to support its retired people but the extrapolations of demographic data are notoriously unreliable (in 1945 a similar doom was predicted).

New France

France has been a society of immigrants since the first workers arrived to work in the nascent industries of the nineteenth century. In today's France 20 per cent of people born in France have a parent or grandparent who was an immigrant in the twentieth century. Early immigrants assimilated and learnt to become French, aided by informal mechanisms such as the Church and the political parties and by the Republican state through the schools and the army. Thus children of the second generation of Spanish, Portuguese, Polish and Italian workers became fully French. This accorded with the Republican view and the unitary state took a neutral position but forged France out of local particularisms. Republicans held that all people were equal regardless of their origins and rejected the principle of the recognition of minority communities within France. There were no 'hyphenated French'. This was the dominant Republican view (as it was in, for example, the USA 50 years ago) but it has come under increasing challenge and the idea of the secular Republic has lost support on the left as it gained it on the right. There have been many headline-grabbing incidents which have illustrated the difficulties of the old Republican view (the 'headscarves incident' being the most famous) and the recognition of

Immigrants

France has attracted large numbers of immigrants since its industrial development started in the nineteenth century but the most recent wave of immigration
was the result of the post-war expansion. In the 1950s the immigrants were
mostly from neighbouring European countries but they ceased to come in large
numbers (Portugal excepted) when European growth took off. In the 1960s the
gap was made up mainly by former colonial subjects, mostly Algerian, who came
to do the unskilled work that other workers would not do. In the early 1970s there
were about four million overseas workers (one million Algerians) in France but the
crisis of the mid-1970s caused the demand for labour to dry up and many became
unemployed. In 1990 there were 3.5 million people of foreign extraction living in
France: 650,000 Portuguese, 614,000 Algerians and 573,000 Moroccans. The
concentration of immigrants in the run-down estates and their lack of skills as
well as their inability to find jobs has led to tensions which have been exploited
politically.

the diversity of French community life is relatively recent. With the rise of more
diverse cultures and larger numbers, the question of whether the old
Republican state can cope has been raised.

Mainly this is a colonial legacy and a result of the economic expansion of the
1950s and 1960s that drew in large numbers of (mainly North African)
workers. In between 1956 and 1972 about two million people came to France,
drawn by the jobs. They concentrated in the industrial areas of the Paris region,
the Nord, Lorraine, Provence-Côte d'Azur and Rhône-Alpes. (After the crisis of
the 1970s the rules were tightened and only about 40,000 immigrants arrive
each year.) In 1962 about 53 per cent were from southern Europe and 19 per
cent from North Africa, but in 1999 about 32 per cent came from southern
Europe and 39 per cent from North Africa. It is the second or third generation
of these immigrants from the former colonies, the *beurs* (slang for 'Arabs'), who
have made an impact. Islam, with something like four million adherents, has
become France's second religion.

Yet the *beurs* are not fully integrated into French society, although they were
born in France and are not North African. This alienation has been increased
by a ghettoisation of the suburbs of the big cities like Marseilles and Paris where
the *beurs* are concentrated. France has its middle class 'suburbs' like the UK but
the suburbs in question were built in isolated positions on the outskirts of big
cities. They were the result of the 1960s building boom for the industrial
workers then taking employment and were created cheaply in huge numbers
(at La Courneuve 4,000 units were put together). In the 1980s these run-down
suburbs suffer from the 'inner city' problems familiar elsewhere: high unemployment, crime, drugs and lack of facilities. Unemployment is much higher for
the young in these areas than amongst the young in general. They feel that they

are excluded from the opportunities in society and that they are not a presence in the economy – although they are in sport and music.

Although the multicultural World Cup winning football team was cele- brated in France, and hip hop (a distinctive French version of rap and street culture) is widely popular, especially amongst the young, there is an underly- ing hostility to the *beurs*. Polls and the success of the National Front attest to the rejection of immigrants, and successive governments in the 1990s have been pressured by this opinion. Conservative governments have preferred a tough response to immigration. The 'Pasqua-Debré laws' ended the 'droit du sol' (restricting access to French nationality) and the rights of foreigners to join their family members in France were limited. In 1996 the expulsion of immi- grants who did not have the required documents to stay in France from Saint- Bernard's Church where they had sought sanctuary became a *cause célèbre*. For the liberal left it was an attack, but for the right it was justified (the action was supported by public opinion). Jospin's governments from 1997 tried to remove the issue from the political arena and to integrate people as citizens of the Republic.

Religion

Religion no longer structures political debate. France has always been a Catholic country, but there has been in France, as elsewhere, a decline in church attendance and religious observation as society has become increas- ingly secular. Indications of this include the crisis of recruitment of priests in France: the priesthood is ageing and not being renewed. About 80 per cent of French people define themselves as Catholics but the importance of faith in society has diminished and the Church is no longer seen as the arbiter in morals or as providing the moral tone. It should be noted, however, that the old cleri- cal/anti-clerical divide persists in shadowy form in the tendency of practising Catholics to vote for the conservative right and secularism to be supported on the left. There are influential Catholic activist groups involved in social charity and these include Third World (Comité Catholique contre la faim), human rights (Action des Chrètiens pour l'abolition de la torture) and welfare associa- tions. These are often widely admired.

Other minority religions, including Islam, have experienced the same erosion of practice and authority. Protestantism in France has always been a minority religion, although it has integrated and contributed disproportion- ately to the creation of the secular Republic. Protestantism is the declared relig- ion of 4–6 per cent of French people, with the practising number about 1.5 per cent. It is a diverse group ranging from the Lutherans of Alsace and the Doubs, to the reformists of the Midi, and with others scattered across the map. There are also over half a million Jewish people in France, mostly (55 per cent) in the Paris region but with numbers in the east (15 per cent) and on the

Mediterranean littoral (15 per cent). They are a group that was reinforced in the 1960s by about 300,000 refugees from Algeria. There are minor exceptions to the downward trend in religious commitment in France. These include various New Age groups but also denominations such as the Jehovah's Witnesses, the Rev. Moon's Church and Scientologists which may number as many as 116 groups and attract half a million people. There was also, in 1988, Mgr Lefebvre's politically right-wing schism from the Catholic Church, whose adherents remain faithful to what they see as a purer Catholicism. Changes in French society in a secular direction have worked against the older values: France has, for example, legalised same-sex partnerships.

Civil solidarity pact

In 2000 France introduced a new form of contract for same-sex couples which will put their partnership in a legal framework. It is a law which was watered down from the initial intention to allow gay marriages after the traditionalists rallied to fight the 'destruction of marriage' in the Assembly (where 550 amendments were tabled and a filibuster took place) and on the streets in demonstrations. The 'pac' gives these couples most of the rights enjoyed by conventional marriages, including the marriage tax rate, but break-up is much easier, they cannot adopt and there are fewer inheritance rights. 'Common law' marriages have been able to draw up a contract since 1992.

Media

France has experienced the development of the mass media as have other western countries, but the experience has been traumatic both for the media, which have undergone a transformation, and the state itself, which has had to relinquish its supervision of many areas. As elsewhere television has expanded rapidly and has become the dominant communications medium. Two state channels were complemented by a third regional channel in 1972, but the main innovation was the Socialist government's liberalisation of the electronic media in 1981–86. Three commercial channels were created: Canal + (subscription), la Cinq and TV6. TF1, the state channel, was privatised in 1987, and there then followed the cable television and satellite channels, so that by the 1990s a very wide variety was on offer. Television has, as elsewhere, had deleterious effects on cinema, which has declined more or less continuously but at an accelerated pace since 1980 (both in numbers of cinema-goers and cinemas).

Radio was also a state monopoly and under supervision until the Fifth Republic. Its heyday was in the late 1950s. Although there were private stations outside French territory, the state's influence was strong. Peripheral stations like Luxembourg and Europe 1 did, however, capture a public and youth audience

Broadcasting

Broadcasting was, at the beginning of the Fifth Republic, a public monopoly under government direction. In 1964 the Fourth Republic monopoly was reorganised as Office de radio-télévision française (ORTF) and continued the government's control of management and broadcasting. The monopoly was progressively lessened after de Gaulle's departure and change in the 1980s was rapid. Some changes were made under Pompidou but Giscard took the most important step of breaking the monopoly of Radio-France and three television channels were established (TF1, A2 and FR3). In 1982 the Socialist government gave the companies considerable autonomy and placed them under a broadcasting authority (a system which continues): currently this authority is the Conseil supérieur de l'audiovisuel. In 1984 private profit-making radio stations were allowed and three private television stations were created (Canal Plus, TV5 and TV6). Then in 1986 the conservative government privatised TF1 and permitted the setting up of private radio stations. In television there remains a public service (A2, La cinquième and FR3). Radio-France is a core national public radio and there are 39 regional public radio stations. There is a myriad of private radio stations including the traditional non-metropolitan radios (Luxembourg, Monte-Carlo and Europe 1) and private television stations Canal Plus (subscription), TF1 and M6 as well as satellite stations (like the Franco-German Arte). The broadcasting regulations are meant to prevent a concentration of ownership and require public service programmes as well as limiting advertising.

that the main stations did not. However, it was the Socialist victory of 1981 that wrought a revolution in French radio. There were pirate radios operating in the cities and provinces but the government legalised private local radio stations and then enabled them to take advertising. This rapidly led to commercial radio networks developing around big companies and the revival of the radio as a mass medium. There remains a public service radio both locally and nationally and paid for through tax. Radio-France is the main station but there are two specialist stations: France-Musique, catering for classical music, and France-Culture, which is the main general culture outlet. Public radio has experienced a growth in the number of listeners as well as a rejuvenation of its audience.

After the war there was an upheaval in the press which saw the confiscation of old collaborationist titles and the rise of a party political press. However, the competition from radio and then from television has led to dramatic changes, and the press has not coped well with falling revenue and rising costs. Since the Liberation the sales of the press have declined, some big names have disappeared and there were only nine national papers in 2000 and only *L'Humanité* remains of the party press. *Le Monde* emerged as a principal serious daily (with a circulation of about 368,856), second to *Le Figaro* (375,000), but below the sports paper *L'Equipe* (388,914). There are about 570 weekly magazines. The end of the Fourth Republic also saw the birth of the American-style weekly papers *L'Express* and *Le Nouvel Observateur* (joined by others in the 1960s). There is also a flourishing equivalent to the British tabloids in *France-Dimanche* and *Ici Paris*, although this sector is tiny compared to its equivalent in the UK. Despite (or perhaps because of) the relative health of the 66 regional daily papers, some of which (like the 786,205 of *Ouest-France*, or the 397,282 of the *Dauphiné Libéré*) still have a mass circulation, the national papers have gone through hard times. Successive governments have aided the minority newspapers but they remain relatively high-priced and ill-adapted to the modern world of media diversity, and further closures might be anticipated.

Newspapers

French newspapers are politically marked but the regional press tends to be much stronger than in the United Kingdom and its outlook depends on its proprietor. At the Liberation the political parties had their own papers (and these had big circulations) but the partisan press mostly diminished when faced with competition from television and radio and better written productions. All the same the political outlook of the papers is usually very evident and reflected in both their comment columns and new coverage.

The main Paris daily papers are:

Le Figaro (450,000): this is the main conservative daily and is part of the Hersant publication group.

Le Monde (350,000): the elite paper which has a world-wide reputation. Nobody would accuse it of being anti-Socialist but it is very open to different opinions in its columns and many of the conservative right have favoured it.

Le Parisien (300,000): this is a tabloid aimed at Paris much as the *Standard* caters for Londoners.

Libération (133,000): this was developed out of the extreme left daily and has since become a left-wing (socialist) paper with an amusing and youthful style.

La Croix (100,000): this is the Catholic daily which tends to support the centre right but is politically eclectic.

Les Echos (70,000): this is the financial daily.

L'Humanité (50,000): this is the Communist Party paper. It has a steadily falling circulation and has been unable to stem its decline. It lives through subsidies and there is doubt as to how long it can continue.

L'équipe, the sporting newspaper, sells about 400,000 per day. There is also a flourishing market of weekly journals (a bit like *Time* or *Newsweek*) and the biggest of these are *L'Express* (centre), *Le Point* (conservative) and *Le Nouvel Observateur* (Socialist), and the satirical and investigative *Le Canard Enchaîné* with a circulation of over 500,000. There is no Sunday paper market equivalent to the UK's. *Le Journal de Dimanche* is the Sunday paper.

Corruption

Recently, since the late 1980s, the problem of political corruption has emerged as a major issue, largely as a result of the persistence of investigating judges. French political corruption, although a prominent issue, is probably not exceptionally bad by international standards. It is difficult (because it was hidden) to

Corruption – the 'ELF affair'

Corruption became an issue in European politics in the 1980s. It is not evident that the decade was significantly corrupt and it may be that investigation became more rigorous, but in France, as in other countries, politicians in general have been spattered by widespread allegations. No party is completely free of suspicion. Over the 1990s magistrates have investigated some 30 ex-ministers, two former Prime Ministers and over 100 mayors and many deputies (though not charged). Public funding of political parties cut down the extent of these practices (which were not for personal enrichment but for the political machines) but they have not been entirely eliminated. The 'ELF affair' is a long-running and bafflingly intricate series of revelations including the allegation that President Mitterrand gave £10 million (equivalent) to help finance the re-election of Germany's leader Helmut Kohl in 1992. ELF was a state oil company (now privatised) set up in 1965 under de Gaulle's presidency and may have been seen as a milch cow by successive French administrations to be used to ease the solution of political problems – mainly in sub-Saharan Africa. Some 49 people received salaries from ELF and the likelihood is that they were deployed to work in politicians' offices (this is a practice wider than ELF and fake jobs for political workers were provided by many nationalised industries). Investigations by the Magistrates Eva Joly and Laurence Vichnievsky uncovered a series of doubtful practices. Some, like the purchase of some £1,100 shoes for a government minister, were greedy, others, like the use of the company jet to ferry politicians (some neo-gaullists as well as Socialists) around the country, seem to have been quotidian, and some appear to have been rather lavish bribes.

ELF used its privileged access to ask ministers to intervene to place contracts with the company and on one occasion was accused of getting the approval of six frigates to Taiwan on behalf of another company (Thompson). In March 2000 the head of the Constitutional Council, Roland Dumas, was forced to resign while judges investigated allegations about his part in the ELF system. Under this, huge illicit commissions were allegedly paid to French and foreign politicians and parties. Roland Dumas, twice Foreign Minister for President Mitterrand and an influential lawyer, is the biggest figure involved, although many of the President Mitterrand's entourage were under investigation. Alfred Sirven, ELF's deputy head and corporate affairs director in 1989–96, was extradited from the Philippines in February 2001 and also went on trial in France. Roland Dumas was sentenced to six months in prison in 2001.

say to what extent there has been an increase in corruption. However, the intense competition between parties and the decentralisation laws have probably stimulated it in the last two decades. Corruption is often designed to support political campaigns and political parties, but there can also be a degree of personal enrichment. To some extent state funding of parties has lessened the pressures on parties to find funds from clandestine sources, but there is still a question mark over what does happen. Even though the scandals mainly concern events a decade ago and not contemporary practices, they are a continual discredit of the political class, of parties and of politics.

The sleaze factor

Country	Score (1999)
Italy	4.7
Greece	4.9
Belgium	5.3
Spain	6.6
France	6.6
Portugal	6.7
Austria	7.6
Ireland	7.7
Germany	8.0
Britain	8.6
Luxembourg	8.8
Netherlands	9.0
Sweden	9.4
Finland	9.8
Denmark	10.0

Note: Transparency International rates countries on a scale of corruption from one (worst) to ten (best) and this index is published. Its score is a rating of how corruption is perceived by the country and outsiders. France is not the worst, but nor it is it exemplary.

Conclusion

Who could govern a country that has 325 cheeses?, as de Gaulle remarked. In social and economic terms, however, the France of extreme differentiation and markedly exceptional social structure has dissolved in the post-war years. Regional particularisms remain but the local patchworks are not as diverse as they once were. This homogenisation and social change has worked through to politics and to French institutions and the new France is one very much in the European mainstream. France can be seen to be grappling with many of the same problems as its neighbours and making advances in broad line with them.

However, the end of the protection of industry and the integration of France

into the European and global economy also means that the country is not protected from the shocks of the world downturns as it once was. France no longer
has to export just to live well but has to sell abroad to survive and maintain its
current high standards of living. Thus the open economy and the outwardly
oriented society has made France modern but has also exposed it to the fluctuations in New York, the Far East and, of course, Europe. In this sense, as in the
social one, it is a European society.

Summary

- France was one of Europe's more sluggish economies until the Second World
  War.
- After the Second World War France entered a period of exceptionally rapid
  growth which transformed the economy and promoted the country into the
  front rank of industrial powers.
- Although it has not repeated that performance, France has avoided the roller
  coaster ride of boom and slump experienced by the UK and has grown
  strongly.
- The principal political problem is unemployment, which remained stubbornly unresponsive to various remedies through the 1970s, 1980s and
  1990s until the Jospin government of 1997. The position improved after
  1997 but it remains a political embarrassment.
- France gives the state a much bigger and more active role than in the USA or
  the UK. This can be seen in the state's support for industry as well in its development of such high-prestige projects as the high-speed train (TGV).
- Welfare provision is extensive and costly but is widely supported.

Further reading

Ardagh, J., *France Enters the New Century* (Viking, 1999)
della Porta, D. and Mény, Y., *Democracy and Corruption in Europe* (Pinter, 1997)
Doublet, Y. M., 'Party funding in France' in K. D. Ewing (ed.), *The Funding of Political
Parties* (CLUEB, 1999)
Fenby, J., *On the Brink: The Trouble with France* (Little, Brown, 1998)
Flynn, G. (ed.), *Remaking the Hexagon: The New France in the New Europe* (Westview,
1995)
Gaffney, J. (ed.), *France and Modernisation* (Avebury, 1988)
Mendras, H. and Cole, A., *Social Change in Modern France* (Cambridge University Press,
1991)
Palier, B., 'Defrosting the French welfare state' *West European Politics* 32: 2, 2000, pp.
113–36
Powell, E. R., 'The TGV project: a case of techno-economic *dirigisme?*' *Modern and
Contemporary France* 5: 2, 1997, pp. 199–214

Questions

1 What is distinctive about the French economy?
2 In what ways has French society changed since the Second World War?
3 What are the main features of the new France?

3

The party system

The Fourth Republic

Although it had been hoped that the Fourth Republic would restore government authority, the reverse appeared to be the case. With the onset of the Cold War and with gaullist hostility to the new Republic the potential governing parties of the centre and conservative right proved able to keep the system in being but unable to effect major changes. In 1947 the Fourth Republic survived quasi-insurrectional strikes orchestrated by the Communist Party but its political capital was soon exhausted and it failed to win the allegiance of the French people. Voters returned parties to the Assembly and the deputies then decided on the many governments that came and went over the course of the Parliament. One result was that the link between the voter and the governments was indirect and often a swing at the polls (to Mendès France in 1956, for example) was not reflected in the subsequent governments.

The Fourth Republic evolved into a party system that Sartori (1976) characterised as 'polarised pluralism'. This was one in which a fragmented centre was vigorously attacked from both the right and left wings. In the late 1940s and 1950s the regime was opposed by the big anti-system parties – the Communists on the left and the gaullists (and then the poujadists) on the right – and was held together by a group of fragmented parties in the centre. Neither the Communists nor the gaullists, nor the poujadists later, had any incentive to moderate their opposition but they were at opposite poles of the spectrum and could only rarely form a coalition (and that would be negative – designed to overthrow a government or reject a measure).

The Fourth Republic was kept in being by finding governments from the centre parties and rejecting the Communists and gaullists. The various combinations of the centre parties proved to be very similar and only a few rose from the run of similar figures who ran the governments and ministries. Only the Mendès France government of 1954–55 stands out as decisive and determined, although the conservative Pinay government of 1952 is remembered for its

40

financial orthodoxy. But the need to find coalition governments from the centre led to the choice of leaders who did not disturb or threaten and who could bargain for position without causing disruptions. Authority seeped away as the Fourth Republic faced one crisis after another on a very narrow basis of support.

Eventually the Algerian crisis, for which the Fourth Republic had no solution, caused the fall of the regime. Most governments treated the Algerian insurgency as a law and order problem with the result that policy decisions devolved to the army and control slipped from Paris. Following an army uprising in May 1958 which the Republic was unable to subdue, President Coty called on de Gaulle to form a government. A vote of confidence in the Assembly was accorded to de Gaulle on 1 June 1958 by 329 votes to 224 and the last government organised its dissolution and the founding of the Fifth Republic. Fifth Republic politics was very different and the party system worked in an entirely different manner, new to France, around a left/right polarisation.

Fifth Republic politics: the first phase

One of de Gaulle's intentions was to reform the chaotic party system of the Fourth Republic. His hostility to parties was such that it was felt necessary to guarantee the right of parties to 'operate freely' (Article 4 of the new Constitution). In fact the Fifth Republic was as much a politics of parties as the Fourth, although the form and implications of the system differed. Presidential aspirants have to have the backing of a political party, the candidates become the representatives of the party and the party runs the campaign. After the presidential election the backing of the party is needed to win the general elections and to dominate the Assembly. Even in opposition the party will be needed to campaign and to organise eventual presidential bids. Parties have not been sidelined in the Fifth Republic and because of their importance the Assembly party and the outside party are both involved in presidential consultations.

Fifth Republic politics changed the 'polarised pluralism' of the Fourth Republic into a system of majority coalitions. There were two phases in the evolution of the Fifth Republic party system, both a result of the presidential effect. In the first the presidency was a unifying factor and in the second it was a divisive influence on the parties. In the first phase there was a strong bi-polar tendency as the two camps of left and right lined up behind presidential candidates. In the second phase fragmentation took place inside the parties and as anti-system protest grew outside the mainstream parties. However, initially in place of the fragmented centre, from which the governments were drawn and on which they depended for their support, the party system separated out into two competing coalitions of left and right around the President. This took some time to happen but it became the distinguishing feature of the new Republic. The Fourth Republic had been built to work with disciplined parties and had fragmented whereas the Fifth Republic did achieve the majority discipline of a modern European state. These developments were, in 1958, overshadowed by the giant figure of de Gaulle.

Setting up the system

De Gaulle had split the centre and unified the right. In the elections of November 1958, the new gaullist UNR polled 19.5 per cent and took 199 seats but was divided into the pro- and anti-French Algeria partisans. The Communist Party polled 19 per cent (10 seats), the Socialists 15.7 per cent (44 seats), the Radicals 8.3 per cent (32 seats), the MRP 11.1 per cent (57 seats) and the conservatives 22.9 per cent (133 seats), and there was also a contingent of 71 deputies from Algeria (fierce partisans of French Empire). De Gaulle, who was elected President shortly after, thus lacked a secure majority in the Assembly. However, while the Algerian war continued the public and the politicians gave their full support to the President so that the effective majority was far wider than in times of civil peace. De Gaulle's position was buoyed up by the continuing crisis and by the widespread perception that only the President lay between the Republic and anarchy or possibly a military coup. De Gaulle was for these four years, 1958–62, a 'Republican monarch' who stood above party. This position was reinforced by the four successive referendums at the beginning of the Fifth Republic. It could not last and de Gaulle had to rely on his own coalition of support, which would be, by the nature of his politics, a conservative one.

Gaullist hegemony in the right

The situation was crystallised in 1962 after the end of the Algerian war and the signing of the peace agreements with the Algerian FLN. In October de Gaulle's opponents succeeded in voting a motion of censure in the Assembly. De Gaulle had started in 1958 with a heterogeneous government including conservatives, Christian democrats, Radicals, Socialists and an African Democrat. In the first Debré government of 27 only 17 were from the Assembly and the rest were technocrats. Of the deputies, 8 were gaullists, 5 were Independents and 4 were MRP. This government was reshuffled on several occasions and politicians were removed and replaced with de Gaulle's own nominees, one of whom was, in April 1962, the new Prime Minister Georges Pompidou. In May 1962 the MRP ministers resigned in protest at de Gaulle's European policy. The Assembly was dissolved after the vote of censure and a campaign was run on the back of the peace agreement and the lack of any credible alternative to de Gaulle or the gaullist movement.

The result of the 1962 general elections was a rout for the opposition to de Gaulle and it had a bi-polarising effect and consolidated the conservative coalition around the President. The principal line of cleavage had ceased to be the

Algerian war and had become the action of the President's government. France moved closer to a situation familiar to observers of UK elections in which the voters in effect chose between supporters of the government or the opposition – an alternative government. De Gaulle had monopolised the conservative side of the left/right divide and created a coalition dominated by his own gaullist UNR party. On this side the main victims of the new gaullism were the Independent conservatives who were virtually eliminated, although one small section around Valéry Giscard d'Estaing (the Independent Republicans) allied to the gaullists. De Gaulle's party and the Independent Republicans emerged from the election with 268 seats (a majority), but the centre was torn between the gaullists and the left and remained a possible recruit to the government side (if conditions could be met). This was a defining moment in the Fifth Republic as it brought into being the conservative coalition that was to govern the Fifth Republic until 1981.

The left appeared to be the other victim of the new conservative majority. The Socialist Party, which had co-operated with the centre under the Fourth Republic, found its allies pulled to the gaullist side and reluctant to co-operate with the left. The main reason for this was the looming presence of the big Communist Party on the left and even in the Socialist Party there were hesitations about concluding an alliance with it. It did look as if the formation of a counter-coalition to de Gaulle would fall on the impossibility of concluding an agreement with the Communist Party that would not be too extreme to win an election. The impetus to an agreement was, on the Socialist side, the prospect of immanent defeat and a near elimination from the Assembly. On the Communist side it was the party's determination to work within the system and to seek allies – there was only one serious possibility and that was the Socialists. In the event the Socialists, Communists and Radicals all bettered their totals of seats but formed only a small opposition of 148.

However, the elections for the presidency consolidated the left-wing coalition. Neither the Socialists nor the Communists wanted to put up their own candidate and were prepared to support the independent Fourth Republic figure of François Mitterrand. Mitterrand had a much freer hand for the presidential campaign than a party candidate would have had and he was backed by the Communist Party, keen to enter the political mainstream, despite a pro-NATO, pro-European platform. A wide backing enabled Mitterrand to run a vigorous campaign and the non-Communist left was slowly confederated behind the new presidential candidate. In 1965, because de Gaulle was expected to be a shoo-in at the presidential elections, forcing him onto a second ballot was the making of Mitterrand as the leader of the left. In outline the coalition based on the Socialists and Communists, but appealing to the centre and floating vote, was in place. The 1967 general elections continued the process of confederating the non-Communist left and building the alliance of the left against the gaullists. The opposition made a further notable advance, although the centre was being torn in two by the polarisation of the party system.

This slowly consolidating bi-polarisation was disrupted by the 'events' of 1968. The gaullist party (reformed as the Union pour la défense de la Republique, UDR) swept back to the Assembly with 296 seats – the first time in the history of the Republic that a single party had won a majority. The Communists won only 34 seats and the non-Communist left a mere 57. In April 1969, however, de Gaulle, defeated in a referendum, resigned and Pompidou became President in June. Georges Pompidou, although de Gaulle's close collaborator, did not have the historic stature of de Gaulle and took some time to impose his authority on the gaullist party, but he also enlarged the coalition to bring in the centre parties. In 1969 the old SFIO Socialist Party was refounded (becoming the Parti socialiste, PS) and then in 1971 Mitterrand became its leader. In 1972 a manifesto was agreed between the Communists and Socialists and a split in the Radical Party enabled a small group of Left Radicals to join them. With the incorporation of the centre the gaullist hegemony over the conservatives was almost complete, as was bi-polarisation.

President Pompidou's conservative coalition won the 1973 general elections comfortably with 268 seats to the left's 176. However, the centre had been almost entirely absorbed into the conservative coalition and the left had consolidated its gains. Within the left the balance was shifting in favour of the Socialist Party, which was making more gains than the Communist Party. Things might have evolved slowly had President Pompidou not died unexpectedly in April 1974. This plunged the conservatives into confusion whereas the left, although surprised, united behind the candidature of François Mitterrand. In a hard-fought election the centrist candidate Giscard became the conservatives' choice and won the presidency by a narrow margin on a promise of reform and a rejection of the radicalism of the left. In both cases the success of the coalition depended on the effacement of the stronger partner. On the right the gaullist party had to give way to the centrists to enable a clear break with the past, a change with continuity, and for a more liberal regime to be instituted. On the left the Communist Party had to avoid provoking any sense of danger or menace and to leave the Socialists to the limelight. These were relations of potential instability.

Gaullism undermined on the centre right

But in 1974 there began a mutation in the Fifth Republic party system that has not quite ended. Within both camps the balance of forces changed. President Giscard d'Estaing started by minimising the gaullist role in the coalition and promoting centrists. Gaullists were angered by this displacement from 'their' Republic; they were still the larger force in the Assembly and were reorganised into the 'neo-gaullist' Rassemblement pour la République (RPR) by the Prime Minister Chirac. In response the centrists were organised into a new confederation, the Union pour la démocratie française (UDF), as a presidential force and a struggle for pre-eminence started between them and the gaullists. On the left the Communists had been displaced as the largest party of the left by the Socialists, who seemed to be reaping all the benefits of the left's advances. A fraternal war on the left also opened up with the Communists accusing the Socialists of betrayal and bad faith. This has been known as the 'bi-polar quadrille' of four parties roughly equal in size: on the one side the Socialists and Communists and on the other the gaullists and the centrists.

The competition between the two blocs was intense. It was ideological, with the nature of society itself seemingly at stake, and the intensification of the Cold War made the Communists' potential entry into government a threat. The conservatives were united behind the President in the urgency of the challenge and the expansion of the new Socialist Party occupied the space on the non-Communist left. The competition between the two blocs left little room for other challenges, be it from traditional conservatives or the ecologists or extreme left or extreme right. In the 1978 elections the left had been expected to win but the Communists had decided six months before to break up the alliance and went into the campaign bickering with the Socialists. It was the conservatives who won the election with 290 seats to the left's 200. But the internal tensions of each camp were to prove determinant – in both cases they got considerably worse.

On the conservative side the gaullists opened a war against President Giscard and the government in the Assembly which, while stopping short of voting a censure motion, was debilitating and undermined the conservative right. On the left there was a quarrel between factions in the Socialist Party but the Communists entered a sullen inveteracy prepared – if necessary – to see the conservative right win again rather than concede Socialist dominance. However, the Communist polemic backfired. This was partly because it showed the voters that the Socialists were autonomous and not in the pocket of the Communist Party. By illustrating the Socialist Party's domination of the left the Communist Party contributed to its own decline.

The 1981 elections were a continuation of the internal competition in the camps and of the confrontation of the two blocs that had developed since 1962. The difference was that after nineteen years of patient coalition-building the left now constituted a credible and victorious challenge. That the Socialists were the leading force in the left became evident in the 1981 elections at which Mitterrand for the third time stood for the presidency. There was no other credible left-wing presidential candidate and no challenge on this front was forthcoming from the Communist Party, which fielded its unprepossessing leader Georges Marchais. President Giscard faced three gaullist candidates all hostile to him and was also hampered by both a late entry and a lack of party support. But there was a feeling that – after 23 years of conservative government – it was time for a change, and Mitterrand, who had been a moderate Fourth Republic minister, filled the role.

Mitterrand's entry into the Elysée on a vote of 51.76 per cent caused no revolution but it was the beginning of a period of political turbulence. In part the

Socialist Party had promised too much (in particular it was unable to keep its promises to reduce unemployment) and in part uncertainty generally increased in the system. Parties and presidential candidates jockeyed for position and the ensuing competition made for changes of government and mismatches between public opinion and party political power. Presidential candidates could be popular in the polls yet unable to impose themselves on the party competition. There was also the rise of Le Pen's extreme right National Front. In addition the failure of cohesion in coalitions led to government changes whose reasons were not altogether clear to the public.

Mitterrand's dissolution of the Assembly immediately after his victory magnified the presidential victory and produced a Socialist landslide of 285 seats to the conservatives' 159 (the Communists held 44). The Communist Party, which had overshadowed the system since the Liberation, had been removed. It was easy, in the circumstances of Socialist hegemony, for the President to offer the Communists four ministerial portfolios. They had no leverage and took what was offered without, however, completely dropping their hostility to the Socialists and running several pro-soviet campaigns. Within the government and the Socialist Party fissures began to appear when unemployment proved not amenable to treatment and the balance of payments worsened as a result of expansionary policies.

The second phase of the system

The 'ferments of dispersion' were already inherent in the party competition before Mitterrand's victory but the fissionable nature of the party system became actual in the 1980s. The five years of the Socialist legislature from 1981 to 1986 were the point of change for the Fifth Republic. The Mauroy government finally crumbled in 1984 in front of demonstrations against measures to integrate the Church schools more closely into the state system. The Communist Party, which had become increasingly dissident, did not join the new government, which inaugurated a new style of 'modernising' and technocratic government under the young Premier Laurent Fabius. It meant that the Socialist Party was still dominant on the left but that the coalition Mitterrand had laboured to bring into being had shattered. The party competition from 1984 revolved around the Socialist Party which dominated the left, the RPR's hegemony on the conservative right, and the emergence of the National Front as a negative pole on the extreme right. Those years of 1981–86 were the end of the enduring and robust majorities that had governed France for most of the Fifth Republic. They also ended the years of presidential supremacy in which the majorities were at the behest of the Elysée. Majorities were returned but they were more fissionable and less pliable and the Republic entered a period of governmental instability which, although not comparable with the Fourth Republic, was in contrast with the 1960s and 1970s. The mainstream parties of the left and conservative right began to lose their authority and credibility as people turned from them and the anti-system parties rose in the polls. This included the ecologists and various 'flash' phenomena (like the ephemeral Bernard Tapie), but in particular the National Front.

Coalition instability

From inauspicious and unnoticed beginnings, Jean-Marie Le Pen's National Front burst on the scene in 1983–84 and exercised a divisive and sapping influence on the right as well as imposing itself on the national debate. Conservative politicians at first hesitated about how to handle the National Front. Initially it appeared, like the Communist Party on the left, to be assimilable with the mainstream parties. It was then rejected but continued to appear available for coalition and to feed its ideas on law and order and immigration into conservative politics through, in particular, the party activists on the right. It also united the left against a common enemy at a time when the Socialists had lost their impetus. The National Front's challenge was made more immediate by a change in electoral system from the Fifth Republic's usual constituency-based one to a partial proportional representation based on party lists in departments. This meant that conservative gains would be limited and the National Front would win seats. On the other hand the Socialists would not have to negotiate with the Communists for second round support.

The rise of the National Front to win 9.8 per cent (35 seats), taking votes from the conservative right, was not enough to prevent the right from winning the general elections of 1986. The outgoing government had introduced proportional representation and this limited the Socialist defeat as well as boosted the National Front's representation. Overall the right polled 42 per cent but their vote had not increased although they had 291 seats and a working majority of 20. On the left the Socialists polled 32.1 per cent and the Communists 9.7 per cent to take 251 seats. Although it was the first time in the Fifth Republic that a majority hostile to the President had been returned to the Assembly, the result was neither a clear repudiation of the Socialists nor a ringing endorsement of the conservative coalition led by Jacques Chirac. President Mitterrand was able to stay in office and 'cohabit' with the Prime Minister Jacques Chirac, who led a fragmented majority. Prime Minister Chirac had two problems: he had to hold together his coalition of centrists and neo-gaullists and he had to face presidential elections in 1988 but was lagging behind the centrist Raymond Barre in the polls. In addition President Mitterrand owed him no favours and the National Front threatened the conservatives from the right.

Haste, and over-optimism about the results they could achieve, led the government into mistakes very quickly. There were demonstrations and a general strike and the government split. The Prime Minister did not, as had been calculated, become the presidential front-runner and President Mitterrand's re-election had a look of inevitability about it. Mitterrand was supported by a

Socialist Party that remained well-organised and effective, and he was able to occupy the centre ground effectively as a non-executive President. Jacques Chirac also had the advantage of party support that enabled him to lead the conservative candidates on the first ballot of the 1988 presidential elections. However, President Mitterrand had an easy victory in an election which confirmed the decline of the Communists (their candidate polled only 6.7 per cent) and the rise of the National Front (Le Pen polled 14.39 per cent). The split on the conservative right was confirmed by the 16.5 per cent for Raymond Barre, and Chirac's crushing defeat by the outgoing President touched off a dissidence inside the RPR (a usually disciplined party).

There was a dissolution immediately following the presidential election but the subsequent legislative elections did not have the same unambiguous result. There was a high rate of abstention (34.3 per cent) in the first round but a determined response (organised by former President Giscard) enabled the conservatives to pool resources, avoid run-offs and put up a single candidate. The Socialist landslide of 1981 was not repeated and the Communist Party remained hostile to the Socialists. The conservatives polled 40.5 per cent, the Socialists 37.5 per cent, the Communists 11.3 per cent and the National Front 9.9 per cent. On the second round the Socialists and their allies won only a relative majority with 277 seats to the alliance of the conservative right's 270 seats, while the Communists held 27 seats and the National Front held 1. Although the government was unlikely to fall to a censure motion, the majorities for legislation were not (as they had been in the Fifth Republic until then) automatic. Michel Rocard's government reacted by trying to bring the centre parties into the coalition (some politicians entered government) and avoiding Communist blockages. As a consequence there was a continual negotiation between the government and the Assembly over legislation, some surprising majorities were found and there was frequent recourse to the package vote.

The Socialist collapse

But President Mitterrand's second septennate saw a further fragmentation of the party system. Michel Rocard's government proved popular but the President summarily dismissed him and replaced him with Edith Cresson who was not. In addition the Socialist Party began to spiral down into factional fighting as rival presidential contenders fought openly for the succession. Worse was to follow as details of party funding scandals became known, party headquarters were invaded by the judicial authorities and the party treasurer (later convicted) was put under investigation. Instability in the governing party led to a series of leadership changes but no sense of direction. Its one-time ally, the Communist Party, was in even worse shape. Dissidents quit the party or contested its policies as it clung to an old leadership and to pro-soviet positions even as the USSR itself was collapsing. This should have been to the benefit of the ecologists, who were credited with 20 per cent in the polls at one point, but they were also split and were so badly organised as to be unable to make use of their opportunities. This confusion on the left benefited the conservative right without their having to do much. They had revived somewhat from their drubbing in 1988 but had made no significant progress nor had a new presidential front-runner appeared within their ranks. In 1992 Mitterrand's referendum on the Maastricht Treaty had split the conservative right into pro and anti factions and had given courage to the anti-Europeans in the RPR (Séguin and Pasqua) and UDF (de Villiers).

The 1993 elections were a well-trailed defeat for the left but disillusioned voters did not turn to the mainstream conservatives – they went to small parties and the National Front. It was a general failure of the big political parties of the Fifth Republic, although this was disguised by a massive majority for the RPR/UDF, who took 448 seats out of 577. The Socialist vote fell, in the first round by almost half, to 17.6 per cent (53 seats), and the Communist vote fell to 9.18 per cent (25 seats). The ecologists' main parties were the Greens (Verts) (4.01 per cent) and Génération écologie (GE) (3.62 per cent) but the divergences between the parties deprived them of any seats. The conservative vote was divided between the RPR (20.39 per cent) and the UDF (19.08 per cent), while the National Front vote rose to 12.41 per cent (though it won no seats).

There then followed two years of further disruption running up to the presidential elections of 1995. Jacques Chirac, still leader of the conservative majority, declined to become Prime Minister for a second 'cohabitation'. President Mitterrand, unlike in 1986, did not intend to run again and was (although few knew it) gravely ill. The former Finance Minister Edouard Balladur, who had the support of the conservative coalition, became Prime Minister of a centrist-inclined government. Unexpectedly, Balladur's exercise of authority made him a popular Prime Minister and the conservatives' preferred presidential candidate. A competition started with his party leader Jacques Chirac for the conservative vote that further divided the mainstream right and the government. On the left the Socialist Party further discredited itself and failed to find a presidential candidate, while it began to be challenged by a revived Left Radical Party.

These trends came to a head at the 1994 European election. At these the anti-system lists led by Tapie (Radical), de Villiers (anti-European right) and Le Pen (National Front) polled 12.03 per cent, 12.39 per cent and 10.57 per cent respectively but some small groups also polled a total of 9 per cent. On the other hand the conservative RPR/UDF alliance polled only 25.5 per cent and the Socialists a humiliating 14.5 per cent (the Communists took 6.9 per cent). If the Communists, then still hostile to the Socialists, are classed as an anti-system party, the elections were a rejection of the political mainstream and a registration of underlying discontent. The Socialist Party leader Rocard resigned (ending a long political career) and the party drifted without sense of direction and without a candidate for the 1995 presidentials. In the conservative ranks the reaction was not so immediate or brutal but the anti-Maastricht right was encouraged and the persisting scandals of party funding also began to hit the UDF parties (and then later the RPR). De Villiers began to reform a Eurosceptic conservative right but the Tapie bubble was soon pricked (he ended in jail). The ecologists drew another lesson which was that they should join the left coalition and seek alliances with the parties of the left to win positions of power (or they would remain excluded).

With the Socialist Party out of contention for the presidential elections and Prime Minister Balladur the front-runner in the polls, Jacques Chirac's campaign took on a leftist aspect in the hope of staying in the race. This proved a successful strategy and Chirac's campaign began to revive. The Communist Party leader Robert Hue also began to campaign and was also able to profit from the Socialist Party's absence from the field in late 1994. In the Socialist Party there was no consensus. Some, committed to municipal politics, had given up on the 1995 presidential elections and others hoped that Jacques Delors, who was due to step down as President of the European Commission, would stand. Delors, no doubt feeling that the task of rebuilding the left was impossible, declined to stand and at the beginning of 1995 Lionel Jospin, former Education Minister and former Socialist Party First Secretary, stepped in. Jospin was overwhelmingly supported by the party's members in a ballot.

The Socialist Party: the soufflé that rose twice

In 1995, following the Socialist Party's severe problems, there was a vacuum on the left that Jospin eventually filled. But Jospin's presidential campaign started late in the day and the main battle was initially on the conservative right where Prime Minister Balladur was faltering and Jacques Chirac was recovering his campaigning zeal. There was a big rhetorical difference between Chirac's barn-storming and organised call to action and Balladur's slow-moving conservatism. Chirac attacked the 'social fracture' and the indifference to unemployment and flirted with anti-Europeanism, but he also wove in themes of a free market and anti-state nature, which were in implicit contradiction to his main message. The conservative right was badly split by the battle and the RPR party, normally outside such struggles, was also a victim. Jospin crept up on the two main contenders in a campaign that was slow to start and concentrated on more modest claims and emphasised 'realism'.

The first round was the main surprise. Jospin headed the poll with 23.3 per cent, ahead of Chirac with 20.84 per cent and Balladur with 18.58 per cent. This was a poor result for the mainstream candidates (and the abstention rate was high for a presidential election) but 'protest candidates' with no chance of winning polled strongly: Le Pen polled 15 per cent, the Trotskyist Arlette Laguiller 5.3 per cent, Voynet 3.32 per cent, de Villiers 4.74 per cent and Hue 8.64 per cent. The combined protest vote reached 37 per cent and in the working class these candidates polled 53 per cent. Chirac won comfortably on the second ballot with 52.64 per cent but it had been the lowest first round poll for an eventual winner.

The presidential campaign was the making of Jospin. It enabled him to repeat Mitterrand's pattern of success in 1965. Nobody had expected the Socialist to win but a creditable showing in the circumstances was regarded as a triumph. It was enough to make Jospin the titular leader of the left and made him the only potential President on the left. He was able to take over the Socialist Party, remake it and rebuild the coalition of the left around his leadership. In the year following the presidential election Jospin was elected leader of the Socialist Party and brought together groups to reformulate policy with an emphasis on realistic, deliverable promises. His new leadership, and the promotion of women, marked a break with the past and introduced politicians unimplicated in the dubious practices and corrupt finances of the Mitterrand years. Jospin, who was a well-known figure on the left, negotiated agreements with the other parties, bringing back the Communists and the Citizens' Movement (Mouvement des citoyens, MDC) and developing a 'special relationship' with the Greens. An election was due in 1998 and Jospin worked unhurriedly to that date.

Jacques Chirac's victory had not been followed, as was usual, by a coat-tails effect, and in the local elections soon after the presidential elections the conservatives made no notable gains. Chirac had nominated as Prime Minister his close ally Alain Juppé. Juppé's government also began to get into trouble and proved unable to convince its supporters after a brusque U-turn on policy announced on 26 October 1995. Rather than change Premiers and develop new support, the President redoubled his support for his beleaguered associate. The conservative right was being dragged down by the failure of the government.

On 21 April 1997 President Chirac announced a dissolution of the Assembly. A dissolution before the end of the legislature is not regarded as normal in France and this one was not explained. It might have been intended to profit from a window of opportunity (the polls showed a chance of victory) and to provide a working majority for the remainder of the septennate. But it was a demoralised and leaderless conservative right that went into the elections in disarray. The left, on the other hand, was not as badly disorganised as had been imagined and pulled together quickly to produce working agreements and agreed platforms. Two years of an equivocal government record and no effective campaign resulted in a rejection of the conservative parties at the polls.

At the first round the revival of the Socialist Party was already marked and the force of the National Front was evident. The conservative parties obtained, with 36.16 per cent, the worst results of the Fifth Republic: the RPR polled 16.81 per cent, UDF 14.7 per cent, de Villiers's movement 2.8 per cent and other independents on the right 1.85 per cent. On the left the first ballot results were unexpected and the total for the so-called 'plural left' was 42.1 per cent. The Socialist Party and its Radical-Socialist allies polled 25.5 per cent, the

Electoral sociology 1997 (first ballot) percentage vote

Vote	Extreme left	PCF	PS+allies	Other left	Ecologists	RPR/UDF	Independent right	FN+extreme right	Other
Total	2.5	10	26	2	7	33.5	3	15	1
Gender									
Men	1	11	26	2	6	31	3	18	1
Women	3	9	26	2	8	36	3	12	1
Age									
18–24	4	11	28	1	8	31	3	16	0
25–34	2	10	28	2	9	25	2	19	2
35–49	4	11	29	3	9	25	2	15	1
50–64	3	10	23	2	4	39	3	15	1
65+	0	8	22	2	4	48	4	12	0
Occupation									
Farmer	0	3	29	0	0	54	6	4	4
Artisan	0	8	15	5	8	32	6	26	0
Management professions	5	7	29	2	12	33	5	4	3
Middle management	2	14	29	1	9	29	2	11	3
Employee	5	6	32	4	10	21	4	17	1
Worker	2	15	28	2	8	20	1	24	0
Retired inactive	2	9	23	2	4	42	3	15	0
Religious practice									
Catholic	0	2	14	1	6	62	6	7	2
Occasional practising	1	4	28	2	7	30	3	18	1
Non-practising	1	10	28	2	7	30	3	18	1
No religion	5	20	32	3	9	12	1	17	1
Other religion	0	11	32	2	7	33	2	13	0

Source: Adapted from D. B. Goldey, 'The French general election of 25 May–1 June 1997' *Electoral Politics* 17: 4, 1998, pp. 536–55

Communists 9.9 per cent, the Greens 3.59 per cent and Chevènement's
Citizens' Movement 1.05 per cent. The outcome on the second ballot was a
working majority for the coalition of the 'plural left' with 320 seats to the conservatives' 257. The Socialists and their allies won 246 seats, the Communists
37, the Radical-de Gauche 13, the ecologists 8, the Citizens' Movement 7 and
others on the left 9 (see Figure 2).

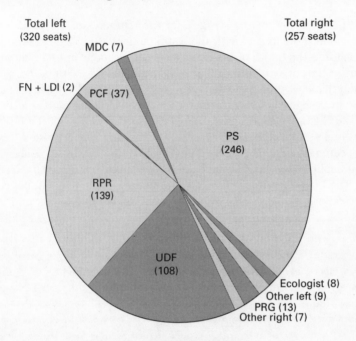

Figure 2   The Assembly elected in 1997 (577 seats)

Source: Le Monde.

In the conservative camp the RPR remained the biggest component with
139 seats to the UDF's 109 (plus de Villiers's own seat) and there were 7 other
independents. The National Front, despite staying on the ballot on the second
round to provoke 'triangular contests' to the detriment of the mainstream
right, took only one seat. President Chirac had no alternative than to nominate
Jospin, the leader of the 'plural left', as Prime Minister for the third 'cohabitation'. It did not look a stable coalition and was confronted by issues such as the
Euro and budget deficits, as well as long-running persistent unemployment,
which would cause it to fail at the first hurdle. But it persisted and proved both
enduring and popular, allowing President Chirac no real purchase on it. It was
consolidated to no small extent by the exercise of government office, which was
unexpected and welcome, and it was skilfully kept united by the Prime
Minister's collegial approach to Cabinet decisions. The government was aided

by a surge in economic growth, which also began to make inroads into the unemployment figures. Jospin's government thus survived, although it hardly incited wild enthusiasm either amongst floating voters (who moved rightwards in 1998 regional elections and 1999 European elections) or the left-wingers (who voted for the Trotskyists in 1998 and 1999). But Jospin was assisted by the collapse of the conservative right, which was in no position to offer an alternative.

On the right there was a struggle for the remnants of the parties and a dispute about how to deal with the National Front. President Chirac's RPR party fell into the hands of his rivals after the elections but he had enough support in the party to prevent it from taking initiatives without the Elysée's accord. Philippe Séguin, who had taken over as RPR leader, frustrated at this constraint, resigned in 1999 during the European elections and the leadership passed to Michèle Alliot-Marie. The RPR also suffered a split by anti-Euro groups in 1999. In the UDF things were made worse by the rise of the free market campaigners in the Liberal Democracy faction (Démocratie libéral, DL) and they split from it in 1998 over the issue of how to confront the National Front. The UDF, amputated of its free marketeers, polled only 9.2 per cent in the 1999 European elections: respectable but not enough to present itself as

---

Michèle Alliot-Marie 'MAM'

In December 1999, Michèle Alliot-Marie was elected President of the neo-gaullist RPR party. A law lecturer with a Doctorate in Law from Paris University, born in the Basque country (she is mayor of St Jean de Luz), she was a deputy for Pyrénées-Atlantiques (6th – Biarritz) from 1986 and an MEP. She worked in the private office of the Giscardian Minister of Education (Alice Saunier-Seïté), then became Secretary for Education in the RPR from 1985 as well as a member of its Central Committee from 1984 and of the Executive Committee from 1985. She was a junior Minister for Education in 1986–88 and then Minister for Sport in 1993–95, but cannot be said to have made much impact in those, probably suffering from trying to bridge the gap between the Prime Minister Balladur and the RPR's leader Chirac. In 1995 she organised a gaullist group to try to overcome the divisions in the RPR between the Chirac and Balladur supporters and contributed to the Juppé government's parliamentarians reporting to the Matignon. MAM's opportunity came when Philippe Séguin resigned when he fell out with President Chirac and then the Elysée tried to run the unimposing Senator Jean-Paul Delevoye for the RPR leadership (who owned to 'neither personal nor presidential ambition'). President Chirac's need for a compliant party was at odds with the desire of the RPR membership to attack the Socialist government and see vigorous opposition to its measures in the Assembly. A more vigorous opposition was established with the rejection of the government's bid to reform the magistracy at the beginning of 2000. Opposition caused problems for the President, who had supported the reform.

the hegemonic party on the right. President Chirac retained sufficient authority in the conservative right to maintain his position as the only possible presidential candidate but was not able to impose a winning strategy on the coalition. To make the exercise of presidential power effective a victory at the general elections was required and that needed a wider coalition of the conservative right and a strategy to win support. On the extreme right Le Pen's National Front split and declined in the polls, breaking the feeling that its rise was irresistible.

Conclusion

The nature of the party system, that is the interaction of political parties, their ideological positions, strengths and weaknesses and their competition and cooperation, are the determinants of political stability. It is therefore important to go behind the events to look at the basis of party system politics as a guide to the possible directions the Fifth Republic might take. The main question is one of coalition fragmentation given the recent past (and the rapid turn over of governments), but the future of the presidency as an executive institution is also at stake. There is nothing, it has been noted, in the Fifth Republic structure which guarantees stability or majorities and to that extent the future is open. In the 1990s there was a rise in the vote for the anti-system parties.

Anti-system votes

	1992 regional	1993 general	1994 European	1995 presidential	1997 general	1998 regional
Abstentions	28.30	27.43	49.94	19.40	28.79	39.83
Spoilt	3.20	3.65	2.80	2.20	3.31	2.68
Other extreme right	0.20	0.27	—	0.28	—	0.12
National Front	13.40	12.42	10.50	15	14.94	15.19
Extreme left	1.20	1.78	2.70	5.30	2.52	4.32
Ecologists	14.70	10.70	4.96	3.32	6.81	5.27

Note: The first two rows are in percentage of registered votes; the remaining rows are in percentage of the vote.

On the right the tripartite division into neo-gaullist RPR, centrist UDF and extreme right National Front has continued; in fact the right was further fragmented. Some developments are inimical to the consolidation of the coalition and others are not. The neo-gaullist party has lost its anti-Maastricht wing (around Charles Pasqua), which has tried to institute its own new party (named the RPF). It is not possible to say whether this has much chance of success or whether it is capable of acting as a spoiler for the chance of the main candidate of the conservative right, nor yet of whether it is capable of drawing votes from the pool of former National Front supporters. The National Front has also undergone a schism with the main cadres departing with Bruno Mégret (to the National Movement). At the European elections of 1999 the National Movement failed to make a breakthrough and must be accounted a marginal force, but the split clearly also hampered the National Front (which polled 5.7 per cent as against 10.6 per cent in 1994). These developments could, for the mainstream conservatives, be helpful: they could free a stock of votes and liberate conservatives from the presence of a radical threat on the right. The UDF has also split, finally unable to subsist even as an electoral clearing house, and the DL works closely with the neo-gaullists. It leaves the remaining UDF unable to rally the centre on its own and vulnerable to the bigger neo-gaullist challenge.

The right as a whole has been in a majority in the polls and at the general elections of 1993 and 1997 as well as at presidential elections and local elections. It has been hampered by its internal divisions and personal disputes, all of which have worked to keep it from power for extended periods. Some of the issues which have beset the political mainstream (like the Euro) have been particularly debilitating for the right and it has been handicapped by the left's astute handling of the French economy. (Growth has been to the advantage of the left.) The continuing occupancy of the Elysée by the RPR's founder is a significant advantage and it is a question of leadership whether the President can unite and inspire the conservative camp.

The left is also fragmented and it has shown a tendency to further splits even since 1993. There have been Trotskyite surges showing the vulnerability of the Socialist Party to a move to the centre (and of its policy in education) and the extreme left has shown no inclination to enter the fold. The Communist Party has been undermined by the Trotskyites (even in its citadels like the Confédération général du travail, CGT) and has been electorally vulnerable to other forces. The decline of Communism is, however, a long-term phenomenon. The Greens may have become the principal pole of the ecological movement but they remain a decentralised and unconventional party with a doubtful governing vocation. Socialist politics is still the centre of the left-wing coalition and is being rebuilt as a governing party.

The government of the 'plural left' has been the beneficiary of the late 1990s economic growth but how it will deal with a downturn is an unknown, especially as much of the left is – by temperament – more comfortable in opposition than in power. The 'plural left' has been held together by the responsibility of government as well as by its opposition to the National Front. How it will fare in the absence of the National Front and confronted by the conservative challenge remains to be seen. The 'plural left' has been astutely led, but its divisions, which had been set aside in the unexpected victory of 1997, had re-emerged after the reshuffle in 2000. The future of the party system itself depends on maintaining unity and on overcoming the continuing divisions of both the right and the left, as well as on the destiny of the National Front's support.

Summary

- Over the Fifth Republic the French party system has been mutable.
- Although at the parliamentary level the system has been bi-polar based on a left/right axis, the system in the country has been characterised in recent years by the fragmentation of coalitions and within parties.
- There have been major disruptive anti-system forces like the Communist Party, the Trotskyists and the National Front. On the right the National Front has undermined the mainstream or orthodox conservatives and on the left the Trotskyite parties have contested the supremacy of the 'plural left' and the Socialists.
- Presidential influence has been a force both for fission and for fusion. Presidents have to bring together majorities but the competition for the presidency has also opened up rivalries, split parties and divided blocs.
- The stability of the Fifth Republic depends primarily on its party politics and not on its institutions. Strong majorities repeatedly returned at the polls have given the backing to leaders for reform and political action in most areas.
- The authority or weakness of the executive depends on its ability to weld together a durable coalition of support. This has been possible in Fifth Republic France but nothing guarantees its continuation.

Further reading

Boy, D. and Mayer, N. (eds), *The French Voter Decides* (University of Michigan Press, 1993)

Cole, A., 'The presidential party and the Fifth Republic' *West European Politics* 16: 2, 1993, pp. 49–66

Criddle, B., 'France. Parties in a presidential system' in A. Ware (ed.), *Political Parties* (Oxford University Press, 1987)

Elgie, R. (ed.), *The Changing French Political System* (Frank Cass, 1996)

Frears, J., *Parties and Voters in France* (Hurst, 1991)

Goldey, D. B., 'The French general election of 25 May–1 June 1997' *Electoral Politics* 17: 4, 1998, pp. 536–55

Lewis-Beck, M. (ed.), *How France Votes* (Seven Bridges, 2000)

Machin, H., 'Stages and dynamics in the French party system' in P. Mair and G. Smith (eds), *Understanding Party Change in Western Europe* (Frank Cass, 1990)

Sartori, G., *Parties and Party Systems* (Cambridge University Press, 1976)

Szarka, J., 'The winning of the 1995 French presidential election' *West European Politics* 19: 1, 1996, pp. 151–67

Questions

1 What typifies the Fifth Republic party system?
2 How has the party system changed in the 1980s and 1990s?
3 What was the impact of the National Front on the party system?

4

The 'plural left'

Fifth Republic politics, shaped by the gaullists, seemed initially to form a conservative republic. From 1958 to 1981 the Assembly had a conservative majority and the presidency was in the hands of the gaullists and centre right. In 1958 the left was divided and the Communist Party was the largest component. This balance of forces inside the left had to be changed before any progress could be made. In the first place the leadership of the left had to go to a moderate, a member of the Socialist Party, and had to determine the direction and programme of any left-wing coalition. A presidential campaign made clear that, in the coalition, the Communists were junior partners.

Over the 1960s and 1970s the relations between Communists and Socialists were rebalanced and the Socialist Party, reconstructed around Mitterrand, the presidential contender in 1965, became the principal party in the coalition. The Socialist Party's presidential candidate became, in effect, the leader of the opposition and the shaping figure of the coalition. Presidential domination of the government served the same purpose and enabled a further sidelining of the Communists and the removal of their ministers from sensitive discussions. Coalition politics around the presidential candidate worked to the benefit of the 'moderate' Socialists and has enabled them to hold power for longer periods than in any previous Republic (1981–86, 1988–93 and then 1997–).

The left's long spell in power necessitated a further restructuring organised around the 1995 presidential candidate Lionel Jospin and his revamped Socialist Party. In 1993 the voters had evicted the left from office and it looked as if the Socialist Party might never recover. Corruption scandals and infighting had destroyed the party but nothing had replaced it as the driving force on the left. Jospin succeeded in bringing together the splinters remaining after the end of the Mitterrand presidency and rebuilt the coalition referred to as the 'plural left'. The plural left has proved, despite tensions and incompatibilities, surprisingly enduring, partially because, in winning the 1997 general elections, it returned unexpectedly to power. There are five components of the left-wing coalition: the Socialists, the Communists, the small left-wing branch of the Radicals, the tiny Citizens' Movement and the Greens. The dominant party is the Socialist Party, the biggest of French parties, but it is far from able to work without allies.

French socialism

The French socialist tradition is one of the oldest in Europe and can be traced back to the work of social theorists like Saint-Simon at the beginning of the nineteenth century. There were many ideas which contributed to socialism, including Christian socialism, utopianism, libertarianism, scientific ideas of planning and organisation, and of course Marxism. In general 'socialism' was an opposition to the unbridled individualism of the new industrial world and a conviction that there was a better way of organising society than through the competition for private profit. Beyond that there was little consensus and it was not, in its early stages, a confirmed ally of the Republican movement or of representative institutions.

French socialism lacked what, in northern Europe, was one of the basic supports for the socialist parties: the industrial unions. Industrialism in France was slow to develop and only small parts of the country (the Nord-Pas-de-Calais and Paris suburbs) were industrialised. Moreover, the French industrial world was suspicious of politics and the unions that did develop were particularly recalcitrant. Unions adopted their own brand of revolutionary syndicalism, believing in the general strike and union action as the way to promote their aims rather than political action. Unions were thus anti-political and revolutionary, unlike those in Germany (for example) which were the backbone of reformist social democracy. French unions created the CGT (their 'Trades Union Congress') in 1895 as a resolutely anti-political organisation.

Once again the influence of the Great Revolution of 1789 provided the justifying cover. Many socialists assumed that the route to a better society would involve a further (socialist) revolution. This strand became predominant in French socialism over the nineteenth century and it was reinforced by Marxism, which gave it an intellectual authority and backing which did not diminish until the late twentieth century. When other European socialists shed their revolutionary Marxism, French socialism remained wedded to it – at least in theory – and the Communist Party reinforced this outlook. The rivalry between the two parties, despite periods of co-operation, has been a constant feature of the French left since the Communists split away at the 1920 Congress of Tours. Reform, gradual change and compromise were therefore not such a prominent strand in the French socialist tradition as they were in northern Europe. On the other hand the Cold War and the hostility of the Communists pushed the Socialist Party into alliance with the centre parties in the Fourth Republic.

In the Fifth Republic the position of the Socialist Party changed. It became the key component in the opposition of the left and the only credible governing party (though others might be accepted as partners). The reduced tension in the Cold War made the Communists available allies and the domination of the conservative right by de Gaulle forced the left either to associate with the President or to unite against the new gaullist coalition. The Socialist Party might have been able to lead the opposition to the President but it fell to François Mitterrand from outside the socialist ranks to do so. This attempt at a regrouping of the left fell apart after the 'events' of May 1968 but the old Socialist Party was itself transformed (from the SFIO to the PS) a year later. Then, in 1971 at the new party's second congress at Epinay, Mitterrand joined with his supporters and became leader of the party. In June 1972 a joint election platform was negotiated with the Communist Party (the Common Programme) and a new dynamic was created turning some centrists towards the gaullists and completing the polarisation of French politics into left and right.

Although the coalition did not win the 1973 elections it was poised for victory and was strong in the polls. It offset the radicalism of the left's message with discreet appeals to interest groups, to the rising middle management and technical strata as well as the working population in French society, and it soon transpired that the Socialist Party was recruiting members. The party's rise was even faster after the 1974 presidential elections at which Mitterrand narrowly failed to defeat Giscard d'Estaing. Members flooded in, most of the remaining non-socialist left joined the party and in by-elections and polls the rise of the new party was confirmed. Party organisation remained relatively weak, though, and the party was characterised by factional struggles throughout this time.

This rise began to dismay the Communist Party and in the autumn of 1974 an argument started between the two parties of the left; the interlude of alliance between Socialists and Communists which had lasted only two years was effectively over. In 1981 the presidential elections enabled the Socialist candidate Mitterrand to outdistance the Communist candidate (its leader Marchais) and to demonstrate the moderate domination of the left. The Socialist Party won the general elections in a landslide with 36 per cent on the first round. In 1981 the Socialist government incorporated four Communist ministers but their party's commitment was conditional and in 1984 they left. It also lost the 1986 general elections and the conservative right returned to power.

What saved the Socialist Party was that President Mitterrand's successful 'cohabitation' enabled him to win a second term in 1988 and the dissolution gave the party a relative, but working, majority in the Assembly. But Mitterrand's second septennate was worse for the party than the first and it was almost destroyed by 1993. Factional in-fighting got worse and in 1991 the President dismissed the popular Prime Minister Michel Rocard and nominated Edith Cresson who was not up to the job. There was a series of scandals: some (like phone tapping) concerned the President's abuse of powers and others (like the funding of the party) were financial. Party headquarters were raided by the police in 1991 and the Treasurer was arrested and banned from political participation. It was clear by 1992 that the general elections were lost but the

President's appointment of another Prime Minister only made things worse when he was implicated in a loan scandal. These factors and the party's inability to find an answer to the most pressing problems of French society (unemployment, crime and growth) led to the Socialist defeat of 1993 by a landslide (winning a mere 18 per cent on the first round).

This was the position when, in January 1995, the former First Secretary Jospin announced his candidature for the presidential elections and was endorsed by the party in a vote. Jospin's stolid, rather than barnstorming, campaign proved successful and a welcome contrast to the style of the departing President Mitterrand. Jospin polled 23 per cent on the first round and came first, confirming the Socialist Party's domination of the left, and his honourable 47.36 per cent on the second round put him in a position to rebuild the party and the left.

Lionel Jospin became the principal figure on the left by stepping forward to run when nobody else could, or would (as did Mitterrand in 1965), and he remade the party as Mitterrand had done. However, Jospin had a different style from Mitterrand. Jospin was cautious, made a virtue of being realistic (no more extravagant speeches) and was untainted by political or financial scandal. But, like Mitterrand, Jospin set about rebuilding the party at the same time as reforging the alliance of the left with the Communist Party in the first place but also with the Greens, Citizens' Movement and the Radicals. Although still distrusted, the Socialist Party began to revive: a new generation not identified with Mitterrand was promoted and the factionalism rampant since the 1970s petered out with Jospin's domination of the party. The party soon repositioned itself as the principal governing party on the left and appeared stable in contrast to the disputing conservatives.

But the recovery of the Socialist Party had only just begun when the new President Chirac called a general election in 1997. Although the Socialists were not prepared for it, the party managed to pull together the coalition, felicitously named the 'plural left', and to work out a platform which enabled them to enter the election relatively united. They won 25.5 per cent on the first round and capitalised on their new-found unity in the run-offs to give them a narrow victory over the conservative right. Jospin had used the defeat of 1993 to renew the parliamentary candidatures and in 1997 30 per cent of them were women. Jospin's Cabinet reflected the new promotions, contained few figures from the Mitterrand years and wove in the representatives of the main coalition partners. It was a government that was forced to hang together in the face of the President's criticisms and the attacks of the conservative parties in the Assembly.

Policy

Over the 1980s the Socialist Party evolved into a party of government. It shed its Marxist, revolutionary outlook and took on a reforming and prudent moderation in its rhetoric. This transformation was aided by the collapse of the Communist Party and the Socialist Party's experience in government. In 1981 the assumption was that the economy could be reinvigorated through a determined expansion and traditional measures (of which extensive nationalisation was the main one) reducing inequalities and depending on government intervention. These efforts did not have the required effect and by 1983 a more modest programme had been implemented designed to help business to create wealth and hence jobs and to invest. The priority given to reducing unemployment (and inequality) was quietly downgraded and the balance of payments and monetary stability were given priority.

Socialist Party members did not reject the party's U-turn in 1983, but neither was it enthusiastically embraced. Most party members had assumed that there was a 'socialist' way to run the economy and that this was better (both morally and materially) than the conservative right's 'capitalism'. This 'lyrical illusion' (as it was called) disappeared in the mid-1980s without being replaced by any new vision. Conservative parties, defending the status quo, have less need of an idealistic (utopian perhaps) motivation than the Socialists, but the left has depended on this aspect to their political involvement. In some respect the rise of Le Pen's National Front made up for the loss of faith in the traditional left-wing outlook as it provided an enemy of choice which animated members and voters and kept the party and coalition together. But the lack of direction in a post-socialist and 'globalised world' is a problem – albeit one they share with other socialist parties.

The fundamental change in party culture and in the position of the left means that there has been a substantial shift in the party's programmes and in those of its presidential candidate. Gone are the long lists of measures and the platforms based on a radical challenge to the 'capitalist' order; they are no longer the forceful and confident pronouncements they once were. Thus the promises to move to a new form of society or to 'break with capitalism' do not feature in the platform or the speeches of top leaders. This has come about partly by design as the leadership of the party has sought to put its reputation for lack of realism behind it and made a virtue of straight talk and reforming (but realistic) ambitions. It is also a result of constraints forcing the left to look to the centre to pick up votes and a Socialist Party freed of the Communist Party's demands made from its left.

Thus the manifesto for the 1995 presidential election by Lionel Jospin was a modest list of practical proposals designed to show prudence as well as a reasoned possibility of dealing with social problems. In 1995 the main proposals were intended to increase employment and to reduce inequalities but the means were more technical than 'revolutionary'. They could have been accepted by a number of the party's socialist partners in northern Europe, although the accent is more state interventionist than new Labour in the UK. For example, the idea of a statutory reduction of the working week has long been a favourite solution to unemployment on the French left. Likewise the use of the state to control employment changes in industry and the use of public companies to steer the economy are unlikely to find favour. By contrast the capping of the budget deficit at 3 per cent of GNP and the freeing of prices from control were key dispositions.

Lionel Jospin's pre-eminence in the Socialist Party is greater than even Mitterrand's was at its height. There is no comparable figure of presidential stature and Jospin started his tenure and his government by promoting people who had little backing of their own. In addition the party leadership has, since Jospin's take-over in 1995, been largely free of factions. The party's diversity is recognised in the leadership but the politicians in top jobs owe their promotion to the First Secretary and not to their factions. In addition the party, chastened by the collapse of 1993, has become markedly more realistic. The party does not want to return to the old factionalism and unrealistic rhetorical excess. There is a left-wing opposition inside the party but it is neither as strong as the opposition to Mitterrand nor as well organised. This *gauche socialiste* is capable

---

Prime Minister Lionel Jospin

Austere, unbending but an unmistakable figure, Lionel Jospin is not the typical politician, but his public persona as the 'ordinary Joe' has been popular. He was born in 1937 and he came from a modest family, but he has the credentials for membership of the Fifth Republic elite. He was educated at the Fondation nationale des sciences politiques (FNSP) and then the ENA (1963–65) before joining the Foreign Ministry. In 1970 he became an economics lecturer at Paris University. In the 1970s he rose in the Socialist Party under the patronage of François Mitterrand and in 1981 became the party's First Secretary, a post he held until 1988. In 1988 he was Education Minister, the key portfolio in that government, and held that post until 1992. He was critical of President Mitterrand and the Mitterrand style of politics and objected to the appointment of Bernard Tapie (subsequently jailed) as a Cabinet minister. He became ill and almost left politics in 1993. However, he proposed a motion of his own at the Socialist Party Congress of 1994 which was critical of the Mitterrand style but set out an alternative vision of politics, and he re-emerged in 1995 as the Socialist candidate for the presidency. Although he polled only 47.3 per cent (14,180,644) at the 1995 presidential elections, he had come first on the first ballot and, in an election at which the Socialists were expected to be given a drubbing, this gave him unimpeachable authority in the party. He used this position to rebuild the party to such success that a party considered unelectable in 1993 won the 1997 elections with its partners. As Prime Minister he developed his distinctive style of straight talk without extravagant rhetoric and carefully crafted reforms depending on political consensus. Former President Giscard summed it up: 'in certain ways Jospin's style responds to some of the preoccupations of French people: honesty of behaviour, sincerity and modesty of approach and a certain prudence of government' (*Le Monde*, 12 July 1977).

of polling 10 per cent or so in internal elections but it is not enough to threaten the leadership's predominance. The social democratic opposition (Rocard and his group) has been incorporated into the leadership and Jospin owes much to the 'rocardians' and their politics.

The composition of Jospin's government was along similar lines. Unlike 1981 when the Cabinet included the main faction leaders, the party archons were not represented in the 1997 government. The big names were absent and only Laurent Fabius (who became Speaker of the Assembly) managed to keep a place in the new structure. Jospin's allies were given key posts and most of the government personnel, with one or two exceptions (like J.-P. Chevènement), were new faces. There was a clear break with the Mitterrand years and ministers owed their portfolios to the Prime Minister not to outside forces. Jospin's key allies, Claude Allègre and Dominique Strauss-Kahn, were made Education Minister and Finance Minister respectively. This government started well and proved popular but it ran into difficulties that necessitated a reshuffle, although this did not mean a big fall in popularity.

However, Dominique Strauss-Kahn had to resign under the cloud of a finance scandal and Claude Allègre's reforms ran into such serious trouble that he also had to depart. In the reshuffle Jospin had to turn to senior figures from the Mitterrand era, Jack Lang and Laurent Fabius, to provide the authority the government needed to survive the crisis. Jospin's second government was thus less his creation and contained more autonomous figures than the first. This altered the balance of the government from a group of equals in a team around the Prime Minister to a Socialist-dominated Cabinet. In the new Jospin government the sense of common purpose and teamwork was lessened and the direction was less well communicated to the public. Prior to the reshuffle the Prime Minister had seemed in touch with ordinary people but that empathy seemed absent in the new government. The government was not, however, able to enlarge its support either on its left or on its right, and the right remained nominally in a majority in polls and at the 1999 European, 1998 regional and 2001 local elections. In the 1970s the Socialist Party had captured the desire for innovation and the youth vote but had become, in the 1990s, a government party like the others.

DSK

One of the biggest names removed from politics by allegations was the Finance Minister 1997–99 – Dominique Strauss-Kahn ('DSK'). Generally credited with restoring France's economic growth as Finance Minister (and one of Prime Minister Jospin's closest associates), DSK was accused of being paid a £60,000 fee from a Socialist-run social security fund for work he never did. Edouard Balladur, Prime Minister 1993–95, introduced the rule that ministers under investigation should leave government and DSK, protesting innocence, resigned in November 1999. He was later absolved and returned to politics.

Under the leadership of François Mitterrand the Socialist Party moved out of its heartlands like the Bouches du Rhône and the Nord-Pas-de-Calais to become a national party with a presence in the whole of France – it even broke through into the Catholic areas of Brittany. However, it was always weakest in the conservative groups like shopkeepers and farmers. This position was almost lost in the lean years of 1993–95 and the Socialist vote remains fragile, but it retains that national presence in contemporary France. Relative to 1988 Jospin's vote fell amongst the young, skilled and unskilled workers, service workers, the unemployed and in the north of the country in Nord-Pas-de-Calais, Picardy, Normandy, Champagne-Ardennes and Lorraine. By contrast Jospin polled best amongst teachers, the non-religious, public service workers, students, middle management, and the 25–49 age group. Despite a long-term secular trend away from the Socialists amongst previously strong supporters, Jospin's electorate was the traditionally Socialist one.

But the defeat of 1993 has not been wiped out. In 1988 the party had polled 37.5 per cent and a number of its voters had not returned in 1997. These votes were missing amongst the under 35s (43 per cent voted Socialist in 1988 and only 30 per cent in 1997), professional people (45 per cent down to 35 per cent), workers (43 per cent down to 30 per cent), unemployed (47 per cent down to 35 per cent), Catholics (42 per cent down to 30 per cent) and the 'sans réligion' (54 per cent down to 35 per cent). This difficulty in rebuilding its vote is partially reflected in the bigger Communist, ecologist and National Front votes in 1997. The Socialist Party has not been able to re-establish itself in the Midi provençal, Languedoc, the north of the Rhône, the east part of the Paris basin or even fully in its strongholds of the Nord and Pas-de-Calais. Thus the party has been rebuilt but remains vulnerable, especially to the competition of the National Front in the older parts of its support. In particular the socialist electorate, which resembled closely the general French social profile in 1997, is split: the party obtained its best results amongst the white-collar and managerial classes (32 per cent), better than amongst workers (25 per cent) or employees (29 per cent).

Left Radicals

The Socialist Party's constant ally since 1972 has been the left wing of the old Radical Party. Their fortunes are bound up and, as they reach agreements not to run candidates against each other, their independent strengths are impossible to reckon. The starting point was in 1972 when the minority left wing of the Radical Party split away to sign the joint platform of the Socialists and Communists – the Common Programme. This breakaway faction was to found the Mouvement des radicaux de gauche (MRG) in 1973 and became the third very small party in the union of the left but never made much progress in organisation or membership despite some areas of strength. In 1981 its presidential candidate, Michel Crépeau, polled only 2.3 per cent, but the party held portfolios in all the socialist governments of 1981–86, 1988–93 and after 1997.

There was a short spell of Radical Party success during 1994–94 when the Socialist Party was in a state of collapse and when its space on the left was vacant. This was the so-called 'Tapie-mania' named after the former Urban Minister of 1992–93 and entrepreneur with political ambitions Bernard Tapie. In 1992, however, he joined the MRG and began to build up the party as a national force based on his exceptional popularity. In the 1994 European elections, and promoted by the Elysée to undermine the President's old rival Rocard, the list led by Tapie with 12 per cent came only 2.5 per cent behind the Socialists. Tapie's unbridled populism had success in the regions like the southwest and Lorrain and amongst the young, the popular class and the unemployed, and the party claimed 25,000 members. In November 1994 the MRG changed its name to Radical. But Tapie was declared bankrupt in 1995 and later condemned to a year in prison for financial irregularities. The bubble burst leaving the party bereft of leadership and substantial debts. It tried to run a candidate in 1995 but then rallied to Jospin's campaign and became again a support of the Socialist Party. It was again renamed the Left radical Party (Parti radical de gauche, PRG) and scaled down its ambitions.

Communist Party

Whatever the impetus was behind the creation of the French Communist Party in 1920, and many of its initial supporters seem to have been uncertain of the commitment they were making, it quickly became subservient to Moscow. From about 1923, after the Kremlin had removed the first leadership, the party was in effect a branch of the Communist movement responding to political developments as interpreted by the leaders of the USSR. During the depression there were many who supported the Communist Party because of its links to the USSR and because it represented, as they thought, a more just, equal and democratic society. However, the people who supported the USSR were probably not big numbers and the Communist Party appealed mainly to the old revolutionary tradition of Republican France.

The Communist Party's hostility to the war effort made it deeply unpopular and the party did not take an anti-Nazi stance until Hitler's invasion of Russia. But it then became active in the Resistance and Communism's Resistance credentials gave it a patriotic legitimacy at the Liberation, an attribute that it retains. During the war it had also managed to gain enough support in the CGT to take over and control the unions and it had a host of satellite institutions like clubs, societies and co-operatives as well as a widely read popular press and publishing empire. French Communism with 28.2 per cent was the biggest party in France during the Fourth Republic and it was also the biggest Communist Party in the western world.

With the advent of the Fifth Republic the political position changed for the worst for the Communists. General de Gaulle found support from amongst Communist voters, despite the fact that the presidency was not an institution the party supported. In the Assembly the Communists might expect to make their weight felt in legislation and in the choice of government personnel but they could not hope to win the presidency and would therefore be excluded from the main institution of the new Republic. The Communists proved unable to use the presidential election to gather protest votes (unlike Le Pen) and were unwilling to oppose de Gaulle directly in 1965 for fear of losing votes to the President. They supported the unity of the left and those in the Socialist Party (and outside) who sought an alliance of the left. When this became really successful in the 1970s it worked to the disadvantage of the Communists and they tried to pull out. However, the momentum of the coalition of the left pulled the Communists along despite their reservations and they found themselves junior partners in the left's coalition with diminishing influence.

French Communism, like other Communist parties, was committed to the Soviet Russian model of society. This was a centrally planned economy with neither private property nor a market and with total control by the centre over production, distribution and exchange. It was described as 'socialist'. This socialism was backed up by a political system controlled from the centre through the instrument of a disciplined, hierarchic Communist Party and the apparatus of a totalitarian state (including a secret police). Elections were bogus and the normal freedoms of western society were non-existent. The Communists promoted this 'socialism' as an ideal and its triumphs were continuously vaunted in the party press and propaganda machine. The advent of Gorbachev's reformism was not welcomed by the French Communists, who remained wedded to the old ideal, and the collapse of the Soviet bloc societies in Eastern Europe was barely noted in the party press.

In 1992 the Soviet Union itself collapsed and Gorbachev was removed from power. There was no recognition in the French party itself that the ideal had vanished or of the viciousness of the socialist regime in the USSR. It preferred instead to ignore the developments of the 1980s and 1990s and to continue as if it had never made a mistake. Communism was therefore not in any condition to make use of the Socialist Party's collapse in 1993. Instead of transforming itself, as did other Communist parties, it maintained a fidelity to what it called 'the Communist ideal' of an equal and just society. This is, as it claims, what socialists have wanted from the inception of their movement, but of course the Communists had been distinguished by their belief that they (alone of socialists) had solved the problem of how to attain that goal.

But the collapse of the Socialist Party in 1993 did enable the Communist Party to reorient itself. This it did by falling back on its patriotic anti-Europeanism and its defence of the welfare state. It claimed that workers' rights and French institutions were under threat from European integration and its supporters (many in marginal agriculture and declining industries) were reassured that their party was taking up their cause. This was an odd position for the internationalist party to find itself in but it was able to maintain a distinctive voice in the political system. The trouble with this new line was that it had to be muted to enable alliance with the pro-European Socialist Party and that was necessary to save the party's last seats in parliament and its position in local government.

It fell to the new leader Robert Hue, who took over from Georges Marchais in 1994, to effect this change in strategy. The 1995 presidential campaign allowed Hue to tour the country presenting a new face and a new message. His detractors dismissed Hue as a 'garden gnome' but this was cleverly taken up as a friendly epithet. Hue, a former nurse, did have a warm presence and portrayed a sympathetic understanding. His message was more egalitarian than 'state socialist' and he animated crowds with calls to fairness and justice rather than the utopia of Communism. This 1995 campaign confirmed the party's status as one of the 'big small' parties of the left.

Robert Hue

Robert Hue was a political unknown before he emerged (to general surprise) as the Communist Party's National Secretary on the resignation of the veteran leader Georges Marchais in 1993. He had been a nurse before becoming a Communist Party full-timer in the 1970s and rising up the local government hierarchy (he was mayor of a small town on the outskirts of Paris). In 1995 he ran a barnstorming presidential campaign which probably saved both his own position and the party from extinction. He faced a difficult task, one of remaking French Communism for post-Cold War Europe, and the party began to factionalise badly. He did bring about the acceptance of governmental positions and a governmental vocation and was a key figure in the coalition that won the election of 1997. He did not himself take office, but remained a deputy.

Little has changed in the functioning of the Communist Party. Though it disowns the term, it is still a top-down 'democratic centralist' organisation. Hue's own nomination as leader in 1994 was announced to the Party Congress in the old style and then voted unanimously as usual. Then Hue was able to use the leader's power of nomination to promote his own supporters and to sideline his opponents. The party still controls the CGT unions, whose leadership is Communist as it has been since the Liberation. But the difference is that Hue's party is more divided than the Communist Party has been since the 1920s. In the Assembly and in the federations recognisable factions have developed.

The Communist Party's rigid Marxism and devotion to the Soviet model of socialism is a thing of the past but the evidence of that rigid thinking is still evident in the party's approach to politics and in its programme. Communist proposals still assume that an egalitarian political will can supersede the working of the market and that a new order of society can be found to benefit the less well off. It assumed that a virtuous circle would create jobs, reduce unemployment and thus reduce welfare pay. Thus intervention by the state was proposed to increase the standard of living of the unemployed and the working poor through a variety of measures. These included requiring equivalent jobs to be created elsewhere before a company could lay off workers, the development of housing for the less well off and a protection of the French market. Meanwhile, doubling the wealth tax and a tax on share income would finance the increased pay-outs to the unemployed and higher family allowances, and relieve the debt of families hit by unemployment. In 1997 the Communists proposed to increase the minimum wage, reduce working hours, give workers the right to prevent lay-offs and establish a new jobs quota for young people in public services. The tax measures were heavily progressive and involved lessening the local rates for minimum wage earners, abolishing death duties for the lower paid, reducing VAT on necessities as well as imposing a tax on financial transactions. The Communists rejected the 'presidential nature' of the Republic, wanted Parliament's primacy recognised, a closer control of government by the Assembly and a non-renewable presidential term. On Europe they were willing to accept a European currency but wanted to keep the franc alongside the Euro and to stop the integration process.

The Communist Party is strong in the areas of old heavy industry in the Nord-Pas-de-Calais, the west of the Paris basin, the Midi Bouches du Rhône and the marginal farming areas around the Central Massive. It has been the representative of a shrinking electorate dispersed by social and industrial change, and the old working-class solidarity (similar to the mining villages in England and Wales) has dissipated. People no longer look to the party and its organisation in the way they once did and those who do are a smaller number. Worse, from its point of view, it has never been able to move out of its areas of traditional strength into the new and expanding industries such as electronics and computing. Hue's electorate is very much an ageing one of the industrial working class and the poor farmers.

In sum the Communist Party has redefined itself as the tribune of the left but also as a partner in the coalition government. These two roles are not easily compatible and there has been a leakage of the left's vote to the extreme left (Trotskyists) and to the ecologists. Communism retains some substantial resources. It is a powerful force in local government, it has a very big, disciplined and efficient organisation and it controls the CGT unions. These factors, and the Socialist Party's weakness, mean that it is an important part of the 'plural left's' coalition and its importance has been recognised with three government portfolios. However, it has yet to remake itself convincingly since the end of Soviet Communism and its main support is still in the declining sectors of the French economy. The party has been tempted to develop an opposition on the left of the Socialists, which would enable it to recruit from dissatisfied groups and retake the ground from the extreme left. This runs up against the now implanted extreme left, the alliances with the Socialists and the party's inability to change.

The left of the left

Competition on the left comes from the small Trotskyist organisations which have always regarded the Communists with suspicion and have existed for a long time. The most important of these is Lutte ouvrière (LO), which is known mainly through its presidential candidate Arlette Laguiller (who has contested every presidential election since 1974) but which is also an important force in the Confédération général du travail (CGT) and Force ouvrière (FO) unions and in factories. In 1995 Laguiller polled 5.4 per cent, a considerable success, and in alliances managed to poll 4.3 per cent in the 1998 regional elections. Alain Krivine's Ligue communiste révolutionnaire (LCR) had some influence in the 1970s but is a lesser force now, although still capable of demonstrations and pressure in union politics. There is also the small Parti des travailleurs, which mainly infiltrates other parties and organisations but is influential in the public service unions and amongst teachers. It is a measure of the decline of Communism that the big Communist Party is willing to engage in joint action with the Trotskyists. Before its decline it regarded them as enemies and to some extent still does.

The rise of the Trotskyite parties confirms the existence of a constituency willing to support the extreme left. These threaten to undercut support for the Communist Party and deprive it of its claim to represent the revolutionary left and the workers. Trotskyism also provided a destabilising dimension to left-wing and union politics in the 1990s. The extreme left reflects a vote which is dissatisfied with the Socialists and with the 'plural left', and disinclined to support them on the second ballot. The Trotskyite left has had substantial success since the 1995 presidential election and there was a joint LCR/LO slate which made progress in the 1998 regional elections. Most of this has been at the expense of the Socialiste Party and Trotskyism has begun to acquire an electorate of its own which will in turn enable it to make stronger protests about the 'plural left's' policies.

Ecologists

In France, as elsewhere in Europe, the ecological movement is a new political force. It is a political cleavage which has developed outside the traditional framework and has different roots from the class or religious parties which dominate mainstream politics. Other politicians have adopted ecological ideas but all the same the movement has progressed steadily since the 1970s and can now be considered a participant in the party system. Ecologists are much younger than other parties, with a good proportion of the post-1968 generation in their ranks and amongst their elected members, and with fewer of the generation over 60. In addition they were more female than other parties, the elected ecologists were educated to a higher level than the mainstream parties and they were also stronger in the professions (especially teaching).

Ecologist vote 1974–99

Election	First round (%)	National Assembly seats
Presidential election 1974	René Dumont 1.32	—
European election 1979	Delarue/Fernix 4.38	—
Presidential election 1981	Brice Lalonde 3.87	—
European election 1984	Greens 3.36 Entente radicale écologiste 3.32	—
General election 1986	Greens 1.2	—
Regional election 1986	2.4	—
Presidential election 1988	Antoine Waechter 3.78	—
General election 1988	Greens 0.4	—
European election 1989	Greens 10.59	—
Regional election 1992	Greens 6.8 GE 7.1	—
General election 1993	Greens 7.8 GE 3.8	—
European election 1994	Greens 3 GE 2	—
Presidential election 1995	Dominique Voynet 3.32	—
General election 1997	Greens 4 GE 2.9	8
Regional election 1998	Greens (part of the left's coalition) GE 3	—
European election 1999	Green 9.8 GE 1.5	—

Ecology, or the preservation of nature, has been a persistent theme in political life but it was not a potent one before the development of green parties. Ecology was not a particularly French theme and many other campaigners contributed to the burgeoning movement in the west of which the French were but a part. There were a number of events which enabled ecology to move to the top of the agenda in France. The first of these was the sinking of the oil tanker Torrey-Canyon in 1967 with devastating effects on the littoral ecology of Brittany. A number of campaigning groups sprung up after this, including, in 1970, the French branch of Friends of the Earth (Amis de la Terre). In 1973 Solange Fernix's Ecologie et survie party started in Alsace and then René Dumont ran a presidential campaign in 1974. Dumont's impact was not big (1.32 per cent) but national networks were created. These presidential campaign networks slowly extended and were consolidated into political parties. Progress in votes was slow in the 1970s, but in 1984 the Greens were founded to federate the ecological movement and soon became the best supported and most organised part of the movement. In the late 1980s the ecological movement split badly between the Greens and Génération écologie and it has a marked tendency to factionalism (see Figure 3).

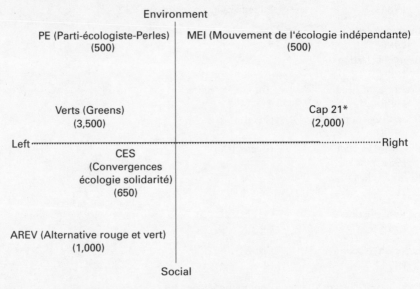

Figure 3 The ecological movement in France

Notes: The ecological movement can be arranged along two dimensions: the standard right/left scale and the environmental/social spectrum. This last indicates the degree to which social concerns (equality, immigration, women's movement issues, etc.) predominate over the environmental issues or vice versa. Not all ecological movements are on the left and some (important groups) find common ground with the conservatives and neo-liberals. However, the Greens – the biggest – are on the left. The numbers in brackets are the approximate size of the party.
* Named after the Rio summit agenda 21.

In 1993 the setback for the ecologists, despite high expectations, led to a change of outlook by many in the movement who began to see the necessity for alliance with the left-wing parties. The Greens became a left-wing party. After Dr Dominique Voynet's campaign for the 1995 presidential election the Greens began to progress at the expense of Génération écologie. In 1997 they polled only 4 per cent but their alliance with the Socialists enabled the Greens to win their first seats in the National Assembly and one government portfolio (Voynet became Environment Minister). The Greens hoped to obtain some governmental credibility by joining the 'plural left' and to overcome their lack of administrative experience. To some extent they were successful, although the Socialist Party had no reason to build up the Greens (as the Communists had built up the Socialists in the 1960s) and there were limits to the extent of co-operation between them. All the same both the Socialists and the Greens had reason to continue their 'plural left' alliance.

Even after government experience the ecologists failed to make much progress in getting local elected members, but they remained popular with the young and the middle classes. Yet the movement as a whole remained as fragmented as before, even though the Greens had become the main component. Their position as part of the coalition for the regional elections of 1998 produced mixed results. Their separate 1999 European campaign (led by Daniel Cohn-Bendit) was a success, however, and their vote increased at the 2001 municipal election campaign. The growing strength of the ecologists and the weakening of the Communists has introduced a tension into the left-wing alliance. The ecologists want a bigger share of the portfolios and the Communist Party does not want to concede anything. This leads to difficult negotiations at each election on the situation of candidates and Cabinet members.

It is difficult to generalise about a movement which is both diverse and decentralised (see Figure 2) and the parties are by no means united nor all distributed on the left. Hence most of the points below apply mainly to the Greens and their allies on the left-wing of the movement (they are mainly on the left but there are centre and neo-liberal ecologists). In the first place, however, the ecological movement campaigns for a respect for nature and this means sustainable development not based solely on the short term. Most ecologists argue that the determination to promote 'scientific' or intensive solutions to society's problems and needs leads to a deterioration in the environment and causes more problems than it solves. Motor vehicles come in for attack under this heading: they pollute, kill and use non-renewable resources (like oil). Intensive agriculture is also criticised for using harmful chemicals and reducing the workforce, while 'organic' agriculture is championed for being environmentally friendly and labour intensive. Nuclear power, which is the principal target of the ecology movement, might provide short-term expensive (and they say dangerous) electricity, but in the long term the problems of decommissioning are unsolved.

In the second place this condemnation of science, profit and individualism tends to be linked in the ecologists view to the unbridled economic expansion of both consumption and production which will lead to a despoliation of the environment. This free market thrust as it spreads and intensifies can only lead to intense competition and dehumanisation. Ecologists therefore propose a self-governing form of new economy not tied to exploitation and growth but more humane and respecting natural limits. Ecologists supported the reduction of the working week for that reason and promoted other measures to render contemporary life less frantic. The movement generally hopes for a new kind of politics of participation and decision-making. Ecological parties, in their ideology, reject the elitism and technocracy of the old-style parties, and have more open and less structured organisations.

The ecologists who are represented in the 'plural left' have matured over the last 20 years and have tailored their programme to electoral and alliance needs. Thus they have proposed to reduce the working week to 30 hours without loss of pay, to help create jobs in small communes, to replace arms industries by humanitarian industries, to establish a programme of public works and to develop tertiary activities. They call for the ending of nuclear power generation and the cutting down of the road building programme. Their platform includes such measures as proportional representation, referendum by popular initiative, a five-year presidential term, guarantees of judicial independence, reinforcing the power of the European Parliament, decentralisation and the right for immigrants to vote in local elections.

The Citizens' Movement

The Citizens' Movement (mouvement des citoyens, MDC) was created at the end of August 1992 inside the Socialist Party to oppose the Maastricht Treaty. Two years later it became a party behind its principal personality, J.-P. Chevènement, a potential presidential candidate. Its principal theme, linking disparate campaigns, was the strong Republican state. It emphasised law and order as well as state involvement in industry (and a touch of protectionism) and a gaullist foreign policy. The Citizens' Movement's initial aim was to create a 'third left' (the term was later repudiated) above the old structures but there was a triple rejection of free market economics, of the Gulf War political alignment and of Europe ('Germany decides, France follows'). Although opposition to Maastricht proved to be the Citizens' Movement's main theme, its European elections list of 1994 made no impact (it won 500,000 votes, a mere 2.5 per cent). However, the Citizens' Movement was sympathetic to the 'Republicans on the other (right) bank' and had a potentially wide audience. Thus Chevènement was supportive of President Chirac's first steps in resuming nuclear testing in 1995 ('costly in the short term would pay in the long term') and later of his Middle East policy, but if the defence of sovereignty was to his liking the 1995 Juppé government's economic policy was not. The Citizens' Movement repudiated the 'Bermuda triangle' of interest rates, Bank of France autonomy, and what they

saw as the restrictive criteria of the 'Maastricht-driven' policies of both the left
and right. At the 1997 Citizens' Movement candidates stood in 164 constituencies – they obtained seven deputies. Its support comes principally from the
intellectual elite and from public service workers.

Jean-Pierre Chevènement

Jean-Pierre Chevènement was born Belfort in 1939 (for which he is deputy and
mayor) and is an ENA graduate. Chevènement is best known for having resigned
as a minister three times and for having an anti-European outlook, a law and order
position and a strongly interventionist economic policy. He joined the Socialist
Party in 1964 and started a 'club' inside the party which supported the alliance of
the left with the Communist Party: the Centre d'études de recherches et d'éducation socialiste (CERES). He supported Mitterrand's accession to the leadership of
the party and was given the task of drafting the party's platform Changer la vie.
When Mitterrand was elected President in 1981, Chevènement was made Minister
of State for Research and (after 1982) of Industry as well. This Ministry suited
Chevènement's interventionist temperament, but that was increasingly out of line
with the Socialist government's market orientation. His demands for a new ministry in the reshuffle of 1983 were judged excessive and he left government.

He was nominated Minister for Education in 1984 and revealed an authoritar-
ian streak as well as an ability to pacify that troubled sector. CERES was replaced by
Socialisme et République in 1986, and in 1988, when the left returned to power,
Chevènement was made Defence Minister but resigned as the fighting started in the
Gulf War in January 1991. Chevènement, who wanted a 'gaullien' French Middle
East policy, accused the USA of promoting fundamentalism at the expense of those
local modernising nationalisms. In July 1992 the Citizens' Movement was started.
Chevènement then campaigned against the 'ultra-liberal' – as it was depicted –
turn taken by the Socialists and quit the party. But Jospin was one of the few politicians whom he was prepared to support and Chevènement became Minister of
the Interior in 1997. He developed as a 'stravian' minister – tough on crime. He vigorously acted to impose 'Republican order' on Corsica and passed an uncompro-
mising bill on immigration. During routine surgery in 1999 he lapsed into a coma
but recovered. In September 2000 he resigned in protest at the government's plans
to devolve power to Corsica.

Conclusion

The coalition of the 'plural left' which emerged in 1997 was not thought likely
to last but proved surprisingly durable. It was formed around the Socialist 1995
candidate Lionel Jospin who negotiated alliances intended to reach out to a
diverse electorate and to construct a governing majority. The old left of the

Communists and Socialists was no longer able to make up a majority and the new forces of the ecologists and the Citizen's Movement had to be brought into the fold. The Socialist decline had been halted and reversed by Jospin's 1995 presidential campaign but the party was still distrusted and too weak to govern alone (as it had done in 1981). French Communism was also a shadow of its former self and had been unable to stem its decline.

The advantage for the ecologists would be constituency agreements enabling them to win seats in the Assembly for the first time. They would also expect a place in the Cabinet (although there had been ecologist Cabinet ministers of both left and right before). The ecologists did not see eye to eye with the Communists on nuclear power and they held views (on hunting, for example) which did not meet the left-wing voters' approval. For the Socialists the ecologists brought the vital extra margin of support, they were new faces untainted by scandal and they provided new ideas. However, ecologists were relatively undisciplined, made increasing demands on the left and proved a difficult partner.

The Socialists' other allies, the Citizens' Movement and the Communists, also proved unsettling partners. The Citizens' Movement provided a technical expertise and in the person of Interior Minister Chevènement, a governmental experience. Chevènement proved to be a tough 'law and order' minister committed to state authority and capable of meeting the conservative right on their preferred territory and besting them. However, Chevènement, a serial resigner, quit government in 2001 protesting at the plans to devolve power to the Corsican assembly which, he estimated, broke the unity of the Republic. In 2001 Chevènement prepared to take his 'Jacobin' case to the public as a presidential candidate.

The Communist Party was not of one mind about participating in government but, under Hue's prompting, it took up the offer of Cabinet portfolios and supported the coalition. Communist Party strength lies in local government where it is allied to the Socialist Party. It therefore had a considerable incentive to accede to Jospin's leadership. On the other hand, as a government party, it was not playing the role as 'people's tribune' which had in the past enabled it to win votes and it was also facing competition from the extreme left for these protest votes. Hue's Communist Party vacillated between opposition and co-operation according to the political tide, and also proved an uncertain, although generally supportive, companion for the Socialists.

Jospin's ramshackle 'plural left' coalition, put together only just in time for the 1997 elections, proved surprisingly popular. It started in a genuinely collaborative mode and undertook a series of reforms which proved to be by and large popular. Jospin's stance as a modest leader of a team was also fruitful and popular with the public. It was, however, a government which ran into problems (there were resignations and street demonstrations as well as a petrol strike) and it was lucky to face a divided conservative right undermined by the competition from the extreme right National Front.

Summary

- The collapse of French Marxism and of the USSR means that the left is without a project for a new society. There at present is no 'alternative' vision and no clear ideological definition to the Socialists or the Communists.
- Since 1981 the Socialists have been in power for nearly fifteen years (and held the presidency for fourteen) so they are now a government party but have had to accept the compromises that government entails. The 'purity' of 1970s socialism has been long lost.
- The Socialist Party is dominant on the left and remains, despite its collapse in 1993, the main party of government on the left.
- 'Plural left' coalitions have been formed around the Socialist Party with Communists, ecologists, Left Radicals and Citizens' Movement parties at local, regional and national levels.
- However, the Socialists are not strong enough to impose their views on the other parties (though they are strong enough to be overbearing) and the coalition is a tense one.
- The 'plural left' is not cemented by an ideology and it is divided on some key issues.
- The small 'plural left' parties find that they have to assert their identities within the coalition and this inevitably means clashes with the Socialist Party and the government.
- The 'plural left's' move to the centre has allowed the extreme (Trotskyite) left to make inroads into the support for the Communists and the Socialists (although the ecologists remain an attractive force and have gained some of this support).
- The Trotskyite challenge is difficult to handle as they stand outside the party system and will not necessarily support the left on the run-off ballots.
- Government in these circumstances has tended to focus on immediate problems, without the overarching ideology that the left once provided.
- Defeat in the 2002 elections could undo the coalition. It might well leave the 'plural left' rudderless and deprive Jospin of a federating power.

Further reading

Bull, M. J. and Heywood, P., *Western Communist Parties after the Revolutions of 1989* (Macmillan, 1994)

Cole, A., 'The presidential party in the Fifth Republic' *West European Politics* 16: 2, 1993, pp. 49–66

Hainsworth, P., 'The return of the left: the 1997 French parliamentary elections' *Parliamentary Affairs* 51: 1, 1998, pp. 71–83

Hoffmann-Martinot, V., 'Grüne and Verts: two faces of European ecologism' *West European Politics* 14: 4, 1991, pp. 70–95

Mair, P. and van Biezen, I., 'Party members in 20 European democracies 1980–2000' *Party Politics* 7: 1, 2001, pp. 5–21

Safran, W., 'The Socialists, Jospin and the Mitterrand legacy' in M. S. Lewis-Beck (ed.), *How France Votes* (Seven Bridges, 2000)

Szarka, J., 'The parties of the French "plural left": an uneasy complementarity' in R. Elgie (ed.), *The Changing French Political System* (Frank Cass, 1999)

Waters, S., 'New social movements in France' *Modern and Contemporary France* 6: 4, 1998, pp. 170–86

Questions

1 In what ways is the French left distinctive?
2 What are the tensions between the parties in the 'plural left'?
3 What do the Communists and Socialists have in common?'

5

The divided right

There is no simple way through the maze of French extreme right and conservative parties. French political modernisation followed a different pattern from the UK and USA and the attitude to the Revolution became the dominant referent on both the left and the right. With the French right the 'Anglo-American' observer encounters an unfamiliar territory. The big 'catch-all' conservative parties that have dominated politics in most twentieth-century western countries have had only weak echoes in France (although their lack has been frequently lamented) and there is a high degree of factionalism. Thus, in viewing French conservative and right-wing parties, it has to be remembered that they often display unusual features. In addition the rivalries between the traditions on the right can be as intense as those between right and left and have sometimes overridden the left–right division (the National Front, for example, was prepared to see the conservative right defeated if its demands were not met).

French right-wing politics, as it currently stands, is divided into three strands (though there are bewildering name changes): these are the extreme right, the centrist (non-gaullist) conservatives and the neo-gaullist conservatives. The extreme right is represented by the National Front and by its smaller splinter group the National Movement led by Le Pen's one-time lieutenant Bruno Mégret. The 'conservatives' are parties in very close alliance and they cover the spectrum of opinion similar to the British Conservative Party. Moderate conservatism is divided between President Chirac's neo-gaullist RPR party and the centrist UDF and Liberal Democracy. The UDF consists of the non-gaullist conservatives (and they themselves are divided) but Liberal Democracy stands outside of the UDF federation. These parties are all centralised and led by a dominant personality but only the neo-gaullist RPR and the National Front have an activist organisation resembling other western European conservatisms. The centre parties are grouped around local notables and are very loosely organised. This continuation of 'notable' conservatism goes some way to explain why France ranks low in the table of party memberships.

The UDF, RPR and Liberal Democracy parties of the mainstream right,

National party memberships in the late 1990s

Country	Year	Total party membership	Membership as % of electorate
Austria	1999	1,031,052	17.66
Finland	1998	400,615	9.65
Norway	1997	242,022	7.31
Greece	1998	600,000	6.77
Belgium	1999	480,804	6.55
Switzerland	1997	293,000	6.38
Sweden	1998	365,588	5.54
Denmark	1998	205,382	5.14
Slovakia	2000	165,277	4.11
Italy	1998	1,974,040	4.05
Portugal	2000	346,504	3.99
Czech Republic	1999	319,800	3.94
Spain	2000	1,131,250	3.42
Ireland	1998	86,000	3.14
Germany	1999	1,780,173	2.93
Netherlands	2000	294,469	2.51
Hungary	1999	173,600	2.15
UK	1998	840,000	1.92
France	1999	615,219	1.57
Poland	2000	326,500	1.15
Mean			4.99

Source: P. Mair and I. van Biezen, 'Party members in 20 European democracies 1980–2000' *Party Politics* 7: 1, 2001, pp. 5–21

referred to here as the 'conservatives' (as distinct from the National Front), are traversed by personality divisions, ideological divisions and fractures relating to presidential contests in the past. Thus there are left and right wings, Euro-sceptics and Euro-enthusiasts, and faction leaders in all the parties and there have been since the monolithism of the neo-gaullists shattered in the 1990s. These can be intricate and difficult to follow and can lead to personalities having more sympathy with people outside their own party than within it. Thus the clash between the supporters of Edouard Balladur and Jacques Chirac for the presidency in 1995 still marks the conservative right, but Giscard sup-porters and Barre supporters are also still identifiable groups. The National Front, despite its pretence to the contrary, also has its factions.

The extreme right

The persistence of the extreme right is one of the features which marks France out as exceptional. Radical right parties took over from the Legitimist anti-Republican right in the late nineteenth century when a restoration was no longer a possibility but when there was still a force to be mobilised. The anti-parliamentary, irrational, romantic and military chauvinism once located on the Jacobin left moved to the extreme right under the Third Republic, starting, notably, with 'Boulangism' in 1886 and then the Dreyfus Affair at the turn of the century. However, at the same time a split began to develop between the nationalist extreme right and the Catholic Church when the Vatican and the Republic made peace. This opened the way for Christian democracy to develop, though not before the extreme right had exploited Catholicism for its own purposes.

This new virulent twentieth-century nationalism was in one way an exploitation of urban mass politics as it appealed to decisive action in troubled times. It was violently polemical, unscrupulous and combative, and unlike the Legitimism of the provincial aristocracy. From this nationalism developed a set of attitudes which had some electoral success but which could never be either a majority or the basis for a majority coalition. It was more a destabilising than a mobilising and rallying force. It seized on political failures and magnified them with debilitating effect for the Republic, thereby undermining the mainstream right (and the left to some extent). In place of liberty, equality and fraternity the extreme right put order, stability and authority but in a modern, virulent form.

If the Vichy regime and collaboration seemed to end the extreme right's political influence at the Liberation, it was in reality only forced underground. Its potential for disruption was confirmed in the rise of Pierre Poujade's small business protest movement which had 51 deputies elected in 1956. This movement was a reprise of many of the familiar themes: anti-Semitism, anti-parliamentarianism and negative rhetoric. The retention of Algeria as part of France became an extreme right-wing cause and reinvigorated many extremist organisations. The extreme right turned against gaullism's decolonisation and the hostility to gaullism has been enduring.

It was not possible for the extreme right to continue on the basis of imperial nostalgia and it had either to retire to the margins of political life or to refound itself. The anti-parliamentary right has reinvented itself and has discovered how to move on from its colonialism. The National Front was founded in 1972 and Jean-Marie Le Pen, who was already a well-known figure on the extreme right, was invited to be its president. Le Pen had been a poujadist deputy and colonial die-hard, and had organised the 1965 election campaign for the extreme right's candidate Tixier-Vignancour. Le Pen had the advantage of having rejected insurrectionary politics and was, in the extreme right's terms, a moderate face for the 'front'. He then set about confederating the groups of the extreme right under his leadership.

But in the 1980s Le Pen apparently rose from nowhere. In the 1983 Paris council elections Le Pen polled 11 per cent; later in the year in the local by-election in the town of Dreux the National Front took 16 per cent and won a seat. Then in 1984 the European elections enabled the National Front's list to poll 11 per cent and win ten seats. But Le Pen's National Front had been ready

Jean-Marie Le Pen

Le Pen, a former paratrooper and street fighter in extreme right gangs, has been in fringe politics since his student days in the Law Faculty in Paris in the late 1940s. He was a 'national orphan' whose father was lost at sea in 1942 and he was given a Jesuit education. His first taste of national politics was his election as a 'Poujadist' deputy in 1956 and he remained a deputy until 1962. He was an ardent supporter of the colonial war in Algeria and opposed de Gaulle's decolonisation of the country, although, unlike many on the far right, he never resorted to illegal activity. He was not re-elected in 1962, but was the motive force behind the extreme right candidate Tixier Vignancour in 1965 and imported American campaigning techniques with some success. There then followed lean years before, in 1972, he was approached to head the extreme right-wing National Front. He quickly turned this into his own organisation and dominated it throughout the 1970s while it worked the streets unsuccessfully. In 1983 Le Pen polled 11 per cent in Paris eleventh arrondissement and then in 1984 Le Pen's list took 11 per cent in the European elections. This was confirmed in 1986 when he led the National Front into the Assembly with 35 seats. Le Pen was not able to retain these seats (the election system was changed) but took a personal vote of 14 per cent at the 1988 presidential elections. Le Pen's abilities as a propagandist and publicist were not enough to bring the National Front near to power and he was not accepted as a partner by the mainstream right even after the conservative débâcle of 1997. Le Pen denies being fascist or racist and is apt to sue people who suggest that he is, but his party combines a variety of revisionists and nostalgics as well as ex-Vichyites and Algeria die-hards. Le Pen's music hall turns have lowered the tone of public debate, however, and in 1997 he beat up the Socialist deputy running against his daughter.

for the take-off when the conditions were right. There is no agreement as to exactly what these conditions were and a variety of factors have been invoked as explanation. The take-off came after the victory of President Mitterrand and the Socialists in 1981 which failed to deliver the promised economic growth or to reduce unemployment. Extreme right-wing parties have flourished during the left's tenure of power and one aspect of the National Front was its extreme opposition to the left. However, it also recruited from the disillusioned by providing a simplistic response to the economic crisis (protectionism) and linked it to a visible presence (immigrants). The mainstream right had already raised the issues of immigration and law and order, thus legitimating the Front's own rhetoric, but they could not compete with Le Pen in outrageous claims. The left was also ambiguous in its response. The Communists had themselves used the issue (famously bulldozing an immigrant hostel) and the Socialists used the Front's presence to divide the conservative right. President Mitterrand had assisted the National Front in 1986 by introducing proportional representation. Le Pen must be reckoned a force in the rise of the National Front. His political ability in

National Front vote 1988–97

Election	First round (%)	National Assembly seats
European election 1984	11.1	—
General election 1986	10	35
Presidential election 1988	J.-M. Le Pen 14.6	—
General election 1988	9.65	1
European election 1989	11.73	—
Regional election 1992	13.9	—
General election 1993	12.41	—
European election 1994	10.57	—
Presidential election 1995	J.-M. Le Pen 15.3	—
General election 1997	14.94	1
Regional election 1998	15.6	—
European election 1999	National Front 5.7 National Movement 3.3	5.7 —

keeping together the disparate groups of the Front is substantial, as is his talent for phrase-coining and for self-presentation. Although Le Pen has been a notorious brawler and displays an astonishing lack of sensitivity, it would be wrong to write him off as a politically naïve street fighter. Le Pen is in fact a skilled operator and a talented demagogue.

National Front propaganda condemns most aspects of the western liberal system: the free market economics, rationality and equality which the extreme right has always abominated. The National Front is a xenophobic movement that has developed its demand for the reimposition of law and order to an extreme pitch. Its politicians call for a society founded on cultural homogeneity and they have developed the idea that each 'culture' is entitled to its own territory but that cultures cannot be combined. Thus France is for 'French culture' and anybody who accepts that can live in French society – those who cannot

should leave. The Front defends the welfare system but for the French in a familiar form of 'welfare chauvinism'. In this manner it appears to be harking back
to a pre-lapsarian past when 'France was French' and when it was a harmonious and homogenous community. It has disclaimed the view that French
culture is superior to other cultures and holds that cultural diversity in the
world is natural and even to be encouraged, but crucially not within the same
territory. Incompatibility of cultures and traditions is the problem, according to
the Front, and mixed cultures can only be a recipe for destruction and disorder.

The National Front has touched on many other issues of popular concern
and has a multifarious appeal. Le Pen's plans to halt the tide of rising crime have
struck a chord and have been taken up by other parts of the political spectrum.
Le Pen has also proclaimed a forthright Europhobia and that, with the mainstream parties pro-European, has opened possibilities. This has been an important issue to marginal groups like farmers and steel or coal workers who fear
competition and who are willing to support Le Pen's campaign against globalisation, the tyranny of foreign capital and the destructive market.

In 1997 the National Front made impressive gains at the general elections
and contributed to the defeat of the conservative right by keeping its candidates
on the ballot for the second round. Its poll of 15.1 per cent at the 1998 regional
elections was another success. These successes were, however, electoral and the
National Front has found itself unable to attain power except (in limited cases)
in a few local elections. However, its strategy of approaching the moderate right
with the intention of promoting its disintegration was stopped by the break up
of the Front itself. In the autumn of 1998 the two principal figures of the
National Front disagreed. Le Pen, because of his attack on a Socialist candidate,
was disqualified from heading the European elections in 1999 and proposed his
wife to lead the list. This was contested in the party and there was also dispute
between Le Pen and Mégret about whether the Front should make alliances
with conservatives in return for support and, prospectively, executive and then
government positions. It was a dispute about the strategy to attain power and
not a difference of right-wing radicalism, on which there was little to choose
between the two. Le Pen maintained control and the main activist base but in
late 1998 Mégret quit, taking with him most of the middle-level functionaries.
It was the first serious setback to the National Front since it burst on the scene
in 1983. This immediately showed in the elections: the National Front vote
declined to 5.7 per cent in the 1999 European elections, its lowest since 1979
(Mégret took 3.3 per cent and his party's future was in doubt). The façade of solidarity had crumbled and the mutual recriminations destroyed both factions of
the party. Le Pen would have no opposition to a presidential bid in 2002 from
within the National Front but the party had lost much of its rising generation.

The National Front's support base has been closely examined: if gaullist
support can be characterised as 'the metro in the rush hour', then the National
Front's electorate was very much a cross-section of contemporary France. The
groups most resistant to the National Front's appeal were students and Catholic

women but the party has picked up significant support in most social groups. The collapse of the Socialists, for example, in 1993 led to the appearance of 'gaucho-lepenism' as working-class voters moved to the National Front. Hostility to Europe and to immigration enabled the party to make inroads into rural areas. But the National Front differs in one respect from the old extreme right in that its voters are masculine and secular. Although it has a strong Catholic Integrist section, it is not a rerun of poujadism or inter-war extremism in these respects.

The centre: non-gaullist conservatives

From 1978 to 1998 the parties often referred to as the 'centre' were grouped together under the umbrella of the UDF. The UDF started as a diverse coalition of Radicals, Christian democrats, Giscard's supporters and social democrats and it served to prevent the self-destructive run-offs which would have allowed the gaullists to profit from their disorganisation. It had been formed as a temporary expedient but its success in 1978 (polling 21.5 per cent to the RPR's 22.5 per cent) was such that it was continued. Yet the UDF was never given a solid structure; it was always a very loose grouping of parties and, crucially, failed to find a presidential victor. It eventually split in 1998 when one of its main components – Liberal Democracy – quit the confederation.

The UDF brought together the small-scale and rural conservatism based on the local notable (a businessman, lawyer or farmer) and it was not a mass activist movement (despite attempts to make it so). It included the social democrats and the Radical Party, neither of which could be said to fit into Rémond's tripartite schema of the right (bonapartists, orleanists and nationalists). The small conservative Radical Party is a shadow of the once-dominant Third Republic party but is determined to maintain itself in existence, although it is largely indistinguishable from its partners. (Its left wing is in coalition with the Socialist Party.) Radicalism does give a strong priority to parliamentary government (and promotes reform of the Assembly) and it does claim an anti-clerical inheritance but the practical effect of these commitments has been negligible. In 1993, its high point in recent years, it was represented by only thirteen deputies; in 1997 this was reduced to three. The social democrats were the small number of former Socialists who repudiated the alliance with the Communists.

But there were two main components of the UDF: the Christian democrats and the Republican Party (parti républicain, PR). The history of the UDF was one of constant struggle between the Christian democrats and the Republican Party for domination over the federation, with minor victories for both sides but neither gaining the upper hand. The UDF's leader in the mid-1990s was François Léotard of the Republican Party, who allied with the leader of the Christian democrats, François Bayrou. Bayrou took over from Léotard as UDF president after the 1997 general elections and in the Republican Party Alain

Mainstream conservatism 1988–97

Election	First round (%)	Seats (National Assembly) of 577
General election 1988	RPR 19.18 UDF 18.43	RPR 128 UDF 130
European election 1989	RPR/UDF joint list 28.87	
Regional election 1992	RPR/UDF 33	
General election 1993	RPR 20.39 UDF 19.08	RPR 242 UDF 206 Other conservatives 36
European election 1994	RPR/UDF 25.58 Other conservatives 12.33	
Presidential election 1995	J. Chirac 20.84 E. Balladur 18.58	
General election 1997	RPR 16.81 UDF 14.7	RPR 140 UDF 109 Other conservatives 7
Regional election 1998	RPR/UDF 30 Other conservatives 6.2	
European election 1999	RPR 12.5 UDF 9.2 Other conservatives 13.1	

Madelin took over from Léotard. The unstable balance was upset at the regional elections of 1998 when four regional presidents accepted National Front support. François Bayrou then demanded sanctions against these presidents. Madelin and his supporters then walked out of the federation and took their chances in an alliance with the neo-gaullist RPR (a return in some ways to Giscard's relation with the gaullists in the 1960s).

This left the Christian democratic party overwhelmingly dominant in the UDF and faithful to the strategy of autonomy from the neo-gaullists. Bayrou then refounded the UDF and started to build it into a more structured party, merging the parties (other than the Radicals) into it. But the UDF federation, lacking one of its main components, did not fare outstandingly well in the European elections of 1999. Running on a pro-European line, it polled only 9.2 per cent and was unable to make any impact on the RPR while the other small parties of the conservative right also rivalled it. Of the smaller components, the social democrats were absorbed into the enlarged UDF along with the Christian democrat movement, whereas the Radicals persisted as a small barely surviving party.

François Bayrou

François Bayrou is one of the most successful and prominent of the new generation of Christian democratic leaders: a 'passionate moderate'. He was born in 1952
into a farming family in the department of the Pyrenées and represented it as a
deputy from 1986. Unlike most of the other leaders he was not a product of the
ENA or Polytechnique but was a graduate in Classics who went into politics very
early in a teaching career. His first steps in national politics were in the campaign
of Raymond Barre and in the ministerial office of the Christian democrat leader of
the 1980s Pierre Méhaignerie, whom he succeeded in 1994. In 1993 he supported
the Balladur presidential campaign. Despite supporting an impetuous attempt to
amend the Church school laws, he was a well-regarded Minister of Education in the
Balladur government of 1993–95 and again in the Juppé government of 1995–97.
His ambition was to open out Christian democracy to make it the dominant force
in French conservatism and he was able to begin that process when he dissolved
the Force démocrate into the UDF in 1999 and took the leadership.

Alain Madelin

Alain Madelin is one of the few politicians of modest origins (a working-class,
Communist family), and entered politics through the student activism of the Paris
University Law faculty. After a brief career in the extreme-right Occident, Alain
Madelin became an enthusiast for the ideas of the free market and a member of
Giscard's Independent Republican Party. He rose rapidly, being elected deputy for
Redon in 1978, and then made a mark in the first legislature of Mitterrand's septennate as a determined opponent of the left. He was Minister for Industry in
1986–88, a position that he saw as a contradiction. In 1988 he supported the campaign of Jacques Chirac and did so again in 1995, providing the free market slant.
He was made Budget Minister in the government of 1995 but left the government
after only two months disillusioned at its lack of enthusiasm for his ideas. In
response he set up a series of 'think tanks' promoting the ideas of the free market
right. In 1997, after the conservative election débâcle, he became leader of the
Republican Party, rebaptised as Liberal Democracy, and turned it into the nearest
thing to a French 'Reaganite' party. In doing so he fell out with the other UDF leaders
and took his party out of the confederation and into an alliance with the gaullists.

The Republican Party/Liberal Democracy

The tradition Rémond refers to as 'orléanist' is the moderate, parliamentary
and constitutional right and broadly fits the current incarnation of the
Republican Party – Liberal Democracy. It is Catholic but parliamentary and
Republican and business-oriented. Fifth Republic politics proved unfavourable

to the old conservative Independents, who were split on most issues and could not agree on the key ones. However, a small group, Finance Minister Giscard's Fédération nationale des républicains independents (FNRI), prospered both in votes, as a part of the gaullist coalition, and in government. This was Giscard's famous 'Oui . . . mais' attitude to gaullism. Giscard managed to associate the party with the gaullists' success (notably economic) while dissociating it from the President's anti-Americanism and anti-Europeanism and from de Gaulle's autocratic manner. Giscard had developed a different approach from that of the gaullist party, one which was more liberal in social matters (like birth control and abortion) but also less interventionist, more *laissez-faire* and reformist, than President Pompidou was.

When Giscard d'Estaing won the presidential elections in 1974 the FNRI was one of the principal beneficiaries. In 1977 the party was reorganised and given a new name (Republican Party) but it was inadequate as a presidential party and when the President's liberal reforms were being promoted it dragged its feet, including, as it did, a large component of authoritarian and traditional conservatives. It did, however, still serve as a recruiting machine for a young generation of conservative politicians and they also moved it in a more free market direction. President Giscard and Prime Minister Barre had started to liberalise the French economy and this was broadly in keeping with the government's thrust.

In the 1980s a young group (the 'bande a Léo') emerged as a new force on the political scene, advocating what was then a novel free market economics and deregulation. However, the consummation of this strategy took place not in the 1980s but in 1997 and not under Léotard but under Alain Madelin, who renamed the party Liberal Democracy and further accentuated its free market approach (to the extent that Léotard joined the UDF). Its free market swing was in keeping with what Madelin had always stood for and made it the *laissez-faire* party of the conservative right. Although it is original, it is not clear that there exists an exploitable space for this party in contemporary France where conservatism has always been attached to state intervention. There are very few figures associated with this political position and those that were have been isolated (like Paul Reynaud) or eccentric. However, to this *laissez-faire* appeal has been added an anti-corruption message led by, amongst others, the reforming Judge Thierry Jean-Pierre.

Yet Liberal Democracy remains a mainly rural and notable organisation with a more secular outlook than Christian democracy although it is still dominated by Catholic notables. Its predecessors always had a free market wing but in Liberal Democracy it became dominant as a result of Alain Madelin's presence. Madelin had made a name for himself on the French political stage by promoting *laissez-faire* solutions to economic and social problems through, amongst other things, his club Idées-action. Madelin, who was briefly a minister in 1986–88 and then again in 1995 has made this neo-liberal ideology central to his approach and to a presidential campaign.

Christian democracy

Christian democracy has a long pedigree in France although the country has not been very receptive to the party and it had only a brief period of domination (at the Liberation). Its roots go back to the liberal Catholicism of the nineteenth century. Christian democracy was derived from the papal encyclicals at the end of the nineteenth century. The philosophy had a more positive attitude to the state (which it saw as the instrument of the community) than did liberalism or *laissez-faire*. At the same time Christian trade unions and political education were encouraged (with some small success), though not 'class war', which was deprecated. Because the Church defended private property and market economics and, where appropriate, non-intervention, the advance of socialism and then communism led to an interpretation of Christian democracy as right-wing. It was, however, torn between right and left wings and many of its leaders were more left-leaning than its voters were. The big issue with which Christian democracy is identified is European integration and that, although still a feature of the movement's programme, is less distinctive amongst centre parties than it once was.

There were advances in party organisation and philosophy in the twentieth century and the Christian democrats were a significant – though small – presence in the Third Republic. This small beginning enabled the Christian democrats in the Resistance to organise the new political party – Mouvement républicain populaire (MRP) – in November 1944. MRP had a dramatic success at the national elections after the Liberation, mainly because there was no competition on the right, and some success in the local elections of April 1945; in June 1946 it was (for four months) the biggest party in France with 28.2 per cent. MRP politicians were influential in forming the politics of the Fourth Republic and very important in the creation of European institutions at all levels. One of the features of French politics was the lack of a big Christian democratic party as existed in Italy or Germany. One reason must be because the party found itself rivalled by de Gaulle's RPF as a moderate centre party and as a bulwark against the Communists. After 1947 MRP lost members and voters to the new gaullist party with the result that it had fallen to 11.5 per cent in 1956.

In the Fifth Republic gaullism further squeezed Christian democracy but it had a remarkable renaissance under the impetus of the 1965 election campaign by Jean Lecanuet. Lecanuet, attacking gaullist authoritarianism and defending Europe, polled 15.9 per cent and in the 1967 general elections 14.1 per cent. Lecanuet used the opportunity to build a new party, the Democratic Centre (Centre démocrate, CD), but found it unable to create a big enough centre space for itself. President Pompidou, looking to the future, increasingly brought some of the Christian democrats into the gaullist presidential coalition and by 1973 the movement as a whole was a participant in all but name. It hoped to be able to move the President in a more pro-Atlantic direction, to step

Mouvement républicain populaire (MRP)

MRP was a growth from the resistance organisations and the long line of Christian democratic movements that were lively but not influential before the Second World War. It represented a 'third way' between the free market liberals and the state-oriented socialists, supporting a market system but leaning to welfare state keynesianism in its social outlook. It became identified with the cause of European integration in which it played a big part in the early years. It emerged at the Liberation as a new force and was untainted by the collapse of the Third Republic and Vichy France, polling 23.9 per cent in 1945 and then in June 1946 becoming the biggest party in France with 28.2 per cent. It lost its top position in November 1946 to the Communists when its vote fell to 25.9 per cent. It broke with de Gaulle, who it had been identified with, and then became one of the principal props of the régime, and participated in most of the governments of the Fourth Republic, keeping both the Communists and the gaullists at bay. However, the gaullists undercut the MRP's electoral support in particular at the municipal elections of November 1947 and that deprived the MRP of the ability to consolidate support at local level. In 1956 support fell to 12.6 per cent and the MRP was torn between left and right wings and by decolonisation. It supported de Gaulle's return to power and joined the first government of the Fifth Republic. However, it did not favour the concentration of power and it was opposed to de Gaulle's European policy and went into opposition. It joined Jean Lecanuet's Centre démocrate (CD) in 1966 and Force démocrate (FD) is in direct descent from that party.

up the pace of European integration and to incorporate a more active social policy into gaullism.

In 1974 Giscard's victory in the presidential elections opened out new vistas for the Christian democrats and they became prominent in government. Christian democracy still, however, remained confined to a relatively small audience in rural Catholic France. Without the ability to reach out beyond a core support it was destined to remain a small – if important – grouping.

In 1995 it was recognised that Christian democracy needed to be given a new impetus and new leadership. Its new leader, François Bayrou, was a product of the Christian democratic movement but not from one of its traditional political dynasties. Christian democracy has been dependent on rural notables and its leaders are often the sons and daughters of previous leaders. However, the problem for the movement remains one of finding a way to dominate the mainstream of conservatism. Bayrou's Europeanism enabled the UDF to keep its share of the vote in the European elections but it is far from clear that the same stance can pay off in other elections. As the leader of the new UDF Bayrou claims to offer the only credible 'third way' between 'rampant capitalism' and state socialism but his social and economic outlook is at odds with the UDF's essentially conservative electorate. Bayrou was a deputy until 1999 but as leader of the UDF European list he opted to sit in Strasbourg in preference to Paris and is thus absent from the Assembly group's deliberations. Bayrou was Education Minister in the Balladur government of 1993–95 but he is not well known to the general public. When questioned in 2001 22 per cent of voters had no view of the party and 23 per cent could not place it on the political spectrum; 30 per cent had no conception of Bayrou's message (only 3 per cent had no view of the Socialist Party). Worse, the same survey indicated a lack of UDF legitimacy on the conservative right: 62 per cent of conservative voters thought the UDF ought to support Jacques Chirac on the first ballot and only 23 per cent believed Bayrou should run. Some 54 per cent of UDF sympathisers thought that the UDF should support Jacques Chirac on the first round and only 35 per cent wanted a UDF candidate. Although the UDF has tried to increase its presence on the ground its membership is probably only about 66,000 it has 68 deputies, 80 senators (in 3 groups) and 8 MEPs.

François Bayrou dominates the UDF but not sufficiently to eliminate its factions. There is a four-way split but the main divisions are between Bayrou's supporters, a free market wing (associated with François Léotard) and a large number of deputies around the figure of Dr P. Douste-Blazy (mayor of Toulouse). Blazy is close to President Chirac and speaks for those who do not want a separate UDF presidential candidate.

Neo-gaullism

Heroic leadership is another feature of French politics. Both gaullism and bonapartism, which some observers see as similar, were the result of crisis conditions, which engendered a determination to restore order and focused on charismatic leaders. De Gaulle's view was not narrowly partisan and the vast gaullist movement reached out beyond the normal electorate of the conservative right, repudiated the existing regime, deplored the domination of France by the political parties and political class, and called for a new constitution. Gaullism, like bonapartism, favoured a strong and centralised state which actively intervened to modernise and to promote the national interest. The two approaches also resembled each other in their nationalism and foreign preoccupations: gaullism emphasised the notion of 'grandeur' and bonapartism that of 'glory'. Gaullism comes close to bonapartism in its advocacy of the use of the referendum, the direct election of the President and the creation of the executive presidency.

But they are not the same. De Gaulle restored the Republic (on two occasions) and did not, like Napoleon III, abolish it. And the Fifth Republic did not inaugurate a dictatorship. Moreover, de Gaulle's anti-parliamentary rhetoric did not lead to the elimination of parties or of the extinction of representative institutions, and gaullism had a strong social side as well as a distrust of unregulated market capitalism.

De Gaulle's first political party was the Rassemblement du peuple français (RPF) founded in April 1947. De Gaulle wound up the RPF in 1955 and retired to his home in Colombey-les-Deux-Eglises to write his memoirs. However, the unexpected brought de Gaulle back. After a military coup in Algeria in May 1958 the government of the Fourth Republic, unable to impose its authority on the colony, made way for de Gaulle. In 1958 de Gaulle's new political party, the Union pour la nouvelle République (UNR), polled 19.5 per cent and took 199 seats. It was this party which, in its various make-overs, was the central spine of the conservative coalition which governed France from 1958 to 1981. Other parties of the right have had to place themselves in relation to it. Gaullism stared with a wide appeal but after 1962 became a more conventional conservative formation, and, although it dominated the other parties of the right, de Gaulle was forced down from the heights into the political arena along with other politicians.

In 1967 the gaullists and their allies won the general election but had only a narrow margin over their opponents from the centre and left. They began the search for allies in the centre, a process interrupted by the 'events' of May 1968. The student troubles were to reveal a gap between the distant and haughty President and the public, and for a few days it looked as if the regime itself might be a victim to the streets as was the Fourth Republic. However, the 'party of order' swept back to power in hastily called general elections in June with a record 294 seats out of 485. De Gaulle, severely damaged by the 'events', lost the referendum in April the following year and resigned. De Gaulle's successor at the head of the movement, President Pompidou, imposed a more cautious conservatism.

Modern neo-gaullism emerged in the 1970s in unpropitious circumstances after the presidential victory of Giscard d'Estaing in 1974. A movement which had been devoted to one man found itself without a leader and at considerable odds about which direction to take – to support the President or to strike out on its own. General de Gaulle's close associates had been routed and were not part of the new President's system. While gaullism drifted, Giscard's new Prime Minister Jacques Chirac quickly organised his supporters, sidelined the old guard and took over the gaullist party. He was fully in charge of the gaullist party before he resigned as Prime Minister in 1976.

Thus the gaullist party became the neo-gaullist Rassemblement pour la République (RPR) in 1976 and was a vehicle to put Jacques Chirac into the Elysée. It showed, on Chirac's take-over, a new dynamism and immediately increased its activist base to some 276,000 members. Its vocation was to become a mass party and it put great effort into recruitment and mobilisation of its membership with rallies and meetings. Jacques Chirac launched the new RPR with a speech at Egletons which depicted a non-partisan 'rally' of all the French people and a defender of the traditional values of gaullism through a French 'Labourism'. Its inaugural meeting was held in Paris in December 1976 and Jacques Chirac was elected its president by its assizes by 96 per cent. In 1977 Chirac became mayor of Paris. By the end of the 1970s the party was claiming 760,000 members.

President Jacques Chirac

Jacques Chirac has been one of the leading conservative politicians for a generation. He was born in Paris, but his family came from the Corrèze where he won a
seat in the 1967 general elections. He had climbed the ladder into the elite through
the Institut d'etudes politiqes and then the ENA before being brought into the
government Secretariat by Prime Minister Georges Pompidou and then made
Secretary of State for Employment in 1967. He was then made Budget Minister,
Minister for Relations with Parliament, Agriculture Minister and then, just before
Pompidou's death, Minister of the Interior in 1974. He was the organiser of gaullist support for Giscard d'Estaing in the 1974 presidential elections and was
rewarded with the Prime Minister's post. He remained for two years despite being
cut out of the decision-making by the President and resigned in 1976 in protest at
the direction of policy and the overweening presidency. This began one of the long-
standing and most personal of disputes in French politics which tore apart the conservative right and cost them the presidency in 1981 and probably the general
elections of 1988. Jacques Chirac took over the gaullist party and it was rebaptised
the RPR in 1976, becoming in the process Chirac's own organisation and the
vehicle for three presidential bids. Jacques Chirac was an indefatigable campaigner
and also persistent. In 1981 he stood for the presidency, and then again in 1988,
before winning in 1995. In between time he had been Prime Minister again
(1986–88) and had been almost been counted out of the campaign in 1994 before
he rallied round and won against the Socialist Lionel Jospin in 1995. President
Chirac's unexplained decision to hold a snap election in 1997 (which his supporters lost) has been one of the principal causes of the disarray of the contemporary
conservative right. President Chirac was unpopular before the 1997 dissolution
but as a non-executive President he has scaled the heights of popularity.

The subsequent history of the RPR is of a party aiming to put its leader into
the Elysée. Jacques Chirac ran in the 1981 and 1988 elections before his
success in 1995. His RPR was pragmatic, taking various positions in response
to party competition at the time, and well organised. Thus the RPR has vari-
ously emulated the UK Labour Party, promoted the neo-liberalism of Reagan
and Thatcher, and espoused anti-Europeanism and populist themes (law and
order, notably). It has animated the war dividing the conservative right and has
fomented further divisions in the 1990s.

Current divisions go back to 1993 when the RPR was the big winner in the
general elections and, with 242 seats, dominated the conservative coalition.
Jacques Chirac decided not to go to the Matignon for the third time and instead
allowed his former Finance Minister Edouard Balladur to take the premiership.
This proved for Chirac a miscalculation as the Prime Minister became a popular
figure and soon led the polls as the conservatives' preferred presidential candidate. The conservative right was split by the new rivalry.

RPR	
November 1994	Chirac resigns as RPR President, Alain Juppé takes over
May 1995	Jacques Chirac elected President
October 1995	Alain Juppé elected RPR President
July 1997	Philippe Séguin elected RPR President
December 1998	Séguin elected RPR President
January 1999	Pasqua's group splits to form the RPF
April 199	Séguin resigns and Sarkozy becomes RPR President
June 1999	Sarkozy resigns
December 1999	Michèle Alliot-Marie elected RPR President

Edouard Balladur

Edouard Balladur has a phlegmatic disposition and is a hesitant public speaker, but he emerged from a stint as Prime Minister in 1993–95 as of 'presidential timber'. He was born in Turkey in 1929 and graduated from the ENA to join the Council of State. He worked with Georges Pompidou as both Prime Minister and President before entering business when his patron died. He was the architect of the RPR's economic policy and was Economics Minister in the 1986–88 government and the key adviser to Jacques Chirac. His cautious and solid if unadventurous middle-of-the-road government was popular and in 1995 he was a conservative favourite in the polls, but he failed to campaign strongly and was pushed into third place by his party leader Chirac on the first ballot. However, his campaign had enthused a new generation of conservative politicians. Much of this large group remained loyal to him and his outlook of Europeanism and fiscal prudence.

In the 1995 presidential elections Jacques Chirac campaigned against the 'conservatism' of the Balladur government but from both a free market and interventionist standpoint. His principal campaign advisers were the anti-Maastricht gaullist (with a state-oriented message) Philippe Séguin from the RPR and the free market evangelist Alain Madelin from the UDF. Although Chirac's message was very mixed, what most people remembered was the campaign's social emphasis and its priority on economic growth and jobs. These promises, at a time when the Socialists were demoralised, gave Chirac the edge and a narrow first ballot lead over Prime Minister Balladur (20.84 per cent to 18.58 per cent), and enabled him to win on the second ballot.

On the first ballot the right was exceptionally fragmented between candidates. Jacques Chirac's electorate was at core an RPR vote but he was able to gain an edge with the young (18–24 years old), workers, and unemployed (where he gained relative to his 1988 vote). On the second ballot he was well ahead of Jospin amongst the young (55–40 per cent) and amongst private sector workers (52–40 per cent). Although the National Front voters did not transfer to Jacques Chirac on the second ballot in as great numbers as in 1988 (51 per cent as against 65 per cent), the supporters of the other conservative candidate moved strongly to support him. There was, however, the biggest abstention rate since 1965.

As a new President, with the weakest first round support of any President of the Fifth Republic, Jacques Chirac might have sought to widen support and bring over the disaffected, but instead he narrowed the basis of the new Cabinet. He nominated his long-time but uninfluential supporter Alain Juppé as Prime Minister and excluded the Balladur supporters as well as Séguin and some other major figures on the conservative right. The government immediately implemented a deflationary policy (contrary to what had been expected) and thus suffered from the outset from disappointed expectations. It would have needed strong backing to take a U-turn but it had none. Its popularity fell as it faced a general strike and a series of setbacks. President Chirac chose to keep on the failing Prime Minister and his popularity also fell, so even after the landslide victory of 1993, the conservative right looked likely to be defeated in the next general elections (scheduled for 1998).

But President Chirac used the constitutional prerogative to call a snap election in 1997. This election, with an unpopular Prime Minister and a panic dissolution, was never properly justified and nothing was done during the campaign to mobilise the presidential coalition. The RPR, which normally would have been expected to rally the conservative camp, found itself directionless under the unpopular Prime Minister. It was a defeat for the President's party, which polled 16.81 per cent and took 140 seats. The RPR remained the biggest party on the right but the conservatives had lost their majority to the left.

Dissolutions

Date	Cause	Legislature
9 October 1962	Censure motion	30 November 1958–18 November 1962
30 May 1968	May 1968 'events'	11 March 1967–23 June 1968
22 May 1981	Presidential elections	21 March 1978–14 June 1981
14 May 1988	Presidential elections	16 March 1986–12 June 1988
21 April 1997	Snap election	28 March 1993–1 June 1997

This time the RPR's losses led to a change of party leadership and to the President losing control of his own party to Phillipe Séguin and Nicolas Sarkozy. But behind the scenes the struggle with the President for the diminishing party went ahead and the new leadership was itself ousted in 1999. The President's supporters then ran the RPR group in Parliament and prevented the implementation of any strategy conflicting with the President's own. Jacques

Chirac effectively remained leader of the weakened RPR and its candidate for
the 2002 presidential elections. As President, Jacques Chirac was unable to federate the conservative right into a winning coalition but prevented other figures
from doing so (who might have challenged his position as the conservative's
candidate). The RPR is the party best placed to federate the conservative right,
but a defeat in 2002 would leave the RPR in a precarious position.

Gaullism is a patriotic nationalism but it does not amount to a coherent
ideology. It has none of the hard edge of Marxism or liberalism and was

---

From de Gaulle's *War Memoirs*

All my life I have had a certain idea of France. This is inspired in me as much by sentiment as by reason. The affective side of me naturally imagines France, like the prin-
cess in the fairy tales or the Madonna in the frescoes, as called to a high and
exceptional destiny. Instinctively, I have the feeling that providence has created her
either to achieve absolute successes or suffer exemplary misfortunes. However, if in
spite of this, mediocrity shows in her acts and works, it strikes me as an absurd
anomaly, the cause of the faults of French people, not the genius of the nation. But
the positive side of my mind also convinces me that France is not really herself
unless she is in the first rank; that only vast undertakings are capable of countering
the ferments of dispersion inherent in her people; that our country, such as it is, surrounded by others, such as they are, must, under pain of mortal danger, aim high,
and remain upright. In sum, for me, France cannot be France without grandeur.

This faith grew as I grew, in the place where I was born. My father was a man
of strong opinion, a cultivated, traditional man steeped with the feeling of the
exalted nature of France. He made me aware of her history. My mother had a right-
eous passion for her country, as strong as her religious faith. My three brothers, my
sister and myself had a certain anxious pride in our country as a second nature.

As a young Lille born boy living in Paris, nothing appealed to me more than the
symbols of our glories: night falling over Notre Dame, the majesty of the evening at
Versailles, the Arc de Triomphe bathed in the sun, the colours won quivering in the
vault of the Invalides. Nothing touched me more than the evidence of our national
triumphs: the enthusiasm of the crowds when the Czar of Russia came, the Review
at Longchamp, the wonders of the Exhibition, the first flights of our airmen. Nothing
saddened me more deeply than our weaknesses and our mistakes, as revealed to me
when I was a child by the way people looked and by the things they said: the surren-
der of Fashoda, the Dreyfus affair, social conflicts and religious dissension. Nothing
moved me more than the story of our past misfortunes: my father recalled the
unavailing attempt to break through at Le Bourget and at Stains, in which he had
been wounded when the attempt was made; my mother evoking the despair she had
felt, when a girl, at the sight of her parents in tears: 'Bazaine has surrendered'.

Source: translated from *Mémoirs de Guerre: L'Appel* (Plon, 1954), pp. 1–2.

couched by its originator in deliberately cloudy, if poetic (and attractive), language. Gaulle's impact on French politics was, of course, massive and some observers are content to say that gaullism is so pervasive that, 30 years after de Gaulle, everybody in France is now a gaullist. There are many features of gaullism which are now accepted: the independent deterrent, suspicion of the North Atlantic Treaty Organisation (NATO), the institutions of the Fifth Republic (though not their presidential working), the legacy of the Resistance and the gaullist interpretation of the past (mostly). Other claims are more dubious but there are few precise prescriptions and no unique routes mapped out by gaullists. In that sense it now belongs to history.

In the neo-gaullist RPR the legacy of gaullism is equally difficult to pin down. There is a continuation of rituals like the visit to Colombey to commemorate de Gaulle's call to Resistance on 18 June, and the ceremony to commemorate the death of de Gaulle on 9 November. Party symbols like the Phrygian bonnet and the cross of Lorraine have maintained the party's gaullist reference and the leadership has cultivated these marks. The party had a tradition of loyalty and a common sense of 'companionage', of association in a joint and patriotic endeavour, but the squabbling after 1988 and the splits in 1993–95 have made it in this way much like other political parties.

Jacques Chirac's platform for the 1995 presidential elections showed the extent to which the RPR is a pragmatic party of the conservative right in its main outlines. A welfare policy was fashioned to appeal to the former socialist voters. Thus the platform proposed to alleviate unemployment by reducing business' 'red tape' and reducing taxes on enterprise. It also proposed to reduce tax (principally to promote investment) and to introduce a back-to-work initiative. There were also measures to reform the hospital system and to help the least well off. In defence the reshaping of national service was proposed (a move to de Gaulle's professional army – long overdue) and a modernisation of nuclear weapons but also an acceptance of the nuclear non-proliferation treaty. Gaullists since Pompidou have supported European integration and Jacques Chirac continued in that vein but the emphasis was placed on reforms to increase the roles of the states through the Council of Ministers and national parliaments. Although the platform looked to pursue economic and monetary union, it would protect state sovereignty rather than increase the power of the EU's institutions.

French 'exceptionalism'

The French right is split in a way that is unusual in Europe. Were it not for its divisions the French conservative right would have been returned to power on several occasions after President Mitterrand's victory of 1981 (in fact the divisions contributed to that victory). In the polls and the local elections (of 2001) the conservative right has held a nominal majority but it has been unable to capitalise on this at the legislative elections. Presidential rivalries are a main part of these divisions but they are underlain by ideological and organisational disputes. The split between the supporters of President Giscard and the RPR leader Chirac mainly ran between the UDF and the RPR (with some exceptions). However, the more recent split between the Prime Minister Edouard Balladur and his party leader Jacques Chirac ran through the RPR and divided the UDF. Thus the parties are further factionalised into Chirac supporters, and Balladur supporters cleavages which date back to 1993–95 and which have still not been overcome. Were the conservatives able to overcome these divisions they would be better able to exploit the mistakes of the 'plural left'.

Hence, the splits on the right are ideological and personality-driven. They have prevented the right from capitalising on its majority in the country at large. For example, the conservative right has been unable to cope with the challenge of the National Front that has taken both voters and activists from the mainstream parties. It has also divided in itself and the propensity to fragment has increased inside both the RPR and the UDF. Thus the outlooks on substantive issues such as the EU serve to divide the conservative parties into pros and antis. But the salient differences in recent years have crystallised around individual politicians who are of 'presidential timber'. More importantly the National Front remains unavailable to the main conservative parties as an alliance partner. It has been off-limits to mainstream politics despite – on an arithmetic count – giving the right a majority in most polls. This has been a major factor inhibiting the conservative right since the mid-1980s.

For the conservative right there are some signs of hope. It has been able to use its majority in the country to win a majority in the local and cantonal elections of 2001. The only plausible conservative presidential candidate is Jacques Chirac and the President is well placed to win a second term. The conservative right has also been handed an unexpected gift in the internal splits of the National Front. The National Front has declined and that has made it more difficult for it to split the right-wing vote on the second ballot as happened in 1997. Moreover National Front supporters have started to move to conservative candidates on the second ballot in a 'tactical' vote against the left.

Summary

- Conservative politics in France has suffered from its divisions since 1981 when Giscard d'Estaing lost the presidency. These divisions, mainly based on personality but also programmatic and ideological, have enabled the left to win in many cases unexpectedly.
- Presidential politics has intruded into all the conservative parties, dividing them between the supporters of Balladur, Chirac and Giscard. As the ideological space has narrowed, these divisions have become increasingly personal.
- Conservative politics, to govern with conviction, will have to surmount these divisions.

- Opinion polls and local elections have indicated that the conservative right has had a potential majority since 1993 and possibly before. The main-stream right has been unable to consolidate this at national level because of its divisions and the influence of the National Front.
- The conservatives of the UDF, RPR and Liberal Democracy are difficult to differentiate but have separate traditions, organisations and loyalties. They remain committed to their independence and, on the second ballots, are capable of combining to capitalise on their potential majority.
- The National Front's split reduces its potential for divisiveness and has diminished its threat.
- The National Front's issues of immigration and law and order remain the 'dark matter' of the French political system exerting their influence across the parties.

Further reading

Cole, A., 'The return of the Orleanist right' in A. Cole (ed.), *French Political Parties in Transition* (Dartmouth, 1990)

Elgie, R., 'Christian Democracy in France' in D. Hanley (ed.), *Christian Democracy in Europe* (Pinter, 1994)

Grunberg, G., 'Why did the right lose?' in M. S. Lewis-Beck (ed.), *How France Votes* (Seven Bridges, 2000)

Hainsworth, P., 'The right: divisions and changes in *fin de siècle* France' *West European Politics* 22: 4, 1999, pp. 38–75

Hanley, D., 'Compromise, party management and fair shares: the case of the UDF' *Party Politics* 5: 2, 1999, pp. 171–89

Knapp, A., *Gaullism since de Gaulle* (Dartmouth, 1994)

Knapp, A., 'What's left of the French right: the RPR and UDF from conquest to humili-ation, 1993–98' *West European Politics* 22:1, 1999, pp. 109–31

Knapp, A. and Le Galès, P., 'Top down to bottom-up: relations and power structures in France's gaullist party' *West European Politics* 16: 3, 1993, pp. 271–94

Marcus, J., *The National Front and French Politics* (Macmillan, 1995)

Mayer, N. and Perrineau, P. 'Why do they vote for Le Pen?' *European Journal of Political Research* 22, 1992, pp. 123–41

Rémond, R., *The Right Wing in France: From 1815 to de Gaulle* (University of Pennsylvania Press, 1969)

Schain, M. A., 'The National Front and the legislative elections of 1997' in M. S. Lewis-Beck (ed.), *How France Votes* (Seven Bridges, 2000)

Shields, J., 'The French Gaullists' in J. Gaffney (ed.), *Political Parties and the European Union* (Routledge, 1996)

Questions

1 Why has the French right been unable to unite in the 1980s and 1990s?
2 To what extent are French Christian democracy and gaullism like British Conservatism?
3 What accounts for the rise of the National Front?

6

Local power

Devolution has been a feature of the Fifth Republic. Centralisation and the commitment to the Jacobin state, which characterised both the conservative right and the Communist and non-Communist left before 1958, were watered down and ceased to be priorities in policy-making. The 'one and indivisible' central Republican state, the conquest of the Revolution, had been intended to ensure unity, equal treatment and equal opportunity within France. In the Republican tradition the state ensured a standardisation of treatment and ironed out local differences (mainly by levelling up). Local government was constrained within well-defined limits to ensure this Jacobin equality. Uniformed viceroys bearing the imperial title of prefect guaranteed Republican democracy at a local level by supervising local government and preventing divergencies from the norm. France was, and is, characterised by a fear of federalism.

However, although France is a unitary and not a federal state, its local government is of particular importance. It would not be too much to say that national politics is built of the blocks of local government and that attachments to the commune and department are strong. There are more local government units in France than in the rest of Europe put together. France has three local tiers: approximately 36,000 communes at the base with 96 metropolitan (plus four overseas) departments (3,530 cantons) and 26 regions each with its councillors. The departments (60 per cent), followed by the communes (30 per cent) and then the regions (10 per cent) make local expenditure. In the distribution of competencies, however, it is more of a marble cake than a layer cake. Communes deal with primary schools, departments with secondary schools and the regions with sixth-form schools and colleges, but the policies interact and are not easily separable. In addition the structure of local government with its central government prefects and sub-prefects is distinctive; to the English-speaking world it is odd but it is the model, exported by Napoleon, for local government elsewhere in Europe.

There is a continuous tension in French politics between the central state and the independence of localities. The French nation was made by an active central state over the nineteenth century, which whittled away local particular-isms to forge a modern nation. At the beginning of the century France was a linguistic and social patchwork and in 1863 about a quarter of the population spoke no French. There were different languages spoken in areas like the Basque country, Alsace, Brittany, Corsica, Roussillon and Provence, and the local patois of some parts of the country hardly resembled French. Under the Second Empire, perhaps as many as 50 per cent of the population did not speak stan-dard French and the country was composed of small local districts – in some cases circulating their own money. Over the century the state slowly created a national community by extending communications to create a French market and a national system, developing a national education system (in the medium of French language) and to an extent also through army conscription. All this was achieved by the central state and was sometimes actively resisted by the local populations affected by this forced modernisation.

Basque lands

There is a feeling in the Department of Basse-Pyrenées (which regroups three his-toric Basque provinces) that there ought to be a Basque region. This is not, however, a nationalist issue and nor is it particularly political in contemporary France. Basse-Pyrenées is a sparsely populated area and mainly rural and small farming in its economy. The Basque region of France is in fact Catholic and conservative in inclination and has inclined to support the centre Christian democratic parties (and gaullists); parties expressing nationalism have struggled to get onto the second ballot and have mostly failed to do so.

The 'deputy mayor'

On the other hand local sentiment and local politics remained vital even after the state's action to create a unitary Republic. France remained essentially rural and a country of small communes and small towns, not, as in the United Kingdom or Germany, one of massive industrial cities. French people related to the state principally through local institutions and particularly the mayor or local council. National society was built from the base up. That meant that the deputies and senators represented their communities first and depended on their local implantation to ensure their national status. The parties, which in the UK provided the ladder for a career in politics, were weak and government discipline was feeble. (Only the Communist Party, the better to ensure leader-ship from the top, enforced a separation of local and national functions.) Local issues were taken seriously and deputies' careers depended on their handling of problems in the constituency. This local government focus was lampooned in Gabriel Chevallier's comic novel *Clochemerle*, in which a government crisis (and eventually a European one) was caused by a dispute in a village about the location of a public convenience.

One of the features of French politics (known as the '*cumul des mandats*') is the simultaneous holding of numerous elected offices by politicians. This has been steadily restricted in recent years and is limited to two (by the Defferre reforms), but being a deputy and a mayor is still a common combination. In fact those figures who had no local political base are exceptional. De Gaulle is one of the few politicians of stature who was not a local politician, although Lionel Jospin was only a departmental councillor for Cintgabelle between 1993 and 1997 and Raymond Barre was, for a long time, only a deputy (before becoming mayor of Lyons). Other figures who have had distinguished local careers include Jacques Chirac (who was the mayor of Paris 1977–95), Jacques Chaban Delmas (mayor of Bordeaux 1947–95), Gaston Defferre (mayor of Marseilles 1953–86), and Pierre Mauroy (mayor of Lille 1973–). Mauroy is one in a succession of prominent Lille mayors which started with Roger Salengro then Augustin Laurent (the 'Pope of Socialism') and may be continued by Martine Aubry in the near future. President Giscard was mayor of Chamalières (a suburb of Clermont-Ferrand) and President Mitterrand was mayor of a small town in the Nièvre (Château-Chinon). Of Prime Ministers, Laurent Fabius was mayor of Grand-Quevilly, Michel Debré was mayor of Blois, Pierre Messmer was mayor of Sarrebourg, Michel Rocard was mayor of Conflans St Honorine, Edith Cresson was mayor of Châtellerault and so on. The importance of local office was shown in 2001 by Catherine Trautmann's decision to return to local politics in Strasbourg and Martine Aubry's decision to return to Lille politics rather than remain as government ministers.

The phenomenon of the big city mayor is world-wide and not confined to France. The importance of the mayors of New York, Chicago, Berlin, Rome, Madrid, Jerusalem, and London and so on hardly needs underlining. Nor does the usefulness of a city reputation need emphasising as the way to launch a national career. Many politicians have been able to start as local politicians and become national figures on that basis, like David Blunkett or Herbert Morrison in the UK and Willy Brandt in Germany. What is odd about the French situation is that politicians remain city mayors (or department or regional heads) at the same time as pursuing a national career. The combination of offices in this way is unusual in the western world.

It might be thought that local government would be the loser in this situation and that the politician would concentrate on national office to the detriment of the city or region. This does not seem to be the case. There are absentee mayors but the main mandate is often the local one. Although it is becoming rarer, many politicians choose to devote their careers principally to their locality. The national positions these local politicians obtain enable them to know their way round the Paris ministries. Their national positions are used as a way of levering concessions out of the central authorities and influencing the Ministry of the Interior (which deals with local government). In previous

Republics a long succession of Ministers of the Interior would ensure that the 'their' friends in local positions were rewarded and they could be persuaded or influenced by deals done at national level. Where deputies took ministerial posts it was often a portfolio that directly affected their area. The mayor of the port of Marseilles, Gaston Defferre, took the Ministries of the Merchant Navy and then the Colonies in 1954 and introduced the decentralisation laws in 1982.

Locally, it used to be regarded as of benefit to a commune if its political head was recognised on a national stage and knew his or her way round the centre. More recently it has become difficult to combine the roles of mayor with national positions. The 2001 local elections resulted in defeats for several ministers who attempted to conquer city halls. The Socialist Elizabeth Guigou and the Communist J.-C. Gayssot both failed to get elected and had their careers set back. Local electors did not like coming second to the national preoccupations of these well-known figures and they found that the sitting mayor devoted full-time to the election campaign had a considerable advantage in a toughly fought election. Major figures of the conservative right found it possible to win or defend city halls unencumbered by national responsibility. The *cumul des mandats* continues but in attenuated form.

The prefect system

Local government in France is set in a formal set of legal rules which, on the face of it, are rigid and unbending but which are in practice supple and capable of accommodating wide divergence. This is the prefectoral system of supervision of local government, known as the *tutelle*, and which has its origins in the Napoleonic Empire (17 February 1800). The prefect is the civil servant in each department appointed by the Ministry of the Interior who is the representative of the central government. Prefects have an allowance and a large staff in a dedicated prefecture (renamed the Hôtel du département after 1982) shared with the department's administration. These 'mini-Napoleons' were intended to impose order, collect taxes and find conscripts, not to be democratic, but the Third Republic adapted the system by introducing elected mayors and councils. The prefect was able to supervise budgets and policy, however, leaving intact many of the system's top-down aspects.

The Defferre devolution laws of 1982 abolished *a priori* supervision by the prefect although an *a posteriori tutelle* remained. Departmental prefects have public order powers and, although no longer officially the supervising *tutelle*, are the active overseers of local government. Prefects are still expected to review all local government decisions and to send them to the administrative courts or the audit courts if needs be after the decisions have been taken. Prefects co-ordinate the field services of the Paris ministries in their area.

Prefects are drawn from a professional civil service department which local government officers join and which has substantial prestige. About 80 per cent of prefects are recruited from the Ecole nationale d'administration (ENA) and come under a different regime from other civil servants, one which allows them to be moved at a whim. Their opinions are documented (it is a highly sensitive post). Many prominent figures in French public life had been in the prefectoral corps or were prefects. A prefectoral career is an excellent training in politics because it provides an introduction to local networks and training in handling them. The Resistance leader Jean Moulin was a prefect, as were, for example, the contemporary politicians Philippe de Villiers, François Léotard and Edgard Pisani. As these examples show, they can be welcomed back to the area they administered and stand for election with success. They have a ceremonial role as the embodiment of the Republic – and a blue and gold dress uniform to go with it. Prefects are thus a permanent presence in the department and are intended to be seen as they take precedence as representatives of the state.

The prefecture has a large staff (its number depends on the size of the district over which it presides) and has the responsibility for co-ordinating the field services of the central state. In principle the prefect should ensure the harmonious working of the local agencies of Paris ministries, of which there are many. All the ministries have services in the provinces but the prefect's control over them will vary from those outside control to those – at least nominally – under the prefecture's supervision. Many local governments deal directly with Paris, however, and a central ministry prefers to deal direct with its local services where it can, so generalisations about the effectiveness of co-ordination are difficult. It is probably the case that co-ordination was more important in the past and that since the war the prefect has been steadily cut out of the main processes of the local field services and is now mainly informed – but not in charge.

The powers of the prefect, still often regarded as a minor sovereign, are in fact highly political. The political nature of the appointments is reflected in the 'waltz of prefects' each time that the government changes from left to right (or vice versa). The prefect has power to command but has to depend on the power to persuade. Local politicians need to be coaxed and cajoled into doing what is required and the delicate relation of the prefect with the local notables can be easily upset. A prefect will have to bear in mind that the big cities are power houses of their own, that the major politicians may well be government ministers in the near future and will certainly have power in Paris. The standard pattern of the relations between prefect and local politician is one of bargaining and help in return for favours that make the system perform efficiently. Moreover any breakdown of harmony in an area will redound to the discredit of the prefect, who is meant to keep things moving smoothly at local level – not to disrupt them. Disruptive prefects, acting with blatant partiality, do exist but run into trouble. In 1995 Jean-Charles Marchiani was nominated prefect of the Var, where the National Front had captured the city of Toulon, and he set out to pound the department into shape. The experiment was ended in 1997 by the new government, who removed him. The prefect's intrusion into active politics had become disruptive and he had already alienated the centrist politicians in the Var. Prefects are political by the nature of their engagement with local politicians and when governments change so do prefects. Prefects too close to opposition figures are moved elsewhere and those who have been too zealous on behalf of the previous government are removed.

In the 1982 reforms the prefects lost control of the budgets as well as of some staff (who transferred to communes and departments), were deprived of their veto of decisions and their control over financial affairs was removed and placed under a regional audit body. The big cities and powerful departments had seen the prefect as an imposition. Cities like Marseilles, Lyons, Bordeaux and Lille had no need of prefectoral bolstering and their administration was well capable of dealing with its own budget. On the other hand the prefect and the prefectoral services were of vital importance to the thousands of small communes which dot the map of France and which are too small to carry out their obligations on their own. For them the prefecture's guidance through law and budgeting and making them aware of the latest missive from Paris was vital. Prefects still negotiate the annual grant from the state with the small communes. Only the existence of the prefecture with its administrative staff enabled the myriad of small communes to survive in modern France. Even so the small communes have probably turned to the departmental council for administrative assistance since the devolution law of 1982. Yet, given the need of the prefect to negotiate with the local politicians, the prefect's supervision role may not have been substantially changed by the laws of 1982, which recognised a *de facto* position.

There was a fear that the abolition of the prefect's supervision and greater responsibilities would lead to the disintegration of local government. That has not proved true but there has been an increase in corruption. Fuelled by the competition between the parties at national level, this corruption has led to the skimming of municipal government contracts to the benefit of the party. Investigations by judges in the late 1980s began to uncover a host of abuses. Most of these involved planning permission (for supermarkets, in particular) and worked through intermediaries. Paris's council, like some Communist councils in the 1980s, was touched by further allegations of vote-rigging in marginal constituencies. All the major parties – gaullists, centrists, Republicans, Communists and even Greens – have had their scandals and this has contributed to the discredit of the political elite in France.

In the past it often suited the local politicians to blame the prefect for preventing them from taking action which they really did not want to take. It was, however, common for the prefect to become the localities' advocate to Paris rather than the means of imposing Parisian orders on the departments or communes. Entering into the game of local politics draws prefects into complicity with the local elites. For that reason, like ambassadors, they are rotated at regular intervals. In today's France they are still powerful figures because of their position at the heart of local networks and as the connection with Paris. They have their dedicated staff with a wealth of technical expertise and they are involved in local politics and administration, enabling them to be strongly influential in their area.

Communes

Communes are the basic 'cell' of French local government. They were created in December 1789 but their roots are old, dating back to the parishes before the Revolution. Loyalties to communes are strong and by most measures they are the most important of local government units. There are arrondissements in the big cities which form a sub-communal unit and there are unions of communes (intercommunal syndicates) grouped together for a specific purpose or to provide services jointly. Of course the exodus from rural France has continued but the small-town nature of France is exemplified by the fact that the bulk of communes are small and rural and have a population of less than 500; there are over 4,000 with under 100 inhabitants. However, most people live in the bigger communes of over 9,000; there are 36 over 100,000 and 5 have over 300,000 people. Many of the communes are too small to provide the services needed but the state's effort to rationalise them has made no headway (although there are some voluntary associations).

Municipal elections are held every six years on a mixed system designed to produce ruling majorities but allow minorities representation. Traditionally there is great interest in local elections and a turn-out of about 70 per cent (in the UK it is about 40 per cent). In general the Fifth Republic local elections have been 'presidentialised' and local systems have been brought into line with the national one. Voters have also taken the opportunity to pass judgement on the national government at local elections. A decline in the standing of the party in power can result in the loss of city halls across France. Thus in 1977, 1983 and 1992 mayors of the party in power received condign punishment. A popular government does not, on the other hand, serve to hoist its party's mayors into office: a rising tide does not lift all the boats.

The municipal elections are personalised because a potential mayor, who is (or becomes) a prominent local personality, heads each list of prospective councillors. The new council whose majority will have been candidates on the list will almost invariably vote the leader of the winning list mayor. In very small communes voters can write in candidates and in those of fewer than 3,500 the electors can cross-vote for members of different lists. In the communes of under 9,000 in rural France (97 per cent of all communes) the confrontation will be arranged on left/right lines but the mayor's personality will be key. (Although they represent 54 per cent of voters this conservative France dominates the Senate through indirect elections to the upper house.) The local elections in the 421 big towns and cities over 9,000 have become left–right confrontations although the importance of the local personality is still very important and the 'swing' at national level does not automatically translate into a local change.

Voters' views of the 2001 local elections
(*Le Monde/Ipsos*, January 2001)

About the forthcoming elections, are you?

	European (1999)	Regional (1998)	General (1997)	Local (2001)
Very interested (%)	15	23	25	32
Rather interested (%)	44	44	43	44
Not really interested (%)	23	17	17	14
Not at all interested (%)	15	14	13	10

What, in your view, should be the three main priorities of the next mayor of your commune? (Chosen from a list)

Security of property and people	56%
Local tax levels	36%
Schools	33%
Traffic and parking	31%
Commune life	30%
New businesses	30%
Air pollution	27%
Housing	17%
Parks and gardens	16%
Businesses	14%

For each of the reasons here, can you say whether it will play a primary or secondary role in your vote in the local elections?

	Primary (%)	Important but not primary (%)	Secondary (%)	Don't know (%)
Record of outgoing mayor	40	40	18	2
Personalities of those heading the list	36	39	23	2
That the list's head lives in the commune	34	38	26	2
The list offers a prime place to women	28	45	26	1
Political allegiance of the list	26	29	42	3
Your opinion of Jospin's government (of the left)	16	28	49	7
Your opinion of President Chirac's action	12	25	57	6

Lists are not always party political; they can be coalition, personal, or non-party (especially in small communes).

There is a two-ballot system and there is a second round if no list wins an absolute majority on the first. Lists have to win 10 per cent to stand on the second but the lists can combine or stand down for the run-off. The composition of the council has been decided (since 1982) by a formula which ensures an absolute majority for the mayor but which gives lists polling over 5 per cent on the second round a voice on the council. In 2001 a new law (applying to all elections) came into force. It stipulated that women had to be represented equally with men on party lists for local elections (in towns over 3,500): there has to be three women for every three men in every group of six from top to bottom. The result was a huge increase in the number of women councillors from under 20 per cent to over 40 per cent; the leaders of the list (the likely mayors), however, remained men. Hence the numbers of women mayors remained at about 8 per cent, although the numbers of women deputy mayors increased and with that the probability that the next generation would see a big increase in women mayors.

Communes have responsibilities for primary and nursery school buildings (though not the teaching), infrastructure, planning, local economic development, public health, some welfare services and culture. Thus they can have active policies of public transport (or experiment with 'alternative' transport), develop roads, build sewers and instal street lighting. Culture is, in many French communes, a matter of local development, some of it very adventurous: sculpture, art, museums, theatre, music and dance are subsidised or given locales and the local libraries are encouraged. Communes also have the power to censor local cinema showings and to decide what to purchase for the library. They have powers over planning and grant planning permission in accordance with the local plan.

Paris, Lyons, Marseilles: 'PLM'

The big cities of Paris, Lyons and Marseilles operate under a different regime which takes account of their size. They are divided into arrondissements (districts) and separate lists stand in each arrondissement for an arrondissement council. However, these councillors were elected on the city-wide list and go from the different arrondissements to form the city council. Paris has twenty arrondissements (each with a mayor) and a council of 163, Marseilles has nine arrondissements and a council of 101, and Lyons has six arrondissements and a council of 73. In these big cities there is normally a big opposition contingent, although Jacques Chirac won a 'grand slam' of all twenty districts in 1989.

Paris merits special mention as France suffers from the 'Goliath's head' phenomenon of the domination of Paris. A major world capital, overshadowing its rivals, the phenomenon of 'Paris and the French desert' has often been

Cities

The move from the land to the cities under the impetus of industrialisation has been rapid in post-war France, but the country is still a more rural one than other European states and has fewer large cities than comparable states. The major cities have quite divergent histories. Nantes and Bordeaux were Atlantic ports, whereas Marseilles looked to the Meditterranean and the African Empire; Lille was a textile city linked to Belgium, and Strasbourg was involved with central Europe and had been part of Germany from 1870 to 1918. One of the legacies of helter-skelter expansion is the creation of a 'suburbs' problem of high-rise wastelands in which the services have deteriorated and in which unemployment is high and crime is endemic.

Lyons

Lyons, the capital of the Rhône region, is the second largest industrial conurbation in France (although Marseilles would dispute this title). It is a city of some 400,000 and a region of 1.5 million and is a major industrial and commercial centre famous for silk (long established) as well as chemicals, metallurgy and banking. Its recent expansion was based on industry and that suffered in the late 1970s, although the service sector continued to expand and a 'science park' has developed in the suburbs around the Ecole normale supérieur. Rapid expansion in the 1950s, 1960s and 1970s has left it with a legacy of suburban estate problems. Its one-time mayor, former Prime Minister Raymond Barre, decided not to stand again in 2001 and started a succession crisis on the conservative right. The centrist Michel Mercier (supported by all the conservative parties) was challenged by the maverick conservative Charles Millon (a former regional president elected with National Front support). This division enabled the Socialist Gérard Collomb to win the city hall in 2001 because a deal could not done between the conservatives and Millon's Liberal Right.

lamented. Yet Paris did not have a mayor before 1977, since governments feared both its revolutionary reputation and its potential power. When President Giscard restored the position, the neo-gaullist leader Chirac almost immediately won it. He then started a feud with Giscard's supporters and turned the city hall into a quasi 'government in exile'. Visiting foreign politicians would normally call in on the mayor of the 'city of light' and, just as naturally, Jacques Chirac would make foreign relations trips abroad. City hall supported the presidential ambitions of the mayor and provided a perfect stage for an ambitious politician. The division of the big cities into districts was, initially, an attempt by the Socialist government of 1981 to discipline their opponent, the mayor of Paris

---

Paris elections

The 163 district (arrondissement) councillors are elected at the same time on lists drawn up depending on the size of the district. Thus the 15th returns seventeen councillors and the small districts of the centre (1st, 2nd and 3rd) return three each. There are two ballots. On the first ballot if a list obtains an absolute majority in a district it takes the majority of seats and the others are distributed proportionately amongst the lists getting over 5 per cent. If there is no absolute majority there is a second ballot at which all the lists getting over 10 per cent can stand. After the second ballot half the seats go to the list with the most votes. The remaining seats are distributed proportionately between the other lists. The system is meant to give the minorities a voice and to enable effective government and it favours the front-runner. At the municipal elections of March 2001 the Socialist alliance narrowly won the city for the first time since the mayor was restored – 130 years after the commune.

Jacques Chirac. This turned against the government when the mayor rallied the people of the city against the naive Machiavellism of the Socialists and carried off another resounding victory in 1983. Paris remained in Jacques Chirac's hands, and a training ground for his younger supporters, until he won the presidency in 1995.

Paris has always been conservative in contrast to (and sometimes in a clash with) its suburbs. Before the war the city council watched, or did little to prevent, the anti-parliamentary riots of 1934 and it was a bastion of the right. De Gaulle's RPF won a majority of votes in 1947 in 14 of the 20 arrondissements and the gaullist UNR won all 31 seats in the 1962 general elections. Since that time it has become the heartland of the RPR. Jacques Chirac won all arrondissements in 1983 and 1988 and came ahead of Giscard in 1981, of Mitterrand at the second ballot in 1988 and well ahead of Balladur in 1995. In 1995, when Jean Tiberi became mayor, Paris suffered from revelations about alleged financial irregularities and the conservatives picked the anti-European Séguin (in a solidly pro-European city) for the elections of 2001. In 2001 the city fell to the left led by the Socialist Bernard Delanoë. This seismic shock resulted from scandals and the divisions of the conservative right.

The mayor

The mayor is the commune's executive 'president' and the state's agent (ensuring that the government's regulations are carried out) as well as the ceremonial head of the city or town. The mayor is not a mere figurehead (as in England) but is the executive head and responsible for the council's work, formally charged with putting into practice the decisions of the council. A mayor is the 'notable' who represents the commune and is also close to the population, better known than the distant deputy and the most popular of French politicians. Most mayors are regularly re-elected and they tend to have long periods of tenure of office. The powers of mayors are in theory extensive and the scope for initiative is wide, especially if they have, as they do in large communes, considerable resources available to them. Mayors in larger communes have adjoints with functional responsibilities for lighting, cleaning, transport, etc., but this should not detract from the essentially personal nature of the post. It is the mayor who calls council meetings (each quarter), proposes the budget to the council and carries out the council policy.

The dynamic and 'building' mayor is a familiar figure in French local government and many mayors have made their mark through adventurous local action (like Catherine Trautmann of Strasbourg or Michel Crépeau of La Rochelle). The mayor is responsible for public order in the commune. 'Public order' is a very broad remit in France and extends from the ensuring of health and safety to the law and order function, which in small communes is assisted by police. Chapman reports that one village mayor, badgered by the Communists to do something about the threat of nuclear war, issued a by-law stating that 'the use of the atomic bomb in the commune is against the law. The *garde champêtre* will ensure that this is obeyed.' But it is a serious power. The National Front mayors have supported police crack-downs in areas they believe to be subject to 'crime waves' and have used the police power extensively.

Departments

Departments are the tier above the commune. These administrative districts are another innovation of the Revolution and might be thought of as rational and soulless units determined for administrative convenience and run by the prefect. There are now 96 metropolitan departments and the 4 overseas departments of Guadelope, Martinique, Réunion and Guiana (with a different status there are also the *Collectivités territoriales* of Mayotte and St-Pierre-et-Miquelon and the *territoires d'outre mer* of Wallis-et-Futuna, French Polynesia and New Caledonia). They were, in 1790, of roughly the same population and their size made travelling round the district, for the prefect, a practical possibility. They were, however, based on old pre-Revolutionary districts and the attachment to the department is strong, much like, in this respect, the old English county. In fact it has long been a view that these essentially unevenly balanced rural departments are the wrong framework for modern local government. But departments gained enormously from the 1982 Defferre laws when they were given extended responsibilities for transport, for middle schools and for social action. They have big budgets and administer many everyday services. Their strength has prevented the development of the regions as more powerful units.

The Third Republic gave the departments their elected general councils but the population changes and the decline of rural areas made the departments very unequal and left some unable to carry out their responsibilities properly. The 1982 reforms revivified the departments by removing their dependence on the prefect and by increasing their powers; the reforms instituted an elected executive president (chair) at the same time as removing the prefect's supervision. General council elections are held every three years but the mandate of a councillor is six years (half are renewed each election). The department electoral constituency is the canton and the system is the two-ballot single-member (like the general elections); elections are contested increasingly along party lines with diminishing non-partisan candidates. It is a paradox that the decentralisation, which increased the powers of the department, drew the national parties into the battle and reduced local significance. However, the cantons still reflect the very rural bias of the departments as well as the under-representation of industrial areas. This skewed representation is reflected as a left/right clash (city versus countryside). There are also sometimes accusations of discrimination against the departments by the cities.

It is the departmental council that elects its executive president. The department president is elected for three years but can be removed by the council if the coalition changes. Department presidents are involved in a process of building and maintaining their support on the council and that involves the usual politics of logrolling and dealing. The president is responsible for taxing and spending and presents the budget to the council, and also for the very large staffs transferred from the prefecture to the department. Another effect of the ending of the prefect's supervision was that the responsibility for helping the small communes passed to the department and to the staff transferred to it from the old prefectures. This is not meant to be a control of the lower tier and is meant to be a co-ordination, but the removal of the prefect's emollient influence and the growth of the council's stature led to fears of political decisions replacing administrative ones.

The departments have been the beneficiaries of devolved grants (no longer as tightly controlled) from the state to cover the services once run by the Paris ministries and they can also raise some taxes. Only the very big cities spend more but departments can spend large amounts and they do spend more than the regions. Departments have a raft of responsibilities for social services and welfare, including children's homes, the disabled and health care such as preventive medicine and health clinics. This is an area where they can make a difference and which is expensive. They are also in charge of some secondary school buildings and the bussing of school children, road building and maintenance, ports and can promote culture in their area. The departments can venture further than their explicitly designated functions and they are active in stimulating economic growth through investment and other measures (though not subsidies).

Regions

Regions came onto the political agenda as a particularly Fifth Republic phenomenon. Departments and communes had been in existence for nearly two centuries but regions are much more recent and have a weaker legal and political status. In 1955, when they were first set up, the regions were planning units and they were the central state's response to the pressure from local officials and pressure groups for the recognition of their special problems. Regional administrative areas were created at the beginning of the Fifth Republic. Regionalism, closely associated with monarchist anti-republicanism, was regarded with suspicion by the left, but the gaullists (like de Gaulle's first Prime Minister, Michel Debré) were also hostile to any weakening of central power. In the 1960s, however, the gaullists developed the role of the planning regions and in 1969 de Gaulle's referendum proposed both Senate and regional reforms (it was defeated). There was during the 1960s and 1970s a growth of regional consciousness that was expressed in many ways such as the attempts to revive languages and the development of cultural circles. At the same time the regional movements became more vocal and swung behind the left as the issue of regional disparities itself began to become more fully debated.

Regions

The Fifth Republic has developed the French regions. They were, in the 1960s, only planning committees that contributed to the national plan but de Gaulle proposed extending their authority in a defeated referendum of 1969. In the 1970s 22 regions were given small budgets and placed under the prefect. In 1982 a new statute making regions directly elected and making the council's leader (president) the chief executive transformed their situation. They were given an increased (though still small) budget and a wider remit over matters such as education and training. Their main activity, however, has been in investment in infrastructure and amenities and they promote regional economic development. Regions have retained their planning role and responsibilities are still being handed down to the regions from the centre.

By the early 1970s the regional aspect to policy-making was firmly established. In 1972 regional planning councils (with no powers) were set up, composed of the deputies and senators of the area and some nominated members. They were made legal entities and given limited powers as well as some small financial resources to a maximum of 55 francs per head, mainly raised through road tax. Leaders of the regions of all persuasions soon became irritated by their lack of autonomy.

The 'Defferre laws' of 1982 effected the main changes to the regions. The reforms created 22 metropolitan and 4 overseas directly elected regional governments and increased their prerogatives. They were not given constitutional status but executive power was transferred to the chair of the region and the prefects' *a priori tutelle* and financial supervision were also abolished. Regions were given economic responsibilities for regional planning, land management and support for the regional economy, and also took over apprentice and vocational training from the state. Regional Councils have power over buildings and investment for high schools, transport and infrastructure. They also have environmental and cultural responsibilities (for languages), as well as for housing, canals and ports, etc. France remains a unitary state and the regions are not the superiors of the communes or departments, which report directly to Paris. In 1986, at the first direct elections, the conservative right's landslide put them in control of all but two of the regions of metropolitan France (Limousin and Nord-Pas-de-Calais). Jacques Chirac's conservative government elected in 1986 did not modify the regional reforms and the consensus on the legitimacy of regional government was consolidated.

However, a struggle between the central government and the regional councils over authority was started at that time. There was also a simultaneous tussle with other local authorities, which felt threatened by the imposition of an additional tier of local government. This rivalry was acute with the departments, which retain the main local government functions. Regions have been given further powers over the years but remain relatively limited (with a small staff). Regional budgets are small and the councils cannot increase them to any great extent. Within the budget the state's grants form a large proportion (perhaps as high as 50 per cent) and that limits the regions' autonomy. They can hardly be said to be at the centre of French political life and they are not always consulted. For example, the Prime Minister announced the abolition of the regional component of the property tax in August 2000 to the complete surprise of the regional presidents and their representatives.

Regions have an elected council and a president. In 1986 a form of proportional representation was chosen for the regions, which fragments the representation and makes coalition government necessary but difficult to manage. Regions, with a few exceptions, were slow to develop a political personality. Some were artificial creations; others had long-standing identities. In the latter case they tended to assert themselves rather more forcefully than the newer units but they have all used their position as representatives to go beyond their original remit. They have developed regional cultural, environmental restructuring and promotional programmes. Regions have made less impact on economic policy than they have on schools. They built new secondary schools and improved others and increased their spending on them.

The regions have yet to emerge as the dominant local government unit and the commune and department remain pre-eminent. The fear that they would spring to prominence and lead to the disintegration of the unitary state has not proved true. They may have contributed to solving some sub-state problems (like Corsica, see below) but they cannot be said to have worsened them. Moreover the prefect, abolished in 1982, returned with increased powers. In fact many of the regions' needs have to go through the prefect, like the applications to Brussels and the regional plan. What was unexpected, however, was that Europe's regional policy would develop and increase the importance of regional representatives in Brussels.

Corsica

Corsica is a special case and the main challenge to the principle of Republican unity. Other regions have had separatist movements, and even violent ones, but nothing has approached that of Corsica in seriousness. There were, for example, some problems in Alsace in the 1930s and Brittany has always been distinctive. Brittany has, however, supported the mainstream parties and its nationalists have been divided and thrust onto extreme wings where they have had little popular presence.

Corsica

The small island of Corsica off the south coast of France has a population of about a quarter of a million and of these only about 140,000 are native Corsicans. It became part of France in 1769 but its language is distinctive and if anything more akin to Italian than French. More or less continuously since 1976, Corsica has been subject to separatist violence. In February 1998 the prefect, Claude Erignac, was killed as he peaceably went to a concert in the capital city Ajaccio. The factional rivalries of the groups and the involvement of criminals in many incidents make violence worse. French governments have tried to stem the island's economic decline by pouring in aid. The demand for independence is limited to about 20 per cent of the voters. Despite the concession of limited powers to Corsica, the violence and bombing did not completely stop.

Corsican nationalists

There are two main nationalist groups: the National Corsican Liberation Front (Historic) and the National Corsican Liberation Front (Regular). In 1991 the 'Regular' faction gave up armed action and the 'Historic' faction continued. They have both warred in the past and one three-month settling of accounts in 1995 led to twelve deaths. Another small group named Sampieru might have been responsible for the death of the prefect Claude Erignac in February 1998. Over the 1990s there were about 400 deaths but many of these were the settling of accounts between Corsican nationalist factions and not directed against the state. In August 2001 the death of the nationalist leader François Santoni was part of an inter-Corsican vendetta but almost wrecked the 'Matignon agreements' on devolution to the island.

Corsica has a population of about 250,000. It is a poor Mediterranean island depending on farming and tourism and it has a language of its own similar to Italian. The island had a brief independence (1729–69) before it was acquired by the French state shortly before the Revolution. Its integration into the Republic has been fitful. It underwent serious decline in the 1950s and 1960s while the rest of France experienced its economic miracle. In the 1960s the independence of Algeria led to the return of settlers to France. Perhaps 500 of these *pied noir* families were helped to buy land and develop tourism in Corsica. The special treatment of the *pied noirs*, and their entrepreneurial business, created a tension that has not been dissipated. In the 1970s Corsican regionalism began to stir. Some of these groups advocated independence and others a more limited devolution but there were also those willing to use violence.

To many this was an issue of law and order and the police were called on to deal with the problem, although the situation of the island attracted some wider attention. With the election of the Socialists in 1981 and the decentralisation laws Corsica's special status was recognised. Corsica was given some control over its economic development and culture. The new Corsican Assembly was to be able to consult the government and it was to be given powers over culture, transport, planning and education. However, other regions were given even greater control over their affairs and the Corsican statute did not enable the Corsicans to deal with issues such as language. In the period 1988–93 there was a further attempt to deal with the island's status. In 1991 the new statute granted a status comparable with the overseas territories but the Constitutional Council struck out the reference to the 'Corsican people, a component of the French people' as undermining the unity of the French nation. This new statute did not stop the continuing agitation or political violence.

In 1997 the Socialist government sought to reimpose order after a further round of violent campaigns. The riposte to this clamp-down was the assassination of the prefect Claude Erignac and there then followed a further tightening of the screw on Corsican illegal activity (lending to the departure of the new prefect under a cloud). Rather than restarting a further spiral of violence, the government promoted negotiation with the extremists. This was not new: previous governments, while vowing never to deal with 'men of violence', had held negotiations in secret. This time, however, negotiations were in the open. The upshot was the so-called 'Matignon agreements' spanning the left and right and including most autonomists. The island's Assembly was given the right to amend laws passed by the Assembly and to set its own regulations. These were watered down from the initial more far-reaching proposals and the lack of direct law-making powers may not meet nationalist demands. However, Corsica would have real autonomy, control of its culture and education, and the Corsican language would be taught in primary schools after 2002.

Internally, Corsica is politically divided and its Assembly is endlessly fragmented. Within Corsica there are those opposed to devolution as well as separatists. The 'nationalists' obtain about 20 per cent of the vote in the regional elections but their influence amongst the Corsicans born on the island is much greater and the population is not willing to disown them (about 65 per cent of islanders did not want independence). Corsica's future depends on the ability of local politicians to find an equilibrium as well as on whether the violence, which has been endemic in the political process, can be controlled. Many politicians in France, notably the Jospin government's Minister of the Interior Jean-Pierre Chevènement (who resigned in protest), fear that the granting of special status to Corsica is the thin end of the wedge that will separate France into autonomous and increasingly sovereign regions. Most French voters, on the other hand, hoped that the problem could be solved with a measure of home rule, although in 2001 about 43 per cent of mainland opinion could envisage independence for the island.

'Confetti of empire'

Created in 1946, the overseas departments (*départements d'outre-mer*, DOM) are Guadeloupe, Guiana, Martinique and Réunion, the remnants of the French Empire that chose to remain attached to France. The three overseas territories (*territoires d'outre-mer*, TOM) chose that status in 1958 and they are New Caledonia, Polynesia and Wallis and Futuna. TOM have a slightly different position under the Constitution, their local authorities can be organised differently, the application of French law can be excluded and they have elected assemblies which are involved in advance with matters which concern them. There have been autonomist movements and demands for greater control in the DOM, but these have often been balanced by a worry that they might be abandoned. They receive subsidies (which may have to be phased out), civil servants working in them get high allowances and social security benefits are the same as metropolitan France. Together the DOM/TOM send 22 deputies to the Assembly.

Overseas France

Known as the DOM-TOM (*départements et territoires d'outre-mer*), France has departments and territories overseas – the remnants of Empire. Overseas departments were, like Algeria was, full departments, and the territories were administered by the Colonial Office, but both returned deputies to the Assembly after 1946. In the Fifth Republic most of the territories (and Algeria) became independent but there are a few remaining scattered enclaves and islands (with a combined population of about 1.5 million): DOM: Martinique, Guadeloupe, Réunion, Guiana; TOM: French Polynesia, New Caledonia, Wallis and Futuna. Some of these have small independence movements.

New Caledonia

This island in the Pacific has been troubled by disputes (often violent) between the indigenous population (the 'Kanaks') and the settlers of French origin who each composed about 40 per cent of the population (the remaining 20 per cent was Polynesian). An independence movement began to develop after 1968 based on the Kanaks' view that they were not being treated equally and that settlers had appropriated the island's main resources of minerals (substantial) and land. In 1981 the election of President Mitterrand aroused expectations of reform which were not met and the situation got steadily more tense and more violent. In 1984 there was an attempt to find a solution but this was scrapped by the return of the right to French government in 1986 and a further deterioration set in. This in turn led to a violent confrontation on the eve of the 1988 elections and an assassination shortly after of the Kanak leader Tjibaou. The incoming Prime Minister Rocard, however, managed to negotiate a solution based on increased aid and a revisiting of the independence question later that enabled a return to normality.

Conclusion

What emerges from this survey of local government is that it is an active and innovative part of the political system taking the lead in projects (such as Giscard's Vulcania Park in Auvergne or commercial developments in communes). It does not, as the legal framework might suggest, wait for central government to take the initiative and meanwhile passively administer local affairs. The relationship between centre and locality is not one of dependency but is characterised by political bargaining in which the give and take is constant and far from one-sided. There is a desire by the Paris centre and by the prefects to get things done and the local authorities have to be brought into a fruitful co-operation. In this process the importance of the local politician, whose position is reinforced by a local elected post, is crucial and the state has to work with powerful 'notables'. These factors are not new – they existed before the Defferre reforms of 1982 – but they have become more important in recent years.

France faces a number of local government problems of which autonomist violence is but a small part. There are still unsolved disparities of wealth and treatment, which the Republicans regard as an affront, and there are pockets of depopulation and decline that are not being tackled by the authorities. But local government is an essential part of the political fabric and no British-style rationalisation is conceivable. A pragmatism and gradualness is required in local reform if it is to gain consent and be a success. On the whole, this is an accepted fact of political life in France, but things have not remained the same. The 'Jacobin' state has been adapted and most Presidents have added their touches to the local and regional framework of government. In particular there were the decentralising Defferre laws of 1982 which changed much while relying on – and sometimes reinforcing – existing structures.

French local government is close to the citizen in its small size as well as in its response to people's concerns. It is the intermediary between the state and the ordinary people and it humanises what would otherwise be a remote and ineffectual bureaucracy. This is an important attribute for any modern country. Local government, with its old traditions, also enables people to identify with their government in a way that is not easily dismantled. These bonds are also important in any political system.

Local government also provides a recruiting and training ground for politicians as well as a means of participation: the sheer scale of local government means that many people can participate in the system through officeholding. This last point is not often made. Politicians can climb the local government rungs and make a career on the back of that structure, so much is well known. But in addition the possibilities for participation by the French people are enormously increased by the numbers of elected posts in local government, which need to be filled. There are something like 500,000 local councillors and that brings French local government as close to a participatory citizens' democracy as is possible in this imperfect world. People take their place as councillors and then, perhaps, return to private life but their contribution is made and their insight into politics is increased. Whether the inefficiencies of French local government, with its tiny communes and dispersed officeholders supervised by a cumbrous state, is a price worth paying is a moot question, but one settled in local government's favour in today's France.

Summary

- French local government is formally rigid but is in reality highly flexible.
- The fiercely defended unitary state makes concessions to territorial entities through the Senate but also in local government and, since 1986, the regions.
- The maintenance of Republican unity has been challenged by the Corsican settlement of 2001. Devolution of power to Corsica has proved difficult. Corsican regionalism borders on a sub-state nationalism and concessions were made by Paris on key points of language and local legislation. These were seen in some quarters as a 'sell out' of the Republic.
- In the absence of strong party structures local government is a key resource for aspiring politicians. Politicians represent the interests of their region, city or town and bargain for these interests with the centre in a non-ideological framework.
- Local powers are unlikely to be relinquished and have been extended in the Fifth Republic (in contrast to the same period in the UK).

- France remains a society of relatively small towns and cities. Attachments to locality are strong and the interaction with the state is very often done through the local politician rather than (or as well as) directly.

Further reading

Ashford, D., *British Dogmatism and French Pragmatism* (Allen and Unwin, 1982)

Ashford, D., 'Decentralising France: how the Socialists discovered pluralism' *West European Politics* 13: 4, 1990, pp. 46–65

Balme, R. and Jouve, B., 'The French region as a space for public policy' in P. Le Galès and L. Hooghe (eds), *Cohesion and Policy and European Integration* (Oxford University Press, 1996)

Kesselman, M., *The Ambiguous Consensus: A Study of Local Government in France* (Knopf, 1967)

Mény, Y., 'The Socialist decentralisation' in G. Ross, S. Hoffmann and S. Malzacher (eds), *The Mitterrand Experiment* (Polity, 1987)

Michel, H., 'Government or governance? The case of the French local political system' in *West European Politics* 21: 3, 1998, pp. 146–57

de Montricher, N., 'Decentralisation in France' *Governance* 8: 3, 1995, pp. 405–18

Schmidt, V., *Democratizing France: The Political and Administrative History of Decentralization* (Cambridge University Press, 1990)

Weber, E., *Peasants into Frenchmen* (Chatto, 1979)

Questions

1 Does the strength of local power mean that France is 'an Empire on top and a Republic underneath'?
2 What changes have been made to local and regional power in the Fifth Republic?
3 Does decentralised power make for national political fragmentation?

7

Interest groups

Pressure groups or interest groups are a feature of western political systems. In societies as diverse as modern Europe the myriad interests of the population are not easily channelled into the political parties and not always fully expressed at national level. People naturally seek other ways of making their views felt and, although tiny political parties are able to form and compete, the interest group is a normal means of pressure on government in western societies. It is not surprising to find them in France, which is as diverse and as competitive as other European countries.

Pressure groups, unlike parties, typically do not want to exercise power; they want to influence government policy on specific issues. Here there is another example of French exceptionalism: in France some interest groups do set up parties of their own or stand in elections. This is an unusual feature of French interest groups, exemplified by Pierre Poujade's mid-1950s shopkeepers' pressure group, which rapidly became an extreme right-wing anti-tax movement

---

Poujadism

Pierre Poujade's ephemeral movement bequeathed a new word to the vocabulary of political abuse: 'poujadist'. Pierre Poujade was a shopkeeper from rural Saint-Céré who led a protest movement which peaked in the mid-1950s (unfortunately for Poujade, not at the 1956 elections) under the name of Union de défence des commerçants et artisans (UDCA). The protest was directed mainly at high taxes but on the back of that came a resistance to modernisation, ordinary people against the rich, attacks on bureaucracy and decolonisation, mixed with an anti-Semitic rhetoric and a populist knock-about style. In the 1956 elections the UDCA campaigned to 'sortez les sortants' and polled 11 per cent (52 seats including the young Le Pen) but Poujade himself was not elected. It then collapsed, undercut by other parties and the lack of leadership as well as by internal quarrels, and Poujade, objecting to de Gaulle's return, returned to obscurity.

121

and won 53 seats in the 1956 general elections. Poujade's party faded rapidly when faced with the exigencies of power (leaving the term 'poujadist' to posterity) but other interest groups have put up candidates and fought elections in the 1990s.

Until the Third Republic the Revolutionary law forbidding the formation of sectional interest groups remained in force and only in 1901 was the law changed, recognising the rights to association and setting out the legal framework for non-profit-making societies. This law enabled groups to register and to be given legal status as well as some local government subsidies; some can employ a small staff. This means that some pressure groups have state support and others (like Chambers of Commerce) have an even more developed semi-public status. But because pressure groups receive public money it does not make them the clients of the government (parties also receive state handouts), as the confrontations over the last two decades show. The state is intertwined with pressure groups in a very large number of committees and through the Economic and Social Council on which the representatives of interests sit. Under Articles 69, 70 and 71 of the Fifth Republic Constitution the Council gives advice on laws. Even so the state, it is assumed on both the left and the right, should be powerful enough to overrule sectional groups and decide on the national interest.

Although French civil society is often said to be underdeveloped and that intermediate associations and interest groups are not as vigorous as they are in the UK and USA, there is a rich culture of lobbies, issue groups and pressure groups espousing the whole range of causes. This, in numbers and diversity, is probably comparable to other western political systems. Groups come and go, and many are ephemeral, so there is no saying what the exact number of active groups is at any one time. Some, like the Municipal Action Groups, which flourished in some big cities in the late 1960s and 1970s, achieve their objectives and are progressively wound down.

However, it is estimated that there were about 700,000 associations in 1999 and as many as 50,000 could be formed each year. A large number of these will be leisure or sporting groups (which are a feature of French local life) but there are also social groups, consumers' groups (there are about 20 of these) and religious groups. Leisure groups, such as anglers and hunters, can become actively political if their interests are infringed, although mostly they are a fixture of society without political implications. In the 1990s hunters felt that their pastime was under threat and they quickly organised themselves as the Chasse, pêche, nature et traditions (CPNT) party (they won 4 per cent in the 1999 European elections). There is a long tradition of association for mutual benefit and for the defence or promotion of interests at a local or national level and perhaps as many as a third of French people are involved in one way or another with these groups. They therefore involve many people and the often-promoted view of France a society of isolated individuals is misleading. Interest groups expressing their concerns through lobbies, on the streets and in direct

---

Chasse, pêche, nature et traditions (CPNT)

This movement, organised around departmental hunting clubs, put up candidates at European and regional elections from 1989. It sprang to prominence with 1.2 million votes in the European elections of 1999. It contests the policies which ecologists promote for rural France and also clashes with the European Union (which restricted the season for shooting migrating birds). It represents the powerful lobby of game hunters who are mainly ordinary people and who exercise a long established right. It may have ambitions to become a full political party but in the main it tries to exert pressure on the established parties (normally conservatives).

---

action are not Fifth Republic innovations and of course the Fourth Republic fell as a result of the actions of the colonial lobby and street demonstrations that Paris could not control.

On a lower level, the numerous private distillers who were allowed to distil a small amount of tax-free alcohol 'for their own use' became notorious in the 1950s. They formed a highly organised and truculent pressure group protecting their privileges and were successful in their defence until the Fifth Republic. The special interests, which were so evident in previous Republics (and so deplored), have not disappeared and remain strong. If French politics has never been confined to Parliament, then neither has the Fifth Republic's creation of the executive presidency succeeded in centralising politics on the Elysée. In 1968, after student riots, the government rapidly produced a bill for the reform of the universities. This was despite de Gaulle's antipathy to organised interests and the Fifth Republic's determination to change the old ways in order to set the national interest as it saw fit. In 1984, 1986 and 1994 the government was also forced to withdraw proposed legislation in response to street demonstrations.

It is clear to many observers that the pattern of interest group activity in France does not fit any particular model of representation. In the academic disputes on models of interest group representation which have pitted the 'pluralists' against the 'neo-corporatists', the French case has been claimed by both sides and claimed to be the proving case by the protagonists. On the one hand there is a view that the French people do not like joining associations and that the diversity of civil society is correspondingly low relative to other European nations (see for example the relatively low party memberships). On the other hand there are extremely close relations between government and business and the influence of unions in some sectors. There are also periodic strike waves and direct action by groups which are unusual (if not quite unique) in western Europe.

As noted, the French state has a different view of its role from its 'Anglo-Saxon' counterparts. The French state sees itself as the general interest above the factions and sectional interests that, given the chance, would distort policy for their particular ends. From this Jacobin viewpoint, there is a dubious legitimacy about the activities of lobbies, pressure groups and unions and they are therefore not brought into the policy-making process as they might be elsewhere. Their exclusion may, possibly, be the cause of protests as interested parties can only influence policy at the point where it is almost implemented. The state should therefore be strong and should not be captured by sectional groups who would then insert their vested interests in place of the general will. However, this, as a generalisation, fails in several areas where political expediency has prevailed over Jacobin state ideology. It is another area in which rhetoric and politics are at odds even though the pretence of the neutral and all-powerful state may be maintained. Bargaining and logrolling are a part of French state activity (as they are elsewhere). Local government prefects are examples of the formally authoritative state which in fact negotiates daily with pressure groups and sub-national powers.

Models of interest group activity

F. L. Wilson (1987) argues that there are four models of interest group representation as applied to France. Each of these succeeds in capturing one aspect of the situation but does not provide a total account. These four models are the pluralist, the Marxist, the neo-corporatist and the protest model. In the 'pluralist' model there is a competition between multiple organisations of interests expressing the demands of groups and individuals with none capable of domination. The state holds the ring for the conflict while at the same time allowing the policy to be followed to emerge. In the 'pluralist' view there is a roughly equal distribution of power through society and the public interest emerges from the conflict of sectional interests. The state in France has been more active than is compatible with this model and its application to French conditions has always been contested.

The Marxist model, which depicts interest groups as expressing either workers' or bourgeois demands, has some attraction because of the strength of the political unions and the division of union activity into political confederations. However, it is not applicable to society as a whole and the interests represented are more intricate than allowed for in the Marxist model – even 'revolutionary' unions do not necessarily support a 'socialist' transformation. It might be noted that the French interest groups are very often also politically split. Often the pattern is socialist, Communist and moderate but in some areas there may be extreme right groups and Catholic groups as well as moderate and radical splits (the radicals frequently having a Trotskyite inflection).

France did undergo a period of 'corporatism' during the war when the Vichy collaborationist regime tried to copy the fascist state of Mussolini's Italy. Under the wartime Vichy regime official unions were set up and these became part of the state structure intended to co-operate with the authorities and with employers. These unions were in fact without autonomy and subordinate to the state so that at the end of the war they were discredited and the contemporary system has no roots in the Vichy regime. 'Neo-corporatism' refers to the tripartite system of state, unions and employers which bargains and makes economic policy for the sector involved. Interest groups are brought into the policy process and allowed a monopoly (or near monopoly) over representation in their sector in return for applying restraints on members. These relationships are outside of the formal political procedures (Parliament and the presidency) and depart from the 'pluralist' model in that such groups are hierarchical and dominate the sector rather than competing for influence.

Yet France is not 'neo-corporatist', even though successive governments have tried to develop the tripartite negotiation between unions, employers and the state (with the state in the driving role) that is characteristic of northern Europe. There is, however, no collective decision-making of a Swedish or Austrian nature in France. The social democratic 'social partnership' through which wages and prices are negotiated and agreed has no equivalent and the trade unions rarely have the near monopoly of representation that would make it possible. Pressure groups retain their independence and so does government. Neither government nor interest groups wish to be constrained by their partners, although they can both gain from collaboration.

Yet there are sectors in France where government and pressure groups are very close, notably agriculture, and these have been called 'meso-corporatist'. In this system the state consults interests but it falls short of a neo-corporatism because the French government sought out a partner to develop and implement its policy. In the case of agriculture the state wanted to modernise agriculture and eventually in the 1960s the farmers' union did become open to collaboration – though it kept its autonomy. All the same the French state is active, not a neutral arbiter, and has shaped the politics of the Fifth Republic. Moreover, the farmers' union is a producers' union (not a workers' trade union) and it has disagreed – sometimes violently – even with the conservative governments which brought it into very close association with the state. There is an understandable tendency for the politicians to listen to and reward the pressure groups on 'their' side of the divide (left or right) and to involve them more closely, and conversely to push out the other side's. What is unusual about the farmers' union has been its ability to remain the privileged interlocutor despite changes in government from conservative to Socialist.

The relationship between the French state and pressure groups is, on the whole, not like the farmers' experience. It is manifest in a number of forms from the antagonistic to the collaborative. Some unions adopt the 'syndicalist' view that the state and the parties are the opposition and so unions should be prepared to depend on their own efforts; other unions are in competition with each other in a 'pluralist' manner. There is, in short, no one form of French pressure group activity in what is an extremely diverse sector of the political system.

Protest

Protest activity in France deserves some particular attention as it is the most spectacular aspect of interest group activity and highly distinctive. Most people will be familiar with the 'events' of May 1968 when student demonstrations were followed after a couple of weeks by a general strike which brought the country to a halt for a month or so. This pattern was repeated in 1986 when student action also led to a general strike and to a government climb-down after an attempt to enforce a tough line had failed. These were not exceptional: although not preceded by student action, there were general strikes in 1936, 1953 and 1995 which forced governments to change course.

Strikes

French strikes tend to be spectacular and disruptive, blocking roads and ports, but going by the number of working days lost per year, striking workers do not wrack France. Over the post-war period as a whole the French record is middling for an industrial country (better than Italy, the UK or Spain but worse than Germany). The days lost have tended to drop, although blips can be caused by particular incidents (like the 1997 truckers' strike which had wide ramifications). It is a feature of French industrial relations, however, that there are periodic widespread almost general strikes like in May 1968 or the winter of 1995–96.

There have been 'interest group' activities at a more local level which are also disruptive. These are outbursts of strike action, occupations (of schools by parents, for example) or blockades which halt certain sectors or even paralyse the country and which often inconvenience people (like travellers) on a massive scale at crucial times. There is a long history of illegal or quasi-legal, but traditional action that goes unchecked, as well as of strikes which become general very rapidly after being touched off by a sectional interest. People will be familiar with the disruptions of ports (around the Channel, of course, but also on the Mediterranean coast), air traffic control strikes, and road haulage barricades which often affect the holiday season, but there are other actions by farmers and factory workers which can be more violent.

Yet France, contrary to the impression given by such incidents, is not particularly strike-prone. Workers, as the statistics indicate, do not go on strike at the drop of a hat. Strike action has been declining since the late 1960s both in terms of the numbers of workers involved and days lost through industrial action. France is one of the least affected countries in the western world, lower in strike action than the UK, but much higher than Germany, the Netherlands or Austria (or Japan). Working days lost by strike action are not high and the level of union membership is very low. It is important not to confuse the situation in France with the UK where (as with other 'northern European' states) union membership is high as a percentage of the workforce and where union discipline is traditionally strong. Many of the strike actions in France are spontaneous or the acts of non-union activists with a particular issue at heart. In May 1968, to take one example, the factory strikes following the student unrest were wholly unexpected. The government, the employers and the unions were taken aback by the rapidity and vigour of the strike wave which soon covered the whole country. Confronted with a general strike the government had to find somebody to negotiate with to end the strikes and the only interlocutor was the unions. The unions were also keen to regain control over 'their' workers and struggled to lead a movement they had not started and which they did not run.

There is a connection between weak unions and low strike rates which is possibly one of the causes of the sporadic and spontaneous outbursts that afflict the country. French unions are split into political confederations (creating, as it were, several different TUCs) and these organisations have difficulty in co-operating. The unions are strong in some sectors (notably the public sector and teaching) but are not, generally, representative of the workforce. Problems can build up on the shop floor until they spill over into spontaneous strike action and they can be set off by action in another sector. Student demonstrations can, for example, indicate to disgruntled workers the possibilities for action, which can then be taken up following the pattern set by previous (and well-remembered) 'wildcat' strikes. Stoppages and strikes can be seen as a sign of workers' exasperation or of the frustration of small businesses rather than of strength.

There is little the government can do when confronted by these broadly supported and spontaneous strike actions. Unions, being marginal, cannot be fined or do much to get people to go back to work, although they usually become intermediaries in negotiations. In the case of fishers and road haulier blockades the intervention by the police (or the army) against 'secondary pickets' would be near impossible. There is safety in numbers and the logistical difficulty in bulldozing (for example) thousands of long distance lorries off the roads and motorways would be too great to make such a 'tough' response possible.

In addition the French public is not as ill disposed to the strikers as those directly hit by the action (holiday makers or exporters) and 66 per cent are prepared to strike themselves (and 36 per cent to occupy factories). Over the 1990s French public opinion has tended to sympathise or even to back strikers. Polls on the strikes in the autumn of 2000 found 41 per cent supportive, 28 per cent sympathetic, 11 per cent indifferent, 10 per cent opposed, 7 per cent hostile and 3 per cent with no view (*Le Monde*, 3 July 2001). In the winter of 1995 the government had no success in opposing the rail strikes. Then it failed in the attempt to turn opinion against the strikers by mobilising the inconvenienced commuters. The public, despite being badly inconvenienced, can see grievances behind the strike action as 'reasonable'. Some sectors, like health workers, pensioners or truckers, get more understanding than others, like public transport workers or the unemployed. One exception to this was the national transport

Unions

There are five main union confederations in France: the Confédération générale du travail (CGT), the Confédération française democratique du travail (CFDT), the Confédération française des travailleurs chrélieus (CFTC), the Confédération générale des cadres et de l'encadrement (CGC) and Force ouvrière (FO). There are some other smaller unions joined together in the Union nationale des syndicats autonomes and the Groupe des dix. According to the International Labour Office France had the lowest trade union membership in Europe in 1997. There were probably only about 2,100,000 members in 1993, some 11 per cent of the salaried workforce. This low membership is a long-term position; it was about 25 per cent in the 1970s and there has been a continuing decline from a low start. Membership is lower than comparable countries and below the rates in countries like Ireland, Italy and Spain. Sweden heads the list with 90 per cent of the labour force in unions but Germany has 29 per cent and the UK 33 per cent.

The Confédération générale des cadres et de l'encadrement (CGC) is a strictly management union confederation which was set up to defend middle management and has affiliates representing those workers. It is strongest in the tertiary sector and in big business but it has about 110,000 members (1995) in commerce, chemicals, food processing, finance, banking and metal working. Its Secretary General is Claude Cambus.

The Fédération de l'éducation nationale (FEN) is the confederation of teachers' unions. Although union membership in teaching is relatively high the numbers have been falling and there was a split in 1992. It has about 140,000 members (1995) and its Secretary General is Hervé Baro.

The Fédération syndicale unitaire de l'enseignement (FSU) is the teachers' unions which split from the FEN and has about 140,000 members (1995), mainly in secondary education where it has a majority. Its General Secretary is Monique Vaulliat.

The Union nationale des syndicats autonomes (UNSA) is the co-operation of seven diverse union organisations from teaching, agriculture, civil service, police, transport and the entertainment world. It has about 300,000 members (1995).

Le Groupe des dix is a very loose association of small unions (including tax officers and posts) and is to the left of the traditional unions. It was important in action against unemployment in 1994 and the strikes of 1995. It has about 60,000 members (1995).

strike in 1999. The strike was a protest against concessions made in the agreement ushering in the 35-hour week.

However, the rapid flare-up and then disappearance of French strikes does pose one difficulty. Strikes are ended by negotiation and an agreement is made. In the absence of any strike organisation the agreement may not be adhered to.

It is then difficult (or impossible) to remobilise the workforce to impose the agreement. A road hauliers' strike in 1996 was repeated in 1997 because the original agreement made with the strikers had not been put into effect. In many cases the main issue might be solved but the attendant problems might be neglected and simmer on as a cause of future discontent.

Types of interest group

French politics hosts a variety of pressure and interest groups. Groups within the state itself will be left aside. These state interests, like local government, nationalised industries and the 'grands corps', all have influence and run lobbies (but they will be dealt with elsewhere), and of course the state itself is far from monolithic. However, the focus here is on private interests in French civil society outside of the state and there are multitudes of them. There are various ways to classify these interest groups and there is no agreement on how to do so. The starting point is perhaps S. E. Finer's distinction between 'occupational interest groups' with a function or an economic good at stake and advocacy 'promotional groups' with an issue orientation of a much broader and more general nature.

Occupational groups

Occupational groups include the unions, the business and owners' organisations (like truckers), farmers and the liberal professions, and are usually well-funded and well-organised. They are active and influential with sophisticated strategies of power and can react quickly to proposed changes in policy that they regard as against their interest. Their importance varies with the political climate but they are involved in day-to-day bargaining in the economy (on wage rates for example) and have an influence beyond their interaction with government.

Union organisation does not fall into a simple pattern. Unions are, for example, much more strongly implanted in the public sector than in the private. There are industries which have been made into virtual 'closed shops', and there are some extremely powerful unions in sectors such as electricity generating and farming. The pattern of French interest group activity does not fall into the ideal known as 'pluralism' in which interest groups compete with each other in an equal manner and on a 'level playing field' with fair play ensured by a neutral state. In the pluralist view interest groups are numerous and competitive, free of the state's control or subsidy and do not hold a monopoly or near monopoly of representation. This has led to descriptions of some French interest group relations with the state as 'neo-corporatism'. It is an accusation which has some truth in some fields and is serious, but in others (as stated) unions are too dispersed and weakly organised to be 'neo-corporatist'.

Only about 13 per cent of the French civilian labour force belong to a union, lower than in the USA and a lot lower than in France's partners in the European Union. In addition the tradition of French unionism is different from that of the main 'northern European' societies where union strength has long been a feature of politics. The origins and outlooks of the French unions are different from those in the English-speaking world, although they have greater affinity with the 'southern' nations of Spain, Italy and Portugal. Union power is not negligible but it does not approach the position of the Scandinavian or German mass-member unions. Unions are important in more than just wage bargaining. There are Social Security Boards, Labour Courts and Factory Tribunals where the unions put up slates of candidates and vie with each other for influence. Non-union candidates also win but the unions are organised for these elections and they are taken as a measure of union strength. The unions did not increase their membership with the arrival of the Socialist government in 1981 because the Communist CGT would have been the principal gainer and the President did not want to increase Communist power. The unions did, however, all suffer from their association with austerity, and unemployment reduced their membership.

The main union confederation is the CGT. It was founded in 1885 and became the focus for *syndicalism*, a form of revolutionary anarchism hostile to capitalism, the state and political parties. In this creed the general strike by the workers would bring down capitalism and they refused to compromise with the 'bourgeois' system. This creed was more rhetoric than action but it had the practical consequence of supporting direct action and keeping the unions at a distance from the rising socialist movement which, in other countries, they would have supported. In 1919 came the first division when Catholic workers founded the Confédération française des travailleurs chrétiens (CFTC), which

---

Confédération générale du travail (CGT)

At its foundation in the nineteenth century this union asserted its independence of political parties. However, since 1947 it has been run by the Communist Party and has always had a Communist majority on its governing committee. It has been strongest in the heavy industries and the nationalised sector but it has been in decline since the 1950s and has struggled to maintain its position as the dominant union. It is the oldest and the largest with 630,00 members in 1994 (480,000 working, the rest retired) and it gets the biggest vote in works elections; it is bigger in the public sector than in private industry. Its biggest unions are in energy, metal work, rail and post but it is virtually absent from the modern sectors of banking, insurance, building and financial services. It is still dominated by the Communist Party, and its leader Bernard Thibault is on the party's national committee, but the party's internal disputes and inconstant line have given the CGT a margin of freedom for the first time since the Second World War.

Confédération française des travailleurs chrétiens (CFTC)

Founded in 1919, this Catholic union federation grew out of the Church's social mission to the working class and its attempt to offer an alternative to Socialist and Marxist unions. The union itself was created in 1919 and sought to expand further its social Catholic view. After the war it was linked to the MRP but, like the Christian democrats, it was torn between its conservatives and left-leaning groups. In 1964 the bulk (about 80 per cent) of the union split to form the CFDT and left behind a mainly white-collar union of marginal importance. CFTC has about 100,000 members and is mainly in private education, employees and middle management in health, rail and local government. Its president is Alain Deleu and its General Secretary is Jacques Voisin.

Confédération française démocratique du travail (CFDT)

This is the offshoot, after 1964, of the Catholic CFTC and is a secular union federation with links to the Socialist Party. It rapidly grew to become the second (by some measures) of the union federations and was a novel institution in the 1960s and 1970s taking up issues that the older unions did not and bearing the banner of 'self-management'. It was able to recruit in sectors like the new technological industries and services which were reluctant to join the CGT, and it was an influential voice outside of the major political parties. It had about 515,000 members (420,000 working) in the mid-1990s but it has lost members since the 1970s. Its main strengths are in health, metal work, local government, rail and transport and education but it also has strength in finance and non-financial services (post, electricity and banks) where it is bigger than the CGT. It has taken a more reformist line than other unions and it approved the Juppé plan at the start of the strikes in 1995. This lost it support and started an internal struggle, although its leader Nicole Notat remained in office.

itself split in 1964 with the formation of the secular Confédération française démocratique du travail (CFDT). The CGT's revolutionary impetus grew, however, under the impact of the First World War and the rising Marxist tide, and after the Popular Front of 1936 the Communist supporters had a strong position in the unions. After the Liberation the CGT had about four million members but this dominant Communist influence became divisive and in 1947 the CGT split into the CGT and the non-Communist Force ouvrière (FO). There is also the teachers' confederation, the Fédération de l'éducation nationale (FEN), which split in 1992, and the Confédération générale des cadres (CGC). In the Fifth Republic the CGT, CFDT and FO were the largest confederations but the unions were deeply divided. Since the split in 1947 the Communist unions

> ## Force ouvrière (FO)
>
> When the CGT was taken over by the Communists this group split off and set up a pro-Socialist but strongly anti-Communist union (its full name is CGT-FO). It is stronger in the white-collar public services like health and post than in private business. Its main strong points are in the Bouches-du-Rhône and the Garonne, the Loire-Atlantique, the Nord and Paris. It has played an important part in the co-management of social security but its new-found radicalism lost it the chair of the social security fund dealing with sickness benefits. It is the third union in size and may have about 400,000 members.

have been the largest but the Communist Party has used the movement for its own purposes. At the beginning of the Cold War the CGT withdrew from participation in negotiations with the state, proclaiming that it wished to have nothing to do with the 'capitalist' system. It has been led by Communists and has a Communist majority on its leadership council; although there have been disputes between the party leadership and the union behind closed doors, it has been a subordinate part of the Communist system. This tie to the Communist Party has contributed powerfully to the CGT's decline, which has been steady through the Fifth Republic: its leaders have supported the Communist Party and it has been unable to develop an autonomous policy. At the beginning of the Fifth Republic the decline had already set in and it probably had fewer than two million members.

In some professions like print and longshoremen the CGT was able more or less to enforce a closed shop, and in others like mining and construction the Communists were predominant. It is, however, a confederation of unions mainly representing the old 'smokestack' industries and manual workers, a sector in decline throughout western Europe. It is also strong in the national-ised industries of gas, electricity and rail. It lost members in the metal industry, post office, ports, textiles, building and education in 1999. Unlike the other unions the CGT has been unable to recruit in the newer industries and it has always been weak in the small business sector. Characteristically the CGT has been involved in a series of rearguard actions trying to delay the closure or restructuring of these older industries and its constituency has diminished with them. Its membership in 1999 was officially given as 653,127 (possibly below the CFDT) and that includes retired members.

At the CGT's 46th Congress in January 1999 its leadership changed. Louis Viannet was replaced by Bernard Thibault, the nominee of the Communist leader Robert Hue, and a more open approach accepting such things as the reduction of working hours and privatisation was adopted. At the same time as trying to gain from its association with government the CGT has tried to recoup losses by working with the unemployed, immigrants and ill-housed. Thibault, like his predecessors, was a Communist leader who had joined the CGT closed shop of SNCF La Villette (in the Paris suburbs) in 1974. He had probably been a Communist Party member since at least 1977 and was nominated to its National Committee in 1995. The announcement that Thibault would take over as CGT leader was made before the Congress, a practice which showed that Communist power over the CGT remained intact and that nomination not election remained the rule. Although not all 86 nominees for the CGT's Executive were elected (four dissidents were dropped), all nominees for the Confederal Bureau (supposedly the choice of the Executive) were elected, pointing up a similar conclusion. However, the usual measure of half Communist and half non-Communist members on the CGT's leadership was changed for the first time. This is an indication of the factionalisation of the Communist Party, whose members can no longer be relied on. Some party members might no longer apply the line and the CGT, once highly disciplined, reflects the party's problems.

The FO since its formation in 1947 has been a moderate socialist-inclined union confederation. It has been fiercely anti-Communist but has been wary of close association with government for fear of being accused of 'class collaboration' and has been chary of entanglements which would allow the CGT to pose as the most aggressive defender of the workers. Marc Blondel has led it since 1988 but it has been pushed leftward by Trotskyite factions (especially the Parti des travailleurs) and has repudiated some of its previously held positions (prioritising negotiation over strikes). It is no longer as hostile to the CGT. FO is mainly a white-collar union and is strong in the civil service.

The principal beneficiary of the FO's radicalisation has been the CFDT. It has sloughed off its revolutionary cast and has become pragmatic and willing to work with governments to find solutions to its members' problems. At its origin in 1964 it was left-leaning and it adopted the slogan of self-management, developing a view of a socialist society and acting, in the process, much like a political party. It played a big part in the events of May 1968 and led some of the more spectacular direct actions in that month. It supported the Socialist Party in the 1970s and the alliance of the left until it broke up in 1977. After that time it sought a less political route by calling for negotiation rather than confrontation. It was distancing itself from the parties, although it supported Mitterrand in 1981 and endorsed the Fabius government's austerity programme of modernisation in 1984. It extended its influence in the new industries without undue competition from the older unions. Its leader Nicole Notat has been outspoken (and attacked by other union members) and supported the Juppé government's unpopular social security reforms in 1995. It was rewarded by workers' votes and took the control of one branch of the Social Security system from the FO. It is possible that it has the largest membership: claimed to be 723,500 in 1999.

The FEN escaped the divisions of the Cold War intact and stayed together despite left/right conflicts and different interests. It represented almost all of the teaching profession at all levels (although other union confederations had their teaching unions) and it has substantial influence. It is closely associated with the state education system and is influential if not preponderant on many teaching issues. Teaching is a very highly unionised profession and the FEN is well organised and powerful. Like many other unions it offers numerous support services (including banks, insurance, tourist agencies, a publisher and retirement homes) and these are much more developed in FEN than other unions. FEN was traditionally close to the Socialist Party and the disastrous plan to bring the Church schools under the state system in 1984 (which led to the fall of the government) came from FEN's influence with Socialist deputies. Any proposal to reform the education system must reckon with the FEN, as the Socialists discovered in 1988 and again in March 2000 (when the Education Minister Claude Allègre had to resign) and as the conservatives had found in 1994. However, as a result of internal disputes and conflicts, the Fédération syndicale unitaire split away in 1993 taking about half of the membership and leaving the FEN minority in most branches of education. The new Fédération des syndicats unifiés was more combative and confrontational and less willing to negotiate and it had a large Communist contingent.

FEN has its parallels in other professions. These include the doctors' Ordre des médicins (to which they must all belong) and the health workers' Centre national des professions de santé, as well as similar bodies for dentists, architects, lawyers, etc., and these often set ethical standards for the profession. Liberal professions are brought together by the Union nationale des associations des professions libérales. In the recent past there have been strikes by medical personnel and even by judges and diplomats. These are not always economic and they may defend other interests of the profession.

Teachers' unions have been brought into the political system through a structure of joint management of affairs between the state and professional bodies or unions. This pattern is repeated elsewhere in France – notably in agriculture. In most countries involvement of agriculture with the state is very high. It is the sector in which the private sector and the state are the most closely intertwined. In France this is probably a consequence of the poor condition of French agriculture at the Liberation. At that time it was unmechanised, divided into plots which were too small, unscientific and badly managed. A great deal of state intervention was needed to modernise French agriculture and that naturally led to the state seeking a partner in the process. In addition the fluctuations of the agricultural market were smoothed out by state intervention from the time of the Popular Front in 1936 in the interests of stability. It is perhaps curious that the corporatism in this area has been so highly developed given the decentralised nature of farming, the dispersed units of production and the traditional 'peasant suspicion' of association and of the state.

The Fifth Republic continued the rapid modernisation and transformation of the French countryside promoted and planned by the state that had started under the Fourth Republic. Modernisation of the small subsistence farms was a disruptive process, deeply unsettling to a traditional milieu, which saw areas depopulated in a rural exodus. The consolidation of the farmers' organisation and rural solidarity was a reaction to these developments through local assistance and attempts to pressure the central state on agricultural issues. These issues included tax reduction, land redistribution or amalgamation of holdings into larger units, rebates on agricultural essentials and a protectionist price policy, which would give farmers a reasonable standard of living. Farmers participated in committees and groups devoted to farming problems and were intimately associated with the solutions.

It was in the Fifth Republic that the farmers became a potent political force, replacing the notorious peasant independence with a determined collectivism and creating a distinctive relationship with the state. Corporatism, usually associated with social democracy, reached a pitch of perfection in conservative France under the first three Presidents of the Fifth Republic. The farmers' union (FNSEA) by the late 1960s constituted an 'Empire within the state'.

There are, as with industrial unions, a number of farmers' unions in France. There is the Communist Mouvement de défence des exploitants familaux (MODEF), the tiny Socialist Confédération nationale syndicale des travailleurs-paysans (CNSTP) and the right-wing Fédération française de l'agriculture (FFA). CNSTP is Socialist-inclined but is concerned to keep the family farms alive and proposes a minimum wage for farmers. MODEF has mainly small farms and is represented best in the marginal farming areas. It is opposed to the modernisation programme, believing that small farms (believed unviable by others) can be saved through government action. These unions are influential in some areas and represent the farmers suffering from the continuing transformation of French agriculture into large-scale businesses, but by any measure they constitute a minority of the farmers.

However, by the 1950s, the biggest (by far) was the Fédération nationale des syndicats d'exploitants agricoles (FNSEA) and its domination has increased during the Fifth Republic. It won most of the seats (90 per cent or so) in the Chambers of Agriculture and was a nation-wide organisation with a big proportion of the active farmers as its members. The possibilities for a close relationship with the state were increased by the FNSEA's hegemony over the farming business community – a domination that has few parallels elsewhere in France. The Chambers, elected in each department by the farmers, were another Fifth Republic development. Although they had existed in the Fourth Republic they were given a much bigger budget and called on to represent farming and facilitate reform.

De Gaulle's new Republic, keen to change France's antiquated agricultural structure by promoting modernisation and the consolidation of holdings (small farms were increasingly less economic) but also to minimise social disruption, cultivated ties with the FNSEA. The FNSEA was drawn into the policy-making process to control the transformation and to ensure minimal upheaval. At first there were farmers' demonstrations (and some violent disruption), notably in 1961, but these were overcome, although they served to underscore the importance of the farmers' organisation to the government if it wanted to implement reforms. This lesson was repeated in the mid-1960s and the rural vote for de Gaulle's Christian democratic opponent Jean Lecanuet in 1965 was a warning of the dangers of alienating the farmers. Despite subsidies and price support, the drift from the land continued and the smaller farms became increasingly less viable. However, by the late 1960s the FNSEA had accepted the transformation of agriculture and FNSEA became the privileged interlocutor using its position not to stem modernisation but to help farmers caught up in the process. It was strongly represented on planning bodies and on the organisations helping create economic units (by buying land to consolidate farms, for example). In the Fifth Republic the FNSEA has tended to be dominated by the larger, and richer, farmers and has been centre-left and gaullist in outlook with virtually no contribution from the left to its governing bodies.

During the years of the conservative presidencies the FNSEA was officially recognised, present in decision-making circles and on state bodies in a unique way – no other unions were so privileged. Thus state policy was formulated with an FNSEA contribution and more importantly the budget for agriculture was administered by bodies on which FNSEA representatives sat. This big union was present on committees dealing with the whole range of agricultural matters and at local level many policies were handled by institutions (like restructuring committees) dominated by the FNSEA. It was an important (sometimes essential) go-between for the ordinary farmer who wanted access to the state. This all amounted to a powerful incentive to join and support the FNSEA, but also a disincentive to join any other union even if farmers disagreed with FNSEA policy. The FNSEA, much more than other unions, also received handsome subsidies from the state. All these advantages led to a 'meso-corporatism' of sorts which, while based on popular support, was reinforced by the state.

That the FNSEA was widely supported was demonstrated by the 1981 Socialist government's ham-fisted attempt to evict it from the centres of power and support the other unions. The new government had made clear its determination not to accept the FNSEA's near monopoly of farmers' representation (and promote the other unions) in the interest of union plurality and democracy. It also proclaimed its ambition to disentangle the FNSEA from the state apparatus, starting with the creation of a Land Board to control the sale of land coming on to the market. (It was thought on the left that the FNSEA's influence on the committees enabled the union to exert pressure on farmers.) The government introduced a package to compensate for the fall in farm incomes but it was less than expected and less than the assistance given to industrial workers. This, along with other mistakes in dealing with farmers and the FNSEA's determination, was regarded as provocative and created a volatile situation. It was not long before the farmers reacted in an explosive fashion with widespread and violent protests, culminating in a massive and peaceful march through Paris by about 60,000 FNSEA members. FNSEA had used the government's hostility to show its importance as the farmers' representative and this was acknowledged. The government backtracked and dropped its most important reforms. It decided that it was better to deal with and through the established networks (even though these were politically conservative) than to go through the disruption of dismantling them.

In March 1983 a new Minister of Agriculture, Michel Rocard, was nominated to reduce the tensions between the government and farmers' union and to rebuild consensus. The Land Board was dropped and the FNSEA became the government's principal partner on agricultural matters once again. When the conservative right returned to power in 1986 François Guillaume was made Minister of Agriculture in an attempt to bind the farmers compliance in government policies. This was successful to some extent (preventing, for, example, the privatisation of the bank Crédit Agricole) and the gaullists won back some of the rural vote; in return the farmers were granted some concessions (notably on tax).

By Mitterrand's second septennate the FNSEA had re-established for itself the monopoly of representation of farmers to government and had recaptured its old positions on committees. However, the status quo ante was not completely restored. The smaller unions gained in importance, as did technical groups representing specific products, and the discontent in the agricultural world with the working of European integration began to grow (and was evident on the referendum on the Maastricht Treaty). In addition the importance of agriculture to the French economy diminished. Governments had been influenced by the size of the sector, but it was increasingly overshadowed by the interests of industry (in free trade, for example).

In the first two decades of the Fifth Republic the left was excluded from power but the centre right became an integral part of the weak corporatism developed by the gaullists. The imperative of modernisation of the French economy was the same for business as for farming. The state did not play a passive role in the development of the economy and sought active allies to participate in regulating and controlling the transition. All businesses are members of local Chambers of Commerce, which represent them and run local developments like industrial zones and ports. But the Conseil national du patronat français (CNPF) was the key body here and it had established its domination within the business sector before 1958. Although big business predominates, it contains within it an organisation of small business – the Confédération générale des petites et moyennes entreprises – as well as the representatives of particular branches (like building or textiles). There is a fair degree of tension between the small and big businesses as well as between different branches of industry, which detracts from the CNPF's effectiveness.

In the Fifth Republic, aided by the continuing growth of the economy and the transformation of industry, the authority of the CNPF (and of the big firms within it) was reinforced. As the Fifth Republic progressed, the threat from the

Communist-dominated left appeared to grow and the CNPF developed its political activity (encouraging support for the conservatives) in response. By the 1970s the CNPF was working closely with the government and had established authority over its members to a greater extent than it had done in the Fourth Republic. The CNPF's closeness to the conservative parties made it unpopular but its effectiveness was also reduced by the determination of the big industrial groups and concerns to make their representations directly and by the sectoral and branch differences within the business class which politicians played on. It remained influential during the Socialist governments of 1981–86 and 1988–93 because it decided to adapt to the new regime, but particularly after the decision in 1983 to 'modernise', which required business co-operation to succeed. The CNPF was changed and is now known as the Mouvement des entreprises de France (MEDEF) but remains the employers' main interlocutor with government.

Mouvement des entreprises de France (MEDEF)

This is the main French employers' confederation set up in October 1998 to replace the Conseil national du patronat français (CNPF). It is representative of big business (small and medium businesses have their own organisations) and there are serious internal divisions amongst its 800,000 affiliates. It co-administers social security with the unions and state and has threatened to withdraw its co-operation in negotiations over the future of social security. Its president is Ernest-Antoine Sellière.

Promotional groups

There is a feminist movement in France that evolved at much the same time as in the rest of the western world. It is, however, divided. There are the older Union féminine civique et sociale, founded in 1925, and the Communist Union des femmes de France, as well as the newer Mouvement de libération des femmes (1970) and Choisir (founded in 1971 by Gisèle Halami and the author of The Second Sex Simone de Beauvoir). Choisir made the running on abortion law and women's legal rights in the early 1970s; although it put up 48 (unsuccessful) candidates for the Assembly in 1978, Gisèle Halami became a Socialist MP from 1981 to 1986. By 1974 the Giscard d'Estaing presidency had already begun to respond to many of their issues with the creation of a Women's Minister (Françoise Giroud) and changes in the laws on contraception, divorce, abortion and domestic violence. These changes continued under the Mitterrand presidency of 1981–95 and included laws on harassment and equal wages.

France, being a country where the Catholic Church is predominant, also has pro-life and family-interest associations. (There is also the pervasive Union nationale des associations familiales, which is represented on most bodies dealing with family issues and jointly manages family allowances.) There are also parents' associations like the Catholic schools defence Union nationale des associations de parents d'éleves de l'enseignement libre, which showed its power in 1984 with huge demonstrations (the biggest since the Liberation) against the government and alive to the interests of the non-state schools. There is a state school equivalent, the Fédération des conseils de parents d'éleves, which, along with other groups like the politically influential Comité national de l'action laïque, lobbies on behalf of schools and students. There are also sixth-form students' unions and one was important in the 'events' of May 1968. Sixth-form students can be brought onto the streets in defence of their rights and when the government in 1986 proposed to change and restrict university entry they were mobilised in large numbers and brought about a back-down and the Education Minister's resignation.

There are several competing university students' unions: although none of them have the membership of the UK's National Union of Students the big two (Communist and non-Communist) are influential. The students' unions were active in the opposition to the government's reforms in 1986 and had links to the Socialist Party and the Elysée. These links helped their cause and some of the leaders later became Socialist deputies. The students were also well represented in the anti-racist group SOS-Racisme that was created in response to the success of the National Front and its effect on public life and discourse. It was close to the Socialist Party in the 1980s and its campaign ('Touche pas à mon pôte') was effective amongst younger people.

SOS-Racisme

This organisation was founded in 1984 by Harlem Désir and rapidly became the principal anti-racist movement and its badge 'Touche pas à mon pôte' (hands off my mate) became widespread. It was in part a reaction to the rise of the National Front but it was vigorous in campaigning for changes in attitudes and better legislation as well as aiding victims of racism. It was very much a youth movement and brought in singers and artists to events and concerts to popularise its message.

There are also environmental and local defence groups that have been constantly active since the emergence of environmentalism as an issue in the 1960s. These groups have lobbied for changes in laws as well as for the protection of particular sites, and have hit the headlines with protests against nuclear power and the despoliation of natural environments. Some of these groups have taken to direct action and others have confined themselves to lobbies of local and national politicians. To these can be added the groups lobbying for the protection of animals and for particular species. France also has Third World organisations and branches of Amnesty International and is the origin of the now world-wide Médecins sans frontières charity.

Conclusion

Returning to the first theme of interest group patterns in France, there is no consensus. France does not conform to either the 'pluralist' or 'neo-corporatist' ideal. Although France has been the object of conflicting interpretations there is no predominant model of interest group activity in the Fifth Republic. The special features displayed by pressure group activity in France cover the pluralist, protest, neo-corporatist and Marxist models mentioned by Wilson. Some French pressure groups do co-operate closely with the state and come close to neo-corporatism; others work in competition in a standard 'pluralist' manner. At the same time the outbreak of protest of various sorts (ranging from the violent, through the sit-in and occupation to the street demonstration) is distinctive and unusual. It need hardly be underlined that the union splits into Communist, socialist and others (often Christian democratic) is not found in 'northern Europe' and has to be taken into account in any model.

Nevertheless France has a large and active set of pressure groups comparable with other societies in the western world – though perhaps smaller. There has been an assumption that French people do not support interest groups and that in this respect the French are different. This may be correct but if so it is probably only in degree. Unions, for example, are much less well supported in France than in comparable societies. The activity of French interest groups covers the same spectrum as those in other western societies and there are no major gaps in the representation. Where gaps appear, pressure groups form to deal with the interest that is under-represented. But it probably remains true that pressure group activity is conducted over the society as a whole with a lesser degree of participation than elsewhere.

Summary

- The pattern of interest group politics in France is distinctive but it is neither clearly 'pluralist' nor corporatist.
- Some sections of the French system are 'neo-corporatist' and others are 'pluralist', with the result that there is a mixture of relations between the state and interest groups.
- Some pressure groups are highly organised and (in education, for example) have to be taken into account and others are very much weaker. This can give the misleading impression that the state is in thrall to powerful sectional interests or, the opposite, that some policies are arbitrarily imposed by the state.
- Unions, despite highly visible and disruptive strikes, are not well organised and do not have big memberships.
- Pressure groups proliferate in a French society that is not devoid of 'intermediate associations' and interest representation is lively. But some parts of society are better represented than others.

- Although it does not fit neatly into the 'pluralist model', France has a viable system of interest representation.
- Interest groups are a permanent feature of French political bargaining and are taken into consideration by all governments. Their strength varies according to which bloc holds power but there are difficulties for the government if they are ignored.

Further reading

Baumgartner, F. L. and Walker, J. L., 'Education policymaking and the interest group structure in France and the United States' *Comparative Politics* 21: 3, 1989, pp. 273–88

Brigford, J., *The Politics of French Trade Unionism* (Leicester University Press, 1991)

Cox, A. and Hayward, J., 'The inapplicablity of the Corporatist model in Britain and France' *International Political Science Review* 4: 2, 1983, pp. 217–40

Culpepper, P. D., 'Organisational competition and the neo-corporatist fallacy in French agriculture' *West European Politics* 16: 3, 1993, pp. 295–315

Duyvendak, J. W., *The Power of Politics: New Social Movements in France* (Westview, 1995)

Keeler, J. T. S., 'Situating France on the pluralism-corporatism continuum' *Comparative Politics* 17: 2, 1985, pp. 229–49

Kesselman, M., 'Does the French labor market have a future?' in J. T. S. Keeler and M. A. Schain (eds), *Chirac's Challenge* (St Martin's, 1996)

Wilson, F. L., *Interest Group Politics in France* (Cambridge University Press, 1987)

Wilson, F .L., 'Alternative models of interest intermediation: the case of France' *British Journal of Political Science* 12: 2, 1983, pp. 173–200

Questions

1 Why are French trade unions divided?
2 Why do agricultural unions have such substantial power?
3 What accounts for the sporadic outbursts of widespread strike action, like August 2000 or December 1995, in France?

Part II

Structures

8

The Republican state

France is a centralised state. Its history is very different from that of the British state. The French nation was forged by a centralising state out of a diverse series of localities first under the French crown and then under the Republics. Starting perhaps as early as the seventeenth century, the resolution of the great state builders like Richelieu, Mazarin and Colbert had established an interventionist tradition for the state in pre-Republican times. Enlightened despotism was not a theory but the practice of the pre-Revolutionary monarchy and it provided France with an infrastructure which, at the time, was in advance of other Europeans.

Jean-Baptiste Colbert (1619–83)

Colbert was Louis XIV's Chief Minister and a principal architect of the centralised state pursuing an economic policy of 'mercantalism' while ridding France of the internal network of tolls which inhibited trade (a job completed by the Revolution). Colbert used the power of the state to build roads and canals and to build up the merchant fleet. 'Colbertism' is used as a shorthand expression for the interventionist state. Intervention by government is both a right-wing and left-wing tradition in France, a country with a large state industrial sector. By contrast, those who believe in *laissez-faire* and a slimmed-down state are a smaller group mainly found in today's Liberal Democracy party (and some in the RPR).

The centralisation of the state was briefly contested in 1789 but the strong administrative structure established on the foundations of the *ancien regime* after the Great Revolution was believed to have prevented discord and to have made France the society it is today. Both the Revolutionary Jacobins and Napoleon sought to ensure a uniformity of treatment for citizens throughout France and that equalisation also became a feature of the state's action. France is a Republican democracy with a highly effective state bureaucracy. The state bureaucracy was reorganised from 1799 to 1804 by Napoleon Bonaparte, who completed what the Revolution had started but was unable to finish. The paradigm Napoleonic state was rational, efficient and powerful and this ideal has influenced the French administration through the nineteenth and twentieth centuries. Napoleon reorganised and extended the state but also placed it on its modern technocratic footing; it began to claim a disinterested position representing 'France' above and outside of the political divisions.

Napoleon remarked: 'I want to create a corporation . . . of Jesuits who have no other ambition than that of being useful and no interest but the public' (Sulieman, 1974, p. 19). Civil servants see themselves as representing the general interest in implicit distinction to the deputies who represent factions of the nation. Only those who saw the state as the creation of a particular regime contested this claim. Over the nineteenth century the state bureaucracy nearly tripled, from 130,000 personnel in 1839 to 350,000 in 1910. As Weber (1979) shows, even as late as 1870, the provinces were politically incoherent and refractory.

To most French political persuasions on the left and on the right the assumption that the state should and can represent the national interest is not challenged. For them the nation remains abstract and without real force unless the state gives it practical expression. Different parties may have had divergent views on what the state should do but they accepted the role of the state in applying the national interest. The idea of the minimal or 'night watchman' state is a minority view and the neo-liberal idea that the state is unqualified to speak for the national or social interest is also not a mainstream one. It is therefore an assumption in France that there is a national interest and that the national will is represented by the state. It was the strong central state that saw France through the several changes of regime and the crisis of the last two centuries and provided continuity in a bewilderingly changing world. The state gained legitimacy, and a reputation for effectiveness, which enabled it to extend its administration into new areas – like industry – where public action was felt to be necessary.

When it comes to industrialisation much the same view prevailed in France. The principal actors in the first industrial revolution in the UK were the individuals, companies and local concerns that became the vectors of social and economic change. All this was in keeping with the tenets of *laissez-faire* and has been seen as the 'right' model of industrialisation. On the continent it was otherwise. The *ancien regime* regarded it as its mission to lead the economy and that task fell to the state. In France, where the state built highways, canals and modernised agriculture but lagged behind in the industrial process, people looked to the state to bring society into the machine age. In order to catch up, the state fostered industry, developed, invested, planned and used its power to establish the backing needed for a modern economy. This was the so-called 'developmental state' which promoted French competitiveness in a world market.

Yet this 'developmental state' was not a Soviet-style command economy which took over and ran everything and which extinguished the market and private sector almost entirely. The French state sought to influence economic activity and to prod the market in the desired direction. Thus rather than concentrating on the areas in which France already had an advantage (mainly agriculture) the state developed productivity in industry and technology. This process involved negotiation, bargaining, enabling and administrative power. The administrators of the state were entrepreneurs who intervened and used their discretion to seek ways to promote society's interest. The Fifth Republic has inherited this state tradition along with the administrative machine created over the centuries.

De Gaulle and his close associates took the view that a strong and centralised state was a necessity. De Gaulle's own philosophy was that the 'ferments of dispersion', the anarchic individualism inherent in the French nation, were given coherence only by the state. French history was, for de Gaulle, one of tension between the state and the nation: the nation was capable of expression only when held together by the state. De Gaulle's close collaborators (such as Michel Debré) did not dissent from this view and were often referred to as 'Jacobin' centralisers. Through the early Fifth Republic the state played its customary role of promoting, leading, driving, redistributing and directing with the intention of modernising France and rivalling Germany as an industrial power. Only recently, with the challenge from Brussels and the search for local autonomy, has this view come under challenge.

Elite 'enarchs'

One distinguishing feature of France is the state elite created through the civil service. The French civil service of something like five million employees is much bigger than the British state but this number includes manual workers, teachers, military personnel, and others who would not be so classified elsewhere. The state is the biggest employer in France (perhaps a quarter of the workforce). The civil service has four grades: A, B, C and D (the last has all but disappeared). Class A are the top 'civil administrators' who make policy, prepare action or carry out orders from ministers and work with the directors in each Ministry. There are about 770,000 in this category. Class B is the 'administration secretaries' who apply policy and who have a technical training. Classes C

Public sector workers

Civil servants in France enjoy privileges that their private sector compatriots do not. They have job security, work shorter hours, get more pay and better health cover and are able to retire earlier. Public sector employment has grown by 20 per cent since 1980 and a quarter of the workforce is in the public sector.

and D are the clerical and secretarial classes who form the bulk of the service and who work under instruction. Within each class the civil servants are divided into corps with similar education and skills (see below).

A small and state-created meritocracy of both great technical competence and rigorous training runs the civil service. The intention was to create a 'technocracy' (though the word was not coined until the nineteenth century) of highly scientifically trained civil servants capable of taking the lead in society. The Ministries run colleges to train civil servants, like the Ecole nationale des impôts and the Ecole des mines; two of the most important will be described below. This is the system of *corps* to which all civil service officials belong and who are recruited and trained through specialist institutions. Civil servants would expect their careers to be within their *corps* and loyalty to them is strong. The *corps* of technical specialists began to be formed in the eighteenth century and others have been added subsequently (mainly by Napoleon). There were *corps* in the Middle Ages but the oldest modern ones are the corps of bridges and roads founded in 1716 and the corps of mining engineers founded shortly after in 1744. Most civil servants have a technical training at the start of their career in one of the dedicated training colleges.

Recruitment is through competitive examination and these examinations are the basis for the claim made that the civil service is a meritocracy. There is a very early and very rigid distinction between the fast track and the bulk of ordinary administrators. This is the big difference within the civil service between the *corps*. The key features of the French civil service are the *grands corps*, which are the most important parts of the elite. They have their own *esprit de corps* and are somewhat isolated from the rest of the civil service and its pressures. There is no official definition of the *grands corps* and how many there are depends on a loose understanding of their status (and some prefer to talk of 'dominant' groups), but at a minimum there are two technical and three administrative ones. In theory they are specialised but in practice they have a broad role and colonise the administration, providing its leadership.

Those in the *grands corps* are almost certain to reach the summit, and this 4,400 or so dominate the state apparatus at the top. These *grands corps* are more dominant than the 'Oxbridge' grip on the British civil service, they are smaller and they have control over their area and their members, which has no real UK parallel. There are, for example, the following *grands corps*: mining engineers, bridges and roads, Council of State, Court of Accounts, and Finance Inspectorate. Although the prefects and diplomats are subject to political pressure and are less autonomous, they are usually added to this list. The Council of State (originally a Napoleonic body) is the highest administrative court and is the government's legal adviser; the Court of Accounts audits public spending; the Finance Inspectorate controls any sector dispensing public money on behalf of the Finance Ministry; the prefects are the local government control officers (see below); and the diplomatic corps form the foreign service.

The prestige of the *grands corps* is such that their members have the pick of the best jobs in the state's service and they colonise the top positions in the hierarchy. They are also sought after by business so that many of the leaders in management are also products of the *grands corps*. The typical curriculum vitae of a French business leader is somebody who has been through a *grand corps*, a ministerial *cabinet* (see below) and then moved to the leadership of a business. Some 45 per cent of company heads have been through either the Polytechnic or the ENA (see below). 'Head hunting' leads to civil servants quitting the public service for lucrative business positions, a career switch known, since the first Polytechnic students switched from military to civilian careers in 1800, as *pantouflage*. Many civil servants leave their *corps* and do not return to it, though this, it should be noted, is a one-way street, as managers do not leave business for the civil service.

But the *grands corps* have the privilege of secondment, enabling members to depart for long periods and then return to the civil service. Members stick together and look out for each other's interests and the interests of the *corps* (recommending their confrères for positions, for example). In the Council of State something like one-third are on leave at any given time and about half have been in ministerial private offices. In the view of most commentators the system of 'leave' is a necessary part of the civil servants' experience and means that they understand how the system works. It also enables them to build up the networks which, by smoothing things over and getting things done, is essential to the French administration. It is equally likely that the civil servants who move round are socialised into the values of the state system more than they realise. This leave also facilitates a political career and many of the top politicians are normally former civil servants. The cross-over of personnel between the civil service and the government, business and Assembly is not like the English experience.

It may be bad for reasons of social justice and equal opportunities, that the political elite system is dominated by the products of the civil service elite to an excessive extent – there is small movement up from below. However, it should not be assumed that France is run by administrators and not by its politicians. There is no unity of outlook between the top civil servants, as the clashes between departments shows. Civil servants who want to enter politics have to leave the administration and run for office. They may have the advantage of the training given by the state but they also know the state structure from the inside and how to use it for their own purposes. There are few examples, in the Fifth Republic, of administrators capturing policy-making and removing their sector from political control.

Grands corps recruit from the civil service colleges the Ecole nationale d'administration (ENA) run by the Prime Minister's office and the Ecole polytechnique run by the Ministry of Defence. The Ecole polytechnique was founded in 1794 as a military college and, although it no longer trains artillery officers, it still works under military discipline. Many of its graduates do not join the civil service. However, it was the principal recruiting ground for the top

---

Grandes écoles

French elite education, originally developed for state service, is highly competitive and meritocratic. At the centre of this system are the so-called *Grandes écoles* and there are a few with an international reputation and educating about 100,000 people. They are outside the university system and have more control over their own affairs than the state universities but they are very small and they provide an intensive course of two or three years leading to offers of high-ranking jobs. The Ecole nationale d'administration (ENA) was founded after the war (and some have been founded more recently) but others go back to the monarchy (like the Ecole des mines) and the Polytechnique is Napoleonic. Graduates of the ENA, 'enarchs', and graduates of the Polytechnique, 'X', are to be found at the summit of French politics.

---

positions in the state until the ENA was founded and it now commands the gates to the technical corps. It recruits from the schools – not the universities – and sixth-formers wanting to sit the exams take an additional two years' training. It provides a mathematical, engineering and scientific education though with no practical placements. The Ecole polytechnique's graduates are ranked and that determines which civil service *corps* they can join. Although there are those who still opt for the army, the main choice is the specialist colleges of the *grands corps* of the mines or bridges and roads.

The ENA was created by Michel Debré in 1945 to unify and modernise the recruitment of top civil servants and it is the gatekeeper of the administrative corps of the state. It creams off the best candidates for the high ranks of the civil service. Its examinations are open to graduates under 28 years of age, those who have been civil servants for five years and wish to advance, and those who have been elected in local government. The number of places is decided by the Minister of the Interior and about a third are kept for civil service candidates. The successful candidates spend two years studying law, economics and management, with periods of placements in industry and in the civil service. Graduates have to spend at least ten years in the civil service and are ranked at their graduation. The higher the rank the more choice they have in their destination. Most opt for the Court of Accounts, Foreign Affairs, and prefectures; the Council of State and the Finance Inspectorate only recruit from the top ten ('la botte' – so-called).

The importance of these royal routes to the heights has been recognised. Their legitimacy rests with their intense meritocracy, which is impossible to gainsay in the current political climate, and the creation of the ENA did break down barriers for the aspiring middle class. ENA graduates are now a principal component of the political elite. Both Prime Minister Jospin and President Chirac are products of the ENA and many of the principal figures of Fifth Republic politics have been 'énarchs'. Most of the senior civil servants are 'énarchs' (a dismissive word) and the top of the civil service is more or less an 'énarchie' with a fair admixture of Polytechniciens. There are criticisms of the Parisian bias of the civil service and of the difficulty of getting onto the fast track (dominated by these early products of elite education) from other positions. The possibility for a career at the top is enormously disadvantaged if a civil servant has not been to the ENA or Polytechnique. Just as crucial, and odd from an outside perspective, is the small world which they recruit from. It is not an aristocracy (in fact the Polytechnic retains an anti-aristocratic and upwardly mobile Republican bias), and it is dependent on drive and intelligence, but the upper-middle-class nature of the backgrounds (and the civil service families) would cause concern elsewhere. In France only the privileged have the educational background to pass the examination barriers and oral exams required to join the elite.

In recent years the numbers of civil servants moving into private industry has increased. This was always a feature of French civil service life: civil servants' government contacts as well as their knowledge of the state machine made them valuable recruits. However, in the 1980s and 1990s the rapidity of leaving has increased and much younger civil servants of the bridges and roads corps have left for industrial careers recruited by companies who want the 'top of the top'. Over 20 years the numbers of civil servants who had 'definitely quit' their corps increased from 6 per cent to 15 per cent; the increased payment is a major consideration.

The Fifth Republic is also characterised by a more pervasive civil service elite. They join politicians' private offices, drop their neutrality, and take up political positions more than in previous Republics. They also enter the political elite with increasing frequency, leading some to refer to the Fifth Republic as the 'Mandarin's Republic'. This in turn has led to the politicisation of the upper civil service and the domination of politics by the civil service. On the one hand the results are a more dynamic civil service and a more informed political class. On the other hand the problems are a destabilised civil service and an increasingly closed political elite.

Administrative law

In France, unlike the UK, public and private law are separate and there is a Court of Conflicts to decide on disputed cases of jurisdiction. Law, and elaborate legal rules, are the frameworks for the French administration. The French civil service comes under the administrative law dealing with the exercise of state power (including local government). It has a much greater extent in France than in other countries and there is a separate system of administrative courts with their own procedures to deal with cases involving the state which, in the United Kingdom, would come to ordinary civil courts. Administrative law and constitutional law overlap to some extent but constitutional law deals with civil liberties and relations between institutions and administrative law deals with negligence, maladministration and other administrative matters. Administrative law courts deal with all state activity except foreign affairs and they can quash any government decree (although not acts of parliament). These administrative courts are organised hierarchically and deal with both general and particular matters and citizens must go to these courts to seek redress (they are inexpensive but very slow). At the apex of the administrative law system is the Council of State.

The Council of State is 'one of the most remarkable institutions of France' and, like many others, has been exported to countries with a Roman law tradition. It was established in Article 52 of the Napoleonic Constitution of 24 Frimaire Year VIII ('Freezy' or February 1799) but it became one of the solid supports of the Republic after 1875. It is nowadays consulted in the drawing up of legislation, the settlement of administrative disputes and the judgement of cases where state officials or services are involved. It is central to the administrative law system because it drafts legislation and acts as the highest court in administration. It is largely an appellate court dealing with challenges in the administrative courts, but the possibility of an appeal is influential on the comportment of the civil service. Within the civil service the argument that 'the Council of State won't allow it' carries weight and ministers are constrained to respect rules and to justify decisions. On the other hand the verdicts of the Council come after a delay of a few years and the judgements are generally more of an embarrassment than a discipline. The executive with a bit of finesse can often get round the law or might be tempted to take its chances with acts it suspects to be of doubtful legality. The Council has used its interpretative latitude to become over time a protection against the over-stepping of authority and about half the decisions fall against the state. Hence its reputation as 'le meilleur juge contre l'état'. It was assertive enough to annoy de Gaulle, who dismissed it in his memoirs as an institution of 'unelected officials holding office by decree'. It has played a role in challenging administrative regulations and it can quash them. It has substantial political effect in the Fifth Republic through the development of policy and civil liberties (though observers disagree about the extent). But it is not a supreme court and cannot quash laws as can the United States Supreme Court.

The Council of State is the legal adviser to the government and this role ensures the quality and uniformity of legislation as well as helping coherence in government and administration by preventing contradictory texts. All legislation is reviewed by the Council (Article 39) before the Cabinet deliberates, and all ordinances are also reviewed (Article 38). (Only decrees relating to the regulation of public administration have to go to the Council.) This 'advice' can be ignored but to do so can be politically difficult. De Gaulle ignored the Council's view that the referendums to change the Constitution in 1962 and 1969 were illegal. But during the 'cohabitation' of 1986–88, when the Council's unfavourable advice on the 'nationality bill' and the 'private prisons bill' were leaked, the public outcry was such that the government had to drop them.

Civil service politics

French government does not operate a spoils system like the USA, but there is more change at the top of the civil service than there is in the UK when the government changes from left to right. As the 'waltz of prefects' after each change of government demonstrates, politicians can chose the tenants of the most important posts and do so.

The General Secretariat of Government is the Prime Minister's administrative office, located in the Matignon. It numbers about 100 civil servants who ensure continuity of the state through government changes. It is divided into four groups each with a function (meetings and minutes; legislation; documentation; relations with parliament). They keep the files, Cabinet minutes and records of the government and they co-ordinate the government's work by following the discussions between ministers and other decision-making bodies including the Cabinet itself. The General Secretariat has the delicate task of preparing the agenda for Cabinet meetings, which has to be transmitted to the Elysée and agreed, making it the link between President and government. It also ensures the publication of the *Journal officiel* (a French Hansard) and its attendant publications. It also has the duty of ensuring the preparation of ministers' bureaux and it has to make sure that decrees are properly published. There are also some 4,000 or 5,000 people who work in one way or another for the Prime Minister's office and this is overseen by the Secretariat. The Secretariat generals themselves are from the Council of State and traditionally have a long tenure. Prime Ministers also have their own private office (*cabinet*) in addition to the civil service's General Secretariat.

The state may have had a reputation for impartiality but the political role of the civil service is well understood by politicians. The power of the impressive machine could not be left to itself and politicians looked for ways to control it. Ministers normally pick the head of section, the *directeur*, from civil servants in the Ministry's administration (rarely from outside). But the main instrument, which began at the Restoration, is the minister's own hand-picked private office (*cabinet*). This institution is well developed in France (and bigger only in Belgium and Italy). It is composed of different numbers ranging from five for a junior minister up to eleven for other ministers and twenty for the Premier. Jospin's government of 1997 had 420 staff in *cabinets*; Michel Rocard's government of 1988 had 600. However, these are the brute numbers and many more in fact participate in *cabinets*. Although Prime Minister Jospin has 55 staff, the Matignon staff can be over 100 (Chaban-Delmas in 1969–72 had 200). Staffs at the Ministries of Foreign Affairs, Interior and Finance are also big. The *cabinet* members are not paid for that function and depend on other organisations for their salaries. Most of these roles would be civil service posts in the United Kingdom, although that is changing, but in France the *cabinet* constitutes a counter-staff set up to influence and control the administration. It also co-ordinates with other ministers, liaises with Parliament and deals with public opinion.

A French government minister appoints his or her own private staff (officially restricted in number) to develop policy, deal with the press, and follow through action in the administration to ensure that the minister's directives are carried out – to be the minister's eyes and ears. They are generally young and are chosen for their competence and their reliability. Most members of the *cabinet* will be civil servants who are politically sympathetic to the minister (Prime Minister Mauroy was mayor of Lille and his staff was very Nord-biased). This makes sense given the need for the private office to know the administration, how it works and how to get round it, and the civil service will continue to pay for the *cabinet* member. This is an important consideration as the money officially allowed does not run to the size of private office that a minister normally thinks necessary.

There are specialist positions within the *cabinet.* The composition and working is the minister's choice, though the key post is the *directeur de cabinet* (usually a civil servant) who has general oversight and is in touch with the Matignon, has the power of attorney and usually helps the minister in Parliament. The *chef de cabinet* is in charge of the minister's diary, relations with the constituency and organisation. But there may be a *conseilleur technique* who is the bridge between the private office and the civil service (Edouard Balladur took this role in Georges Pompidou's *cabinet*). There is usually a member who works on parliamentary business and sometimes a powerful *chargé de mission auprès du ministre* (special adviser) who stands apart. There are likely to be other unofficial collaborators, who make the *cabinet* up to a much larger group than the published figures, and these supernumerary *cabinet* members can be very powerful. Most of the *directeurs de cabinet* come from the *grands corps* and all members of the private offices return to their original jobs once the minister leaves. However, civil servants gain career advantages like nominations to better positions from their time in the *cabinet.*

The main criticism of the *cabinet* system is not, however, this self-promotion but the hidden power the staff members have and use away from the public's view. They are liable to circumvent official procedures and lines of report and intervene where they can. They often do not have clear structures and control of ministerial business can move into unexpected hands. In this view the *cabinet* is liable to move out of its role of dealing with issues submitted by the minister to giving orders and controlling the administration. These things are certainly one of the dangers of the *cabinet* system and there have been some notorious abuses. It has been suggested that the *cabinet* staff ought to be restricted to 100 for the government overall and that they should not be the intermediaries between the minister and the civil service. However, this is not likely to come about.

Many civil servants have a political vocation in France, something they do not have in the United Kingdom. In France civil servants can join parties, express their views and participate in political life. In the Finance Ministry one of Giscard d'Estaing's civil servants was a Communist who wrote under a pseudonym attacking the government. Giscard, feigning ignorance, used to ask his collaborators if they had read the 'extremely interesting article' attacking this or that policy. It remains controversial whether civil servants should be administering a policy in the day and attacking it in the evening. It is not unusual for civil servants to move into politics at different levels and to be politically engaged, although the use of a pseudonym is normal at the top.

In the Fourth Republic members of government with a civil service background did reach a maximum of 42 per cent but in the Fifth Republic there has been a minimum of 52 per cent of former civil servants in governments. In de Gaulle's government of 1958 the figure was 70 per cent, and in Pierre Messmer's in 1973, Jacques Chirac's in 1974 and Raymond Barre's in 1976 the figure was 60 per cent. This reflects, partly, the position of education as part of the administration in France and partly the presidential effect which leads the Elysée to nominate reliable figures with no political standing of their own. However, it also illustrates a change in the Republican political elite, which has come increasingly to include meritocrats promoted up through the state system itself. To date Edith Cresson has been the only Fifth Republic Prime Minister who was not a civil servant at some time in her career.

Fifth Republic developments

A more recent development is the creation by President Georges Pompidou of the Ombudsman (*Médiateur de la République*) with a small office (about 50 staff and a departmental network) in 1973 to bridge the gap between the state and the citizen. The Ombudsman's office contributes to the functioning of the civil service by resolving tensions, but it cannot intervene on its own initiative or be approached directly by citizens; the request has to come through a parliamentarian. The Ombudsman has a six-year term and presents an annual report to the President and Parliament, which is published, but its recommendations to the administration do not have imperative force and there are no sanctions. All the same the Ombudsman's office has dealt with about 20,000 letters each year and has made an impact since its introduction by promoting reforms (22 are currently under review). It is, however, a marginal contribution to the control of the administration because the office does not use its disciplinary powers and these would give more bite to the position. But it has also taken the view that the civil service is a self-correcting organisation that does not need to be constrained by outsiders.

In the Fifth Republic independent bodies have been developed to act as a buffer between the state and the organisation being run. The first of these was the Commission nationale de l'informatique et des libertés to ensure that files and computer records are available to individuals and that they do not contain information about a person's views. Others controlling public freedom have included the Commission nationale des comptes de campagne et des finances politiques (to oversee political spending) and the Conseil supérieur de l'audio-visuel. There are also committees overseeing the economy and competition such as the Conseil de la concurrence or the Commission de côntrole des assurances. And the Commission d'accès aux documents administratifs is intended to ensure that citizens have access to the administration's documents on them. These bodies are given their independence, their personnel are not sackable by the state, and they are not subject to orders from other authorities. They have to regulate and to ensure that the rules are applied in the sector they cover and can impose penalties for non-compliance. They are a pragmatic solution to the problem of regulation of the sensitive sectors where state intervention is no longer regarded as legitimate but where rules have to be enforced.

Judges

Judges are part of the state service in France and the judiciary is viewed as a public service. In addition to the structure and practice being very different, the Republicans have traditionally not interpreted the separation of powers in Montesquieu's way: legislative, judicial and executive. The Revolution proclaimed that there was a separation of powers in their sense that the judges could not bring administrators before them and that the 'government of judges' was unacceptable. There is a Ministry of Justice (as in many continental states) which controls the courts, judges, prosecutors and the police, and investigating magistrates are controlled by the Interior Ministry. Appointments, promotions and careers are decided by the Supreme Judicial Council and are not independent of the executive. The Supreme Judicial Council is presided over by the President of the Republic with the Minister of Justice as vice-president, and nine of its members are nominated for four-year terms by the President and one each by the Speakers of the Senate and of the Assembly. Neither are independent commissions investigating; they also depend on the executive and the civil service staff them on a temporary basis (before secondment back).

French courts are based on an 'inquisitorial' system in which the prosecution investigates and decides whether it is possible to build up a case. The police hand a case to the prosecution's examining magistrate (*juge d'instruction*), who decides whether to prosecute, and if that decision is in favour of prosecution the dossier goes to a prosecuting judge. In recent years the examining judges have become more active and political cases have been pursued with more vigour than before. This is not just a French development – similar determination has been shown in Belgium, Spain and Italy – but the effect has been a spate of political scandals as abuses of power (mostly party funding) have been uncovered. No party has been untouched but the city of Paris has been a centre of concern and allegations have been made against the former mayor of Paris.

Education

Education in France is a state responsibility and a matter of national pride. The Great Revolution proclaimed that the state had a duty to provide education for all its citizens. Hence education administration comes from a different tradition to the English system. The battle conducted by the state to reduce the Church's influence in schools has no parallel in the United Kingdom. In pre-Revolutionary France the Church regarded its role as a teaching one and the religious orders delivered education, although the *Académies* provided higher education. This did not go unchallenged and in the Enlightenment claims were made for the state to organise the instruction of the nation. A system of universal, free and compulsory education surfaced during the Revolution and then Napoleon started to create the framework for a nation-wide system. Napoleon left primary schools to the Church but created the secondary school (*Lycée*) and the University of France (subdivided into seventeen *Académies*). The universities were to serve the needs of the state and were run by the Ministry of Education, which appointed staff, provided the finance and determined the curriculum. The state had a monopoly of degrees and teaching was made the prime concern (not research).

But the problem of the part the Church should play was not resolved even

Church schools

This has been a long-running issue in French politics. Separation of Church and state has been fraught and nowhere more than in education. The Fourth Republic reintroduced secular education after the Vichy interlude but the Church schools continued; in the Fifth Republic the private '*écoles libres*' were offered support if they accepted state standards and inspection. They then continued helping students who had not done well in the state system and enabled parents to move children out of unfavoured state schools (parents escaped large immigrant populations, for example). Alain Savary's attempt in 1984 to bring the Church schools under greater state control met with massive demonstrations and was dropped. The demonstrations were in part at least a testimony to a lack of faith in the state schools as well as to a fear that an escape route might be closed. In 1995 there were about 1,142,000 pupils in state secondary schools and 897,300 in private schools (mostly Church schools).

Education reform

The French education system is notoriously resistant to reform. There were the dramatic 'events' of May 1968 that were occasioned in part by a proposed university reform, that sequence was repeated in 1986 and university students also took to the streets in 1995. Protests in the late 1990s were over poor provision, overcrowding and badly maintained schools. The Minister of Education in the Socialist government of 1997, Claude Allègre, declared his intention to 'slim down the mammoth' of one million teachers and reduce union influence in education by giving parents and students a bigger say and by devolving tasks, but the protests were stepped up. Although Allègre had the support of the Prime Minister Lionel Jospin (they had been associates at the Education Ministry in 1988) he had to resign in March 2000 as a result of disruption and union pressure.

---

though the regimes after the Empire leant to the Church's side. Because the Church was seen as siding with the enemies of the Republic, the Third Republic began the battle for secular education at all levels. Teacher training was brought under the state in 1879 (*Ecoles normales* were set up in each department). In the 1880s Jules Ferry's tenure as Minister of Education ensured that primary school education became free then compulsory in 1882 and that secondary schools for girls were opened.

The clash between Church and state concerned not just education but the French government itself. The question of what the proper role for the state was became one of the critical issues and was defined to the advantage of the state in an enduring manner. Republicanism and state provision became associated in education and in other areas. This had its positive side as well as its negative side. The uniformity of provision and the goal of high standards were positive results of the struggle against the Church. But the rigid system allowed little room for initiative or experiment and the framework was greatly restrictive. Anatole de Monzie is credited with the famous remark that, as Education Minister 1932–34, he knew at any time what was being taught in every classroom in France. The system was also slow to respond to new suggestions and localities were forced to wait for policy decisions from Paris.

Over the Third Republic the rights of the Church in education were steadily restricted. Religious orders were excluded and this became a bitter issue in the 1900s. An anti-clerical government under Combes (moderate in everything except religion) closed Church primary schools and reopened them as state schools, and made education a centralised state service that appointed teachers, paid them and controlled the curriculum. At the heart of this was the secular principle that religion was a private affair and not one for schools. There is no religious participation in the national school system (although anybody qualified can set up a school), which remains centralised under the charge of the Ministry of Education.

Welfare

Welfare also developed from the Revolutionary idea that the Republic ought to provide citizens with the means to participate in society; social legislation thus became part of the expanding idea of the state. The Rights of Man of 1793 stated that societies 'owe subsistence to unfortunate citizens' and the Republic had the obligation to find them work or give them the means to live. Any opportunity for participation, it was felt, would be ineffective if people were too poor or too ill for it to be meaningful, although it would be some time before France was rich enough as a society to fulfil the Republican ideal. The French welfare state is older than the British version (although the first major legislation was passed at roughly the same time) and also has different foundations. There were, in France, different strands of social philosophy (like Catholic social theory) which supported welfare provision and *laissez-faire* liberals never had the influence they did in the UK or the USA. The contemporary system is composed of many elements and is something of a patchwork preventing a truly universal provision, but the heart of it is the National Security Fund put in place by the gaullists at the Liberation. This reform created a number of elected Boards composed of union representatives and business leaders who run the collection of dues and distribute benefits. This system was intended to encourage consensus between the two sides of industry: it was hoped that business would understand needs and unions would understand the constraints.

As with other countries the principal problem has been the spiralling cost of welfare provision and for much the same reasons: increasing medical costs, pension requirements, and unemployment, which have led to many more illness and support payments. At the same time as costs have increased and the deficit in the social security budget has become a major problem, people's willingness to pay taxes to support the burden has diminished. In fact the distribution of benefits and the entitlement regime is the result of a struggle between interest groups and not an administrative fiat. As in the United Kingdom doctors proved a formidable interest group (and negotiation over fees for services is fraught) and other producers like the drug companies have also had an interest in the social security regime.

Unemployment and economic slowdown following the oil shocks of the 1970s have created a new poor in France. These long-term unemployed have been behind the rise in poverty figures since the 1980s. This despair has spilled out in riots in the inner cities as well as into rising crime and drug taking. The Rocard government of 1988–91 took the main step to deal with this by providing a minimum income for those who were looking for work and the administration of it was passed down to departments. At the same time efforts were made to stimulate job creation and to find work for the young unemployed.

Internal politics

Although the French civil service is an impressive administrative machine and may look capable of steamrollering opposition, it is not monolithic and has its own internal rivalries. As Jack Hayward (1986) says, 'the omnipresence of administrative elites should not be confounded with their omnipotence'. The common formation of the civil service elite, contrary to common assumptions, does not lead to a united outlook as, in fact, the top people seek to advance their cause, their ministry or their *corps*. Hence, there are internal divisions and rivalries within the French bureaucracy which often spill out into the public arena and shape public policy more than the image of a rational and remorseless administration might suggest. 'Turf wars' over responsibility and over who will control new developments are a feature of the public service everywhere and France is no exception.

The same is true of the conflicts between the spending ministries and the Finance Ministry which are common in bureaucracies. In France the Finance Minister's status reflects a 'Treasury' predominance and this spills over into ministerial behaviour in government as well where the conflicts are reproduced between the spenders and the getters. There is also the problem with administrations everywhere that the decision-makers are sometimes 'captured' by interest groups. This is notably the case with agriculture, where the Ministry of Agriculture works very closely with the farmers' representatives, but there are many other less well known cases. At a more basic level the civil service has to make allies and rub along with the administered population and this invariably leads to concessions and to bargaining with pressure groups and in turn to divisions in the state. However, the French civil service has a more vigorous role in promoting and instigating change than do administrations in comparable societies.

State spending control

France's Revenue Court (which patrols and audits state finance and spending) reported in January 2000 that the grip on state spending was insufficient. Abuses, it stated, abound in the state system. The Finance Ministry itself was taking liberties with its own budgets and accounts while patrolling the other areas of state spending. Much of the abuse comes from the evasion of the National Assembly and Senate's scrutiny by using 'off-budget' devices, like the systems of bonuses and temporary staff, to get round guidelines and restrictions on staff. One result is that more people are employed by the state than the official numbers: 2.68 million as against the registered 2.3 million. Government employees (other than nationalised industries) in the central and local state and welfare services amount to about 5 million people, which, at 24 per cent of the workforce, is one of the highest in the developed world.

Administration, or bureaucracy, has come under increasing criticism in France, as in the rest of the western world. France has a long tradition of state industries but that has not kept it from following the trend toward privatisation. The background to this is slightly different from in the UK because the state industries in France are more often than not a source of some pride and not, like their UK counterparts, derided as inefficient and wasteful. In 1945 the Liberation settlement installed a big public sector through the control of the capital markets, regulation of the labour market and an active state which, nevertheless, allowed a great deal of latitude to private enterprise. The high speed train (TGV), the rail service, Concorde and air transport are cases in point. In the early 1980s there was a big programme of nationalisation by the Socialist government and, whereas these initiatives can hardly be said to have been the success that was anticipated, they took failing companies which were subsequently turned round and made profitable under the state's control. The state is not viewed in France in the same ideological or practical light as in the UK or USA and there has been a steady advance of state control and take-over over many centuries.

Yet, in recent years the neo-liberal pressure on the state to divest itself of functions, and to remove the shackles from nationalised corporations, has been seen in France as elsewhere in western Europe. The drive to obtain value for money has been evident in the French state as it has privatised the nationalised industries in such hallowed areas as Renault and Air France. The disengagement of the state with nationalised industries had started with the 1984 Socialist government, which also experimented in bringing in private capital and permitted the selling of subsidiaries. Privatisation started in earnest with the 1986–88 conservative government sell-off of fourteen industries and has continued since that time. President Mitterrand's promise in 1988 to freeze the balance between state and private sectors was (broadly) kept while the Socialists held power but the return of the conservatives in 1993 restarted the privatisations (Juppé's 1995–97 government kept up the pace). But the Socialist government of 1997 was, in fact, a vigorous privatiser of hitherto untouched state industries such as Air France, France télécom, Aérospatiale and Thomson. These privatisations have not been without their problems but the main programme has been accomplished, reducing, in that way, the state's involvement in the economy for the first time since the Great Revolution.

Conclusion

France has participated in the 'neo-liberal revolution' which has swept the western world and the reduction of the role of the state is evident in many spheres – as it is in the UK, Germany and Italy, for example. There has been a big change in the French attitude to the economy and to social life. However,

France's continuing 'exceptionalism' in this respect should also be borne in mind. France is still a very state-centred society in terms of the numbers employed by the state (which are relatively large) and where the state is engaged (in industry for example). The reduction in the status of the public services has not gone as far as in the UK and the state enterprises are still seen as positive. The selling of the transport network would not be countenanced in France and the state is still responsible for the provision of basic welfare.

More importantly, the attitude to the state as the shaper of society has not shifted fundamentally. The French state is still expected to take a lead and play a role of promoting developments seen as beneficial to society as a whole – it is not seen as a malevolent force or the cause of malaise. French politicians do not, on the whole, challenge the legitimacy of state activity and the public is likely to look to the state for the solution to problems. As noted at the beginning of this chapter, the idea of the state as the representative of France and as a creative factor in French life has a long history and a long half-life. In this it is closer to the continental tradition than to the UK or the USA.

Summary

- The state is a dominant actor in French political life.
- The idea of the strong state, derived from the ('Jacobin') Great Revolution, is widely supported on the left and the right.
- French free market 'minimal state' forces have been relatively powerless.
- There has been no support for the dramatic 'roll back' of the state as there has been in the UK or USA.
- The separation of powers has not been a major concern of French Constitution drafters despite the eminence of Montesquieu. There is an ambiguity in the relation between the judiciary and politics that is unusual in western countries.
- There is a state-created elite at the top of French political life.

Further reading

Barker, E., *The Development of Public Services in Western Europe* (Oxford University Press, 1944)

Cole, A., 'The *Service Publique* under stress' *West European Politics* 22: 4, 1999, pp. 166–84

Crozier, B., *The Staled Society* (Viking, 1970)

Dyson, K., *The State Tradition in Western Europe* (Robertson, 1980)

Flynn, G. (ed.), *Remaking the Hexagon* (Westview, 1996)

Guyomarch, A., '"Public service", "public management" and the "modernisation" of French public administration' *Public Administration* 77: 1, 1999, pp. 171–93

Hayward, J. E. S., *The State and the Market Economy* (Wheatsheaf, 1986)

Rhor, J. A., 'What a difference a state makes' in G. L. Wamsley *et al.* (eds), *Refounding Democratic Public Administration* (Sage, 1996)

Rouban, L., *The French Civil Service* (La Documentation Française, 1996)

Schmidt, V. A., 'The changing dynamics of state–society relations in the Fifth Republic' *West European Politics* 22: 4, 1999, pp. 141–65

Suleiman, E. N., *Elites in French Society* (Princeton, 1974)

Weber, E., *Peasants into Frenchmen* (Chatto and Windus, 1979)

Wilsford, D., 'Tactical advantages versus administrative heterogeneity: the strengths and limits of the French State' *Comparative Political Studies* 21: 1, 1988, pp. 126–68

Questions

1 What is the nature of the French state elite?
2 Why is the French state traditionally *dirigiste*?
3 Is France a state-dominated society?

9

The President

The Paris residence of the President and site of the presidential staff is the Elysée Palace. The Fifth Republic has been characterised in a number of ways, including as a 'Republican monarchy, a 'super-presidency' and a 'semi-presidential regime'. All these are intended to capture the impressive domination of the presidency in the life of the Fifth Republic. However, the last term, which has become popular, conceals more than it reveals: the Fifth Republic is liable to veer from being a powerful executive presidency to a prime ministerial regime depending on where the majority lies.

The presidential term

Starting in the Third Republic, French Presidents have been elected for a septennate, the longest term in the western world. There has been a persistent questioning of the seven-year presidential term throughout the Fifth Republic and reform was attempted once by President Pompidou but then abandoned. Many presidential candidates have brought up the idea and then dropped it but it became pressing with the fourteen-year term of President Mitterrand and the prospect of a fourteen-year term for President Chirac. In May 2000 the former President Giscard proposed a five-year term (renewable once) to bring the legislative and presidential terms into line and this was supported by both President Chirac (who shortly before had vigorously opposed it) and Prime Minister Jospin. This reform, it is sometimes assumed, would eliminate 'cohabitation' but there is no mechanism linking the Assembly and presidential majorities. The reform was passed in September 2000.

However, once a presidential system has developed, as it has in France, it puts a premium on leadership. A president or presidential candidate can reach out beyond the narrow confines of partisan support and build a wider coalition. Even though a politician campaigning for the presidency must have party backing, that will not be enough and the platform will have to appeal to voters

164

from other sections of opinion. A presidential campaign gives the candidate the opportunity to construct such a platform with less hindrance from party apparatus itself and although it is likely to become a battle between camps (left versus right) it can also promote co-operation within camps.

Presidential politics is also vulnerable to personal failure in that the emphasis is on one personality to carry the brunt of political strategy and tactics. In a party system such as the United Kingdom a party can 'carry' a weak leader and still win elections. There are many examples of voters returning one party while having doubts about its leader: the German CDU/CSU, for example, won elections in the 1980s despite the relatively low poll rating of its leader Helmut Kohl (though that changed, of course). In the French case the presidential system depended on the success of the leaders in mobilising and retaining support. Where this flagged, as it did in 1986, 1993 and 1997, the coalition behind the President fell, and the presidency lost power.

The French tradition

Republicans have been suspicious of the presidency as an institution and the Second Republic was not convinced that there should be an executive President (they were persuaded). However, Louis Bonaparte, who became the President of the Second Republic in 1848 backed by six million 'Republican' votes, took only three years to carry out a coup d'état, thereby abusing presidential power. This was Napoleon III's famous '18 Brumaire' (December in the Revolutionary calendar) and was followed by the establishment of the Second Empire. Republicans who desired a non-partisan figure, or at least a more self-effacing one, rejected Napoleon III's example.

When the Third Republic was consolidated the Presidents, with a few exceptions (mainly conservatives), dedicated themselves to a representative role more like a constitutional monarch than an executive (or American) President. Their main influence came in government formation where some were quite active and selected the potential Prime Minister with some creativity. Yet they did not play a day-to-day role in government and were not executive leaders. Georges Clemenceau, the combative Republican now remembered as the 'Father of Victory' in 1918, dismissed the office out of hand. He had once advised colleagues to vote for the most stupid contender for the presidency. Usually Parliament would follow this advice and elect Presidents who did not threaten the legislature's power (Presidents were elected by parliament).

The first President of the Third Republic, Jules Grévy, explicitly recognised the pre-eminence of the Assembly and kept a low profile as tenant of the Presidential Elysée. President Grévy made no attempt to expand the authority of the institution and on the contrary contributed to its effacement by withdrawing from participation. Grévy was, all the same, a Republican and had strong political views. The President was influential both in manipulating the choice of Prime Ministers and in foreign affairs, which at that time (after the Franco-Prussian War) remained pacific. A year into a second septennate Jules Grévy resigned in a scandal over the sale of honours, and there followed a succession of largely unmemorable Presidents who were distinctly passive in their approach to the office, many declaring that they were non-political.

Presidents took a closer interest in foreign affairs than in domestic matters and travelled to consolidate alliances and advance France's cause, but they also had an influence in the equilibrium of the state and society through successive crises. For example, President Loubet, at the height of the Dreyfus Affair that tore France apart, resolutely refused to take sides and sought only to reduce the divisions. There were strong personalities (like Poincaré who vigorously intervened) who were able to find majority support, but they were liable to find themselves isolated in the Elysée prison unable to organise political support. Prime Minister Clemenceau shut out President Poincaré after November 1917 and President Millerand resigned after a clash with the Assembly. Albert Lebrun, the last President of the Third Republic, sought a neutral role in a turbulent era. President Lebrun made little use of the prerogatives he had and his impact on events was small. In June 1940 Lebrun made no attempt to stiffen resolve and may have contributed to the support for the armistice. When the Republic was dissolved he signed it out of existence. Commenting on this tradition, as de Gaulle noted, the President was only there to 'open chrysanthemum shows'.

After the war, there were proposals to strengthen the executive, and to reinforce the presidency itself, but the mainstream in the constituent assemblies were hostile to an American-style presidency of separate powers. After long and exhausting presidential debates the Constitution adopted in 1946 made the National Assembly the source of executive power and established a presidency of limited powers but with a capacity for influence. In the Fourth Republic there were two Presidents: the Socialist Vincent Auriol and the centrist René Coty. Their influence came about because of the fragmented party system in the Assembly but was felt in different ways. President Auriol faced mounting instability, economic crisis, the beginning of the Cold War which moved the big Communist Party into opposition to the Republic, and the rise of a mass gaullist movement also hostile to the Republic. He was active in trying to solve the persistent Cabinet crises, negotiating with parties, helping produce the government programmes and looking for a Prime Minister (there were some very surprising choices) who could command a majority. The purpose of this intervention was to ensure stability and to provide a centrist majority which rejected the extremes of gaullism and Communism. President Coty is now remembered for the thirteen ballots required to elect him and the role he had in bringing de Gaulle to power in 1958. Coty was discreet and less determinedly interventionist than was Auriol, and was more consensual in approach, bringing, for example, the Communists into consultations. He did, however, dissolve the Assembly in 1956 and then chose the Socialist leader Guy Mollet as Prime Minister and not the coalition leader Mendès France. In 1958

President Coty intervened decisively, telling the deputies to make de Gaulle Prime Minister or he would resign.

This is the background to the Fifth Republic and the framers of the Constitution similarly envisaged the President as a ceremonial head of state. The President of the Fifth Republic in the texts resembles these modest representative figures and does not derive power from the Constitution. The Presidents of the Fifth Republic are meant to ensure the regular functioning of institutions but their 'powers' are to redress the balance by calling in other actors. Thus the President can, *in extremis*, dissolve the Assembly and thus call on the electorate (Article 12), but can also call on the Constitutional Council to pronounce on bills (Article 61) and deliver messages to the Assembly. In addition most of the President's acts under the Constitution have to be countersigned either by the Prime Minister or by appropriate ministers (not those discussed below). Acts often thought of as 'presidential', like holding referendums and dismissing the Prime Minister, are not found in the Constitution. The control of nuclear weapons by the President results from a law of 1963 and is revocable by the Assembly.

The President's ceremonial status explains why there is no provision for presidential accountability in the Constitution as would be expected in a modern state. Thus Article 68 declares that the President is responsible for actions carried out in the course of his or her duties only in the case of 'high treason'. 'High treason' is undefined and 'impeachment' would necessitate a lengthy and cumbersome process which is unlikely ever to be invoked. This effectively puts the President beyond control not just during and after the presidential term but also – possibly – for acts even before taking office. This is a very strong reason for assuming that the President of the Constitution is not an executive President, but this 'irresponsibility' also poses substantial problems of accountability and control.

The President is described in Article 5 as an 'arbitrator', that is an umpire, and the government as responsible to the Assembly and not to the President. This would seem to make the executive presidency as it has evolved unconstitutional. There is some discussion of this Article (the meaning of 'arbitration') but it seems to be an open and shut case. The almost daily presidential violation of this article is not questioned, but it is probably not good for the rule of law.

If the Constitution is read as being a parliamentary one then the presidential roles as 'Head of the Armed Forces' (Article 15) and in 'negotiating and ratifying treaties' are ceremonial and repeat Article 33 of the Fourth Republic. They are counterpoised by Parliament's responsibility to declare war and the government's control over the army (Article 21). The President does not have the support to negotiate treaties (that is to be found in the Foreign Office) and nor do the Presidents control their own budget to redress any lack. In 1986 the President was deprived of information by a hostile government which wanted to keep control of foreign affairs and at times the President did not know what was happening. In 1962 the Constitution was amended and in 1965 the first direct election of the President took place. Direct election, in itself, does not confer power (some directly elected Presidents are not executives) but it makes the exercise of supreme power more legitimate and has enabled Presidents to expand their prerogatives (see below).

But the question thus remains of exactly what presidential powers amount to under the Constitution. What can the President do without countersignature? According to Article 8 (1) they can 'nominate the Prime Minister'. This does not mean that the Prime Minister is responsible to the President, as Article 49 (1) makes clear that the Premier 'pledges the responsibility of the government to the National Assembly'. In practice Presidents have dismissed Prime Ministers and have appointed their choice. It is, however, a presidential practice at odds with the Constitution and disappears if the President's majority in the Assembly is defeated. Thus the 'cohabitation' periods of 1986–88, 1993–95 and 1997– saw the President constrained to chose the Assembly majority's candidate. Where the majority is determined to do otherwise can only lead to a crisis and the President's resignation. This happened in 1924 when the conservative President Millerand was confronted with a victory of the Radical and Socialist left in general elections. There was a 'strike of Prime Ministers'; nobody in the majority would accept any nomination other than its leader Edouard Herriot, so the President nominated Finance Minister Frédéric François-Marsal as Prime Minister. François-Marsal was censured by the Assembly and the President had to resign. However, where the majority is unclear or shifting, the President might play a creative role in deciding whom to ask to form a government. This was the Fourth Republic presidency's important function.

Referendums under the procedure of Article 11 are not subject to countersignature. However, these have to be proposed by the government or by Parliament and are only for a limited purpose not including the amendment of the Constitution. Part of this Article has been respected: the government officially proposed the subject which was then put to the referendum by the President. This procedure was respected even by de Gaulle and despite the appearances. But the amendment of the Constitution in 1962 to introduce direct election of the President was not constitutional (nor was the referendum of 1969). Article 89 lays out the procedure for amendment and Article 11 makes no provision for constitutional matters. De Gaulle's referendums were in reality decided by him alone and endorsed by the government (which might be surprised by the initiative) but that was a feature of political leadership rather than constitutionality. After de Gaulle's departure the referendum has been used three times and those not with success.

Article 12 gives the President the power to dissolve the Assembly after consulting the Speaker and Prime Minister (their advice can be ignored). This Article is, in effect, the right to bring in the people to break a logjam or *immobilisme* in the Assembly through the means of a general election. Dissolution in the French tradition is, however, different from the UK where Prime Ministers are expected to pick the best moment for their side to win. As a rule the French legislature is expected to run its term unless there is a crisis or clear problem. Thus the right to dissolve the Assembly was exercised by de Gaulle in 1962 (when the government was censured) and in 1968 (in the 'events') to resolve political crisis. Dissolution was also used after the presidential victories of 1981 and 1988 to avoid a clash between President and Assembly when the left's President faced an Assembly of the conservative right. In those circumstances, where the President held the political high ground and was able to mobilise support, the dissolution became a 'power' to reinforce presidential authority. However, although there was a mismatch between the Assembly and President, dissolution was not used when Pompidou won in 1969 nor in 1974 when the centrist Giscard won the elections and faced a gaullist majority (although it was contemplated because the gaullists would not necessarily support President Giscard). Both Presidents Pompidou and Giscard represented the conservatives and both had problems from inheriting majorities in the Assembly which were not 'their supporters' but those of the previous President from the same camp.

The right to impel a dissolution, as British Prime Ministers Wilson, Heath and Callaghan found to their cost, does not guarantee your side support in the subsequent elections. Recently in 1997, President Chirac's dissolution of an Assembly with a big majority of the conservatives, one year before the end of the legislature's term, resulted in a rejection of his supporters and the left won a majority. President Chirac's attempt to use a 'window of opportunity' when the polls looked favourable was a warning. This dissolution was misunderstood and badly explained (allowing speculation to grow about possible austerity programmes and so on) and failed to convince the voters to back an unpopular government. If the President's coalition is not returned there is little that can be done and the public would not take kindly to being asked to vote again to get the 'right' answer. Where the President has dissolved the Assembly there can be no dissolution for another year.

The President can instal a 'Republican dictatorship' under the emergency powers of Article 16 where there is a serious and immediate threat to the Republic and with the only reservation that the Constitutional Council has to be consulted on all acts. This Article is quite specific and its use is constitutionally limited to the establishment of order. President de Gaulle used this Article once, when there was an attempted military coup in Algiers in April 1961 (though the emergency lasted until September). Parliament meets during the application of the Article and the Assembly cannot be dissolved during that time. In 1961 the deputies were not inclined to push their own rights against the President who went beyond what was strictly constitutional during the period of April to September. It is clear, however, that Article 16 cannot be invoked to get round political crisis or if the opposition wins an election (that would be a *coup d'état*).

There are other Articles which give Presidents power to act on their own. Article 18 enables the President to send messages to be read to the Assembly and Senate. Article 17 gives the President the right to pardon convicted offenders. Article 54 enables the President (and Prime Minister and any 60 parliamentarians) to ask the Constitutional Council to judge whether an international obligation is in conformity with the Constitution, and Article 61 enables the President to submit ordinary laws for the same judgement. Under Article 56 the President can nominate three members of the nine-strong Constitutional Council and decide on its president. These powers are not significant, although the nominations to the Constitutional Council can affect the shape of legislation and slow down the law-making process and have been used for that purpose.

There remains the disputed question of the presidential 'veto'. To what extent is this a real constitutional power? Under the Third and Fourth Republics it was not for the President to refuse to sign acts and the presidential signature was a formal register. In 1986 President Mitterrand refused to sign decrees prepared by the government (under Article 38), and the Prime Minister, to avoid a confrontation, backed down (the measures were then quickly put through Parliament). This is probably one area where a maximalist interpretation of the President's power became possible as a result of the authority provided by direct election. It remains, however, a judicially untested and highly dubious practice in a country where the text, not the practice, is the law. President Pompidou suspended a constitutional revision after the Assembly and Senate voted it. In June 2000 President Chirac threatened to veto the amendment of the Constitution if the parliamentarians changed the proposal (as is their right).

But France before 1958 lacked executive authority and there were many who had seen the presidency as the way to establish both leadership and stability in France. It was therefore possible to establish an executive presidency on the back of de Gaulle's unparalleled prestige and the Algerian crisis when France was on the verge of civil war. It was a development which, however, went beyond the text and it must be asked where it came from. The answer, unsurprisingly, is from politics.

From de Gaulle's time onwards Presidents have usually been leaders of the majority coalition. They have created and headed a left-wing or right-wing alliance of political parties designed to win them presidential and parliamentary elections. The fates of the parliamentary majority and the President have been the same as the fate of the government and the governing party in a parliamentary system. Backbenchers will save their seats and prosper to the extent that the government is successful and they fall if the government fails. When de Gaulle returned to power in 1958 he was able to dominate the government. This is because a coalition of support in the Assembly elected in November 1958 consolidated behind him and power shifted to the Elysée following his election as President in December of the same year. These two things were not unprecedented, and one could have taken place without the other, but they were the founding political impetus to the Fifth Republic.

Under de Gaulle, Pompidou and Giscard d'Estaing, the first three Presidents, the majority was a conservative one in which the gaullists (or neo-gaullists) were the biggest single party. In 1981–86 and then 1988–93 the majority was a left-wing one in which the Socialist Party was the dominant component and there have been three periods of 'cohabitation' during which the President lost control (and about which see below). There are thus two stages in the development of the Fifth Republic presidency. The first is the period of 'gaullist' presidency: that is of solid presidential majorities (either left or right). The second is one of the reduced presidency: the disintegration of support for the President starting with the 'cohabitation' of 1986–88 and lasting to the present.

The executive ('gaullist') presidency

The 'gaullist' executive presidency includes de Gaulle, Pompidou and Chirac but also the non-gaullists Giscard d'Estaing and Mitterrand. It is the conception of the executive presidency in which authority stems from the President and power is measured in closeness to the Elysée. It is a dynamic institution and provided the impetus for such projects as the nuclear weapons programme, civil nuclear power, the Beaubourg (Pompidou) centre, the TGV and so on. This presidency is characterised by the extreme concentration of power in the hands of one person and the attendant problems of capricious decisions and intrigues between close associates. The Fifth Republic presidency in this mode is the most powerful of chief executives in the western world because there are no countervailing powers nor responsibility to other institutions.

The historical start is with de Gaulle's return to power in 1958. At that time the fear of a military *coup d'état* and the pressing crisis of the Algerian war kept the deputies behind de Gaulle, despite the lack of a majority and a strong gaullist political party. De Gaulle's supporters were organised for the general elections of November 1958 at which the gaullists and their allies won a relative but not absolute majority of 199 seats (with 19.5 per cent of the vote). An electoral college of elected politicians mainly from local government elected de Gaulle President of the Fifth Republic on 21 December by some 79 per cent. This indirect election was sufficient in the context of the continuing war and insurrection in Algeria to give de Gaulle mastery of the executive and, if not quite a free hand, the ability to carry through most of the programme he wanted to.

In April 1962 the Evian peace agreements were endorsed by 91 per cent of voters in referendum. This popular support was the opportunity for the President abruptly to replace Prime Minister Debré with the unknown Georges Pompidou. This was highly significant because Pompidou owed his position entirely to de Gaulle and because the Constitution does not enable the President to dismiss the Premier. De Gaulle's support in the Assembly, however, diminished after the peace settlement and the opposition to de Gaulle in the Assembly grew to the extent that a motion of censure was passed in October 1962. The immediate cause was the undoubtedly unconstitutional referendum to pronounce on the direct election of the President (which was duly endorsed). In the subsequent general election de Gaulle's party and its allies benefited from the presidential dynamic to take 268 seats, a comfortable majority. The voters, who returned a majority supporting the President to the Assembly, confirmed de Gaulle's domination of the political scene. It should be noted that this presidential domination predates the introduction of direct election of the President which first took place in 1965. De Gaulle had declared in a press conference in 1964 that the 'President alone holds and delegates the authority of the state'.

During de Gaulle's presidency the gaullist party dominated the majority and was supported by the smaller Independent Republicans (followers of Giscard d'Estaing) and by the MRP until April 1962, although the centre parties remained critical of gaullism. De Gaulle extended the presidential remit as political expediency dictated. Although the idea of the 'presidential reserved domain' of foreign policy became current, no President accepted a restriction on presidential authority. The 'reserved domain' was contested in 'cohabitation'. Prime Minister Edouard Balladur in 1993 used the term 'shared sector', whereas Premier Jospin said in 1997, 'there is no sector in which the President has the last word'. In foreign and defence policy all the President's acts are subject to countersignature and they are in constitutional terms the Prime Minister's powers. The Premier countersigns even the acts of the President as head of the armed forces and accreditation of ambassadors.

De Gaulle may have been interested principally in foreign affairs, but neither he nor Pompidou (nor Giscard, Mitterrand or Chirac) allowed that there was either a reserved or a neglected sector. Presidential authority was extended to all policy and not just that of high politics. De Gaulle's authority was ultimately dependent on his popular support. This he recognised when the April 1969 referendum was defeated and he resigned immediately.

His successor Georges Pompidou continued the gaullist conception of the presidency, although the centre began to be slowly incorporated into the gaullist majority. Pompidou was concerned, as de Gaulle had not been, that the presidential majority had to be enlarged to bring in the centre parties to the coalition. In addition Pompidou, having none of the historical stature of de Gaulle, had to resituate the presidency on a more embracing appeal. This process was under way during Pompidou's truncated septennate but, while the principal figures in the government were presidential nominees and de Gaulle's partisans were replaced, the gaullists remained in the driving seat. Pompidou, Prime Minister 1962–68, knew the government's business in a detail approached by few others and intervened as he saw fit. He demonstrated his authority over the coalition by dismissing Prime Minister Chaban only a few weeks after he had been given a vote of confidence in the Assembly. There is no telling how far this presidential grip would have been tightened because Pompidou fell gravely ill and died in April 1974.

It was the election of the former Finance Minister Giscard d'Estaing from the minority party in the coalition, and not the Resistance gaullist Chaban Delmas, which started to cause dissension in the conservative right. Giscard had supported de Gaulle but had not joined the gaullist party and his support came from the centre and centre right, including some of the old Fourth Republic parties. Giscard won the presidency by the narrowest of margins (50.7 per cent) against the left's candidate Mitterrand and took the opportunity to place his supporters in prominent positions, ousting many gaullists in the process. Thus was introduced into the politics of the presidency a tension which has yet to be resolved. The dominant part of the coalition, the gaullists, became the junior partner in the government after 1974.

Giscard had started with a more modest concept of the presidency and scaled down its pretensions, but the presidential grip on policy was tightened. The new President centralised decision-making on the Elysée to the maximum and intervened almost whimsically as the mood took him and in detail. He appointed Jacques Chirac as Prime Minister but reduced the role of the Premier, cutting him out of the decision-making at times almost totally. Apart from the fine-grained control of ministerial business which went beyond his predecessors' practice, the concept of the presidency remained much the same: the source of authority.

Although the Prime Minister Chirac was a gaullist, the post was downgraded and centrists took the key ministries. It was the move to the centre and the change of personnel which had enabled Giscard to win the election but the gaullist dismay at being pushed into the second rank in their Republic was to emerge later. When Chirac resigned as Prime Minister in 1976, and was replaced by the centrist Raymond Barre, the gaullist party was reorganised and renamed (the RPR) and the hostility to the 'giscardians' became more overt. In the 1970s the distrust of the left kept the conservative right loyal to the President, though not without open disagreements, and the 1978 elections were won as a battle against the Socialist–Communist alliance. But after that victory the gaullists again felt that their contribution had not been recognised and the guerrilla war on the right stepped up in tempo. It became more envenomed after 1978 and the neo-gaullist Assembly group even refused to vote some government business. This war contributed substantially to the defeat of the outgoing President Giscard at the 1981 elections but still continues to divide the conservative right. Giscard was undermined by the hostility to the centre shown by the gaullists and either dropped measures or promoted some which were not to his liking in order to appease the coalition partner. The presidency itself began to suffer from his authoritarian manner on the one hand and the drift in policy on the other.

The victory of the left's candidate in 1981 was a restoration of presidential pre-eminence and Mitterrand took the opportunity to dissolve the Assembly and win a handsome majority. Mitterrand, who wrote a famous attack on de Gaulle's presidency, seems to have taken the view that the executive presidency was dangerous before he was elected and would be dangerous afterwards but was safe in his hands. President Mitterrand took the presidency back to the 'gaullist' position as the fount of authority and was secure in the backing of a large majority of which 285 deputies out of 492 were Sociaists devoted to him personally. President Mitterrand led the left and had no need of the Communists' 44 deputies but could not count on a majority for the Socialists in the future. Four Communists were brought into the government and a coalition of the left (Socialists, Communists and MRG) was kept intact. The governments of the 1981–86 legislature were as much presidential constructs as the governments of the previous conservative Presidents had been, and ultimately decided policy and tactics. (A French satirical television programme depicted the President as 'Dieu'.) The Communists accepted an alliance with the Socialists (and with reservations presidential government) and Mitterrand's first five years of the septennate could be regarded as in line with the 'gaullist' presidency.

Non-executive presidency

The 'cohabitation' of 1986–88 marks the second phase in the development of the presidency of the Fifth Republic. With a seven-year presidential term, the Fifth Republic President can become unpopular and can lose touch with the public. De Gaulle realised that he had to retain public confidence and resigned when he lost the referendum of 1969. President Giscard anticipated losing the elections in 1978 and declared that, if that were to happen, he would retire to the presidential chateau at Rambouillet 40 kilometres from Paris to signal that it was not 'his' government (but not resign). President Mitterrand did not take this view when he lost his Assembly majority in 1986 and stayed in the Elysée, but the conservative right, by agreeing to form a government under his continuing presidency, opened a new phase in the Fifth Republic: 'cohabitation'.

'Cohabitation' so-called is the situation in which a President of one coalition faces an Assembly dominated by political opponents. The elections of 1986 were the first in which a President could not win a supporting majority in the

---

'Cohabitation'

This is the term now used to refer to the presence at the head of the executive of a President of the left confronting a Prime Minister of the right (or vice versa). It is not a constitutional term and was not used by President Mitterrand (the first to experience 'cohabitation'). There have been three periods each coming after the President's supporters lost an election: 1986–88, 1993–95 and 1997–. The longest 'cohabitation' so far has been between President Chirac and Prime Minister Jospin. 'Cohabitation' is disliked by the political elite, on which it places restraints (although it has worked relatively well), but it is liked by the public, which appreciates co-operation at the summit.

Assembly. By not resigning when his supporters failed to win, the President made possible a change in the nature of the regime. (He was not obliged to resign and the 'repudiation' by the voters was not a massive one.) President Giscard had almost faced this in 1978 but it had been averted by the conservative right's vigorous rally to support the President and the left's internal squabbling which lost it the election. The Socialists touched the depths of unpopularity in 1984 and were unable to recover to win the 1986 general elections, which were a victory for the conservative right led by the neo-gaullist Jacques Chirac. President Mitterrand, faced by a conservative majority in the Assembly determined to see their leader made head of government, had no alternative other than to appoint their choice, Jacques Chirac, as Prime Minister. The Fifth Republic reverted abruptly to being a parliamentary regime in which the Prime Minister and government were responsible to the Assembly on which they depended for power, prestige and authority. Lacking a majority in the Assembly, and without constitutional power, the President is pushed to the sidelines and can rely only on his political wiles to regain some authority.

In 1986 the Constitution was applied for the first time as the framers had intended as a prime ministerial executive supported by the Assembly majority. The position was not politically clear because since 1959 the Fifth Republic had been *de facto* presidential and presidential dominance especially in foreign affairs had become the general expectation. In addition the Prime Minister, Jacques Chirac, had presidential ambitions and had determined to run at the next presidential election to restore the 'gaullist' presidency. As a result the 'cohabitation' of 1986 maintained a façade of public harmony but was a political battle for pre-eminence behind the scenes. President Mitterrand withdrew from the front line of decision-making and policy implementation, becoming in the process a 'Fourth Republic' President but also a popular figure (his poll rating soared). Partially this was forced on the President, since information was withheld from him, and partially it was the tactic of paying out rope to the government, disassociating himself from the government's many mistakes but associating himself with the successes. He used his limited constitutional prerogatives astutely and played on the public perception that the President was supreme in foreign policy matters. It was a paying proposition for the President, who won the 1988 presidential elections against his own Prime Minister.

After winning the presidency again in 1988 Mitterrand dissolved the Assembly but this time, unlike 1981, there was no landslide victory for his supporters. The presidential coalition had a relative majority of 277 to the conservative right's 273 (the absolute majority was 289) and could be defeated if the 27 Communist deputies voted against the government. For the first time since 1962 the President had been refused a majority. The main change was a scaling down of the ambitions of the presidency to a more modest dimension as an international figure (in the 'reserved domain') and as an overseer of government activity run by the Prime Minister. It was left to the Prime Minister to negotiate on a case-by-case basis with the Assembly to find a majority for each measure. The Socialist Party in the Assembly also proved less amenable than in 1981 and the Prime Minister of 1992–93, Pierre Bérégovoy, had to climb down on several occasions. In the second septennate President Mitterrand stood above the political arena and sometimes criticised his own Prime Ministers (during the nurses' grievances of 1988 and the secondary school problems of 1989, for example) and constricted their margin for manoeuvre. The 1988–93 legislature ended in catastrophe for the President with near rejection of the referendum on the Maastricht Treaty in September 1992 and a landslide victory for the conservative right in 1993. In the 'cohabitation' of 1993–95 the President was gravely ill, did not intend to run for a third term and had no support from a potentially governing coalition. The RPR leader Jacques Chirac declined to take the post of 'cohabitation' Premier a second time and it was decided that his close associate Edouard Balladur would. This choice was forced on the President. Prime Minister Balladur had an easier relationship with the Elysée than any previous incumbent and made good use of that freedom to make himself a presidential contender.

Prime Minister Balladur's decision to enter the presidential race made the situation in the conservative majority more fraught. It divided between the partisans of the RPR leader Chirac and those of Balladur, who was a party member but supported by most centrists and some RPR figures. With the left at that time out of contention, the conservative candidates indulged in the luxury of a dispute over who could best represent them. Despite this fraternal rivalry Jacques Chirac won the presidency in 1995, reasserted the 'gaullist' presidency and packed the government with his own supporters. Prime Minister Alain Juppé depended on the President and the Elysée launched a series of personal initiatives, including the restarting of nuclear tests, reintegration into NATO, and the reform of teaching and justice. But the Prime Minister and the President had great difficulty in imposing their authority on the (huge) conservative majority in the Assembly. The government's authority was in free-fall and taking the President down with it when, in 1997, the President called a snap election. This impetuous dissolution was decided in the hope of regaining some ground and a majority capable of governing for the remainder of the septennate.

But the election of 1997 turned out to be a repudiation of the President and he had no option other than to nominate the opposition leader, the Socialist Lionel Jospin, as Prime Minister. After this rebuff the President had to return to a minimal constitutional role for the presidency. President Chirac began to rebuild his popularity as a non-executive President by using his office as a 'bully pulpit' and by encouraging divisions in the government coalition. But Jacques Chirac had lost control of the RPR party he had created as it fell into the hands of his critics Philippe Séguin and Nicolas Sarkozy. There ensued a battle between the President's supporters and the politicians on the conservative right as the President tried to recoup power inside his own camp. This turned out to be a negative power to prevent the emergence of a rival rather than the positive presidential power of building a majority coalition.

It was a less conflictual 'cohabitation' than the first had been because the President had been repudiated by the voters and some ground rules for a peaceful stand-off had been worked out during 1986–88 and 1993–95. In foreign policy the main concern was to keep the image of a united France speaking – as they said – with two mouths but one voice. The Kosovo war allowed President Chirac to appear as the pre-eminent authority in foreign policy and a backstage dispute had enabled the President to predominate at the Amsterdam European Council almost immediately after the 1997 elections. At European Councils the President and Premier appeared together, delegations were presided by the President and the official press porte-parole was the Elysée's. European policy now pervades all government business and ministries and cannot be disentangled from domestic policy. Most ministries (agriculture, transport, etc.) have their European section and deal directly with their counterparts in the EU, making it almost impossible for the presidency to control them. The Elysée is not at the centre of this decision-making, although the President meets the Minister of Defence on Monday, the Foreign Minister on Tuesday and the Prime Minister before Cabinet meetings on Wednesday. Although the President went on official voyages, the Premier could decide which to join and also decided which of his own voyages to undertake (with presidential advice). When the Premier's diplomatic visit to Israel went wrong in 2000 there was a prudent retreat from the front line, though not a concession of this area.

Thus it has emerged from three 'cohabitations' that the President has limited powers. The President is not obliged to resign if the voters reject his supporters at general elections even if there has been a landslide to the opposition (as in 1993). But the new majority will limit the choice of Prime Minister and very likely there will be no choice at all other than to nominate the leader of the new majority. There is no opening for the President to block or veto legislation passed by a parliamentary majority but where there is a need for a President's signature that may be refused. In a certain number of cases the President can bargain over nominations to a limited number of positions and – if required – can refuse them. In foreign and defence policy the President is expected to play a ceremonial role at the front but the substance of decision-making in the 'reserved sector' can become the Prime Minister's. But the President can also act as the leader of the opposition and criticise the government's action from a detached and 'principled' position. In effect the President can become the leader of the opposition during 'cohabitation' but not in the British sense of a parliamentary and constant critic.

Although at the time of the first 'cohabitation' the French people regarded the change with apprehension, they have subsequently proved favourable to 'cohabitation' and with steadily greater enthusiasm. The change in authority from President to Prime Minister was clearly perceived by the public so there was no ambiguity about the response. Before the 1997 'cohabitation' 68 per cent wanted the President to stay and only 29 per cent wanted him to go. 'Cohabitation' was viewed more favourably in 1998 than in 1986 and more of the public saw it as advantageous than disadvantageous. In the third 'cohabitation' the popularity of both the Prime Minister and the President grew, with the implication that both might be re-elected and the presence of two competing politicians at the head of the state could become normal. In the first 'cohabitation' President Mitterrand was far more popular than Premier Chirac was, and in the second 'cohabitation' Prime Minister Balladur was more popular than President Mitterrand was.

The Elysée

To impose presidential authority on government the successive Fifth Republic Presidents built up a presidential system and staff. For the purposes of the executive presidency the Elysée had to become a steering group and overseer of the presidential programme's implementation. Starting with de Gaulle, a close surveillance over the various ministries was instituted. This 'supervision' kept the President informed, promoted policy and ensured compliance so that where some measure met with presidential displeasure it would be rejected. Where there was disagreement a series of meetings had to take place until a compromise was found. For the most part where a minister disagreed with presidential policy or presidential decisions they had to depart (as did Jean-Pierre Chevènement, who dissented from President Mitterrand's Gulf War policy). Under 'cohabitation' the Elysée was reduced to a simpler role monitoring government where it could but not intervening.

Led by the Secretary General of the Elysée, who is an authoritative figure in the executive presidency and who works very closely with the President, is the secretariat. The Elysée secretariat is a relatively small body of about 30 or so composed of elite recruits (mainly from the *grandes écoles*). Each member is responsible for a sector and both follows developments in it and provides information and advice. But there is a tension in the Elysée system which may result in office warfare and resignations. There is also a presidential *cabinet*, or private office, of about 39, which deals with matters to which the President wants to pay particular attention. These invariably include foreign and defence policy and also African policy, but may include any policy area which catches the President's eye. Staff attend government meetings on the topics they cover but the influence of the private office depends on personality (of the President and the office member) and can be greater than that of the relevant government minister. The Minister of African Affairs, Jean-Pierre Cot, resigned after eighteen months because of his lack of influence on policy, and later President Mitterrand made his son Jean-Christoph adviser on African affairs. President Mitterrand liked to gather information from different sources and did not allow associates to 'capture' policy areas; other Presidents have been more managerial and have had straight lines of delegation. In times of 'cohabitation' the President's staffs have no entry into government meetings (defence and foreign affairs usually excepted) or ministries and have no overseeing responsibility. Their task then becomes one of keeping the President informed, looking after the President's image and the media, and ensuring the President's political support. But they are no less crucial and in the third 'cohabitation' they planned the President's return to the fore and concentrated on relations with the conservative right.

The Elysée is not a government. Even under an executive presidency it cannot do more than oversee the conduct of affairs. Presidents compose the music, the Prime Minister conducts the orchestra, and the Elysée staff make sure that the score is being followed, so to speak. This simplification is generally correct but the Fifth Republic executive presidency has led to the development of a court system in which closeness to the President confers power. The 'court' enables ministers (and others) who are dissatisfied, or who have a particular goal in mind, to appeal beyond the formal power system and go to the Elysée. The President's close advisers took many key decisions (over decolonisation of Algeria) and the government and Prime Minister were kept out of the process.

Conclusion

With the reform of the presidential term from a septennate to a quinquennium the future of the executive presidency is still unresolved. There is no reason why a five-year term should ensure the concordance of the presidential and legislative support any more than the septennate. The difficulty for the French executive has always been the mismatch between the President's support and the majority in the Assembly and that problem will not disappear with the new presidential term. The first presidential quinquennium will start in 2002.

The reform of the presidential term introduces a further uncertainty into the relations between President and Prime Minister but it is the simultaneous election which creates a new conundrum for the politicians. If, in the future, the new President and the new Assembly are elected at much the same time, the legitimacy of both will be unassailable and that will open up the battle for position. In the past the dividing line between Prime Minister and President has been settled when the President has lost or been seen to be repudiated at the polls. 'Cohabitation' Presidents to some extent withdrew from the front line bowing to public opinion: Mitterrand in 1986 and 1993 and Chirac in 1997.

If in 2002 a President is elected followed a few weeks later by an Assembly of a different colour, the Prime Minister may not find the Elysée accommodating. The Elysée will be further reinforced if the leader of the Assembly majority has just been defeated at the polls by the President. In the future an executive President could intervene more actively in experimenting with Prime Ministers (depending on the coherence of the majority in the Assembly), bargain over the filling of Cabinet posts and the possibilities for finding coalitions could be enhanced. It is more likely that the President would dispute the foreign policy of the government and retake the 'reserved domain'.

In the future where the French voters elect a President of one side and an Assembly of another it will be difficult to argue that a 'cohabitation' has not been intended. Thus both the President and the Assembly would probably back down from an immediate confrontation (like a dissolution or a refusal to serve by Premiers). Any politician who disturbs the balance will be viewed with disfavour and that will force the battle at the head of the state to be a backstairs one. Thus a 'cohabitation' for five years has not been ruled out but then nor has an executive presidency. The new five-year term merely adds a further twist to the political conflict at the summit.

Summary

- The executive presidency depends on the President building and retaining political power. The key to the continuation of the dominant gaullist presidency is the ability of Presidents to create coalitions of support and that requires constant effort.
- Presidential power comes from those political bases the President can find.
- Presidents Mitterrand and Chirac in the process of three 'cohabitations' have demonstrated that it is not necessary to have an executive President.
- 'Cohabitation', once an unthinkable catastrophe, is now a normal feature of the Fifth Republic and does not lead to social and institutional collapse.
- Neither the institutions nor the ability to dissolve the Assembly guarantee presidential domination.

Further reading

Cole, A., *François Mitterrand* (Routledge, 1994)

Elgie, R., 'The French presidency – conceptualizing presidential power in the Fifth Republic' *Public Administration* 74: 2, 1996, pp. 275–91

Frears, J., *France in the Giscard Presidency* (Unwin, 1981)

Gaffney, J., 'Presidentialism and the Fifth Republic' in J. Gaffney (ed.), *The French Presidential Elections of 1988* (Dartmouth, 1989)

Goldey, D. B. and Knapp, A. F., 'The French presidential election of 23 April–7 May 1995' *Electoral Studies* 15, 1996, pp. 97–109

Hayward, J., *De Gaulle to Mitterrand, Presidential Power in France* (Hurst, 1993)

Northcutt, W., *Mitterrand: A Political Biography* (Holmes and Meier, 1992)

Pierce, R., *Choosing the Chief* (University of Michigan Press, 1995)

Suleiman, E., 'Presidentialism and political stability in France' in J. J. Linz and A. Valenzuela (eds), *The Failure of Presidential Democracy* (Johns Hopkins, 1994)

Weatherford, S. and Weatherford, M. S., 'The puzzle of presidential leadership' *Governance* 7: 2, 1994, pp. 146–59

Questions

1 Presidents have no constitutional power to sack the Prime Minister but they have done so. How?
2 What is presidential power in foreign policy?
3 What is the 'Republican' presidential tradition?

10

The Prime Minister

The title of 'Prime Minister' has a long history in France and goes back to the monarchy but in the Third and Fourth Republics the office was called the 'President of the Council'. Third Republic Presidents of the Council invariably took charge of another ministry as well, to which they devoted themselves and which was at first their principal priority. Clemenceau was, for example, Premier and Minister of the Interior in 1906, and in the longest-running government of the Third Republic Waldeck-Rousseau was President of the Council, Interior Minister and Minister for Church–State Relations. A President of the Council was quite likely to be a political lightweight whose role was to keep the heavyweight politicians in the Cabinet working together. However, over the years the position did grow in importance and the Fourth Republic Constitution was the first to codify its importance, although this was subsequently constrained by lack of stable majorities. In 1958 the title of 'Prime Minister' was restored and the power of the position was reinforced.

As with the President, so with the Prime Minister: authority follows the leader of the majority. In the 'gaullist' Fifth Republic as long as the President leads the majority the Prime Minister is a subordinate in the presidential team and not an independent political power. Some Prime Ministers have been completely self-effacing and others have been more assertive but the generalisation remains broadly true of the Premiers from Debré through to Fabius (1959–86). Yet during 'cohabitation' where the Prime Minister leads the majority in the Assembly authority passes from the President to the Premier, from the Elysée Palace to the Hôtel Matignon.

First, however, a brief constitutional note on why this transfer of power should take place. The authors of the Fifth Republic Constitution created a prime ministerial leadership for the executive. This meant that the government, aided by an arsenal of devices for use against a disruptive Assembly, would provide the leadership the country was thought to lack during the Fourth Republic (and the Third). In this way the Constitution created a new executive but not, as it transpired, presidential.

In the Constitution prime ministerial power is spelt out in two Articles (20 and 21) and these make the Premier, as the British constitutionalists used to say, 'the keystone of the Cabinet arch'. Article 20 states that the 'Government directs and decides the policy of the nation'. This is not qualified. It does not say 'some of the policy of the nation' and it therefore includes foreign and defence policy. Moreover, in the Constitution, the 'Government' is the ministers and Prime Minister but not the President. Article 21 goes on to state that the 'Prime Minister directs the operation of the Government' and is made responsible for national defence. There is no mention of the President in that role and no room for ambiguity. The Prime Minister also appoints people to civil and military posts under the restrictions of Article 13, which gives the President a control of the higher level nominations. The Prime Minister can, under Article 34, use decrees to legislate and this has been extensively used. To this can be added the government's constitutional authority in the Assembly itself. They can decide on the agenda for the Assembly (Article 48), can veto any amendments with financial implications (Article 40) or which go beyond the strictly defined 'legislative domain' (Article 41), use the package vote (Article 44) and use the special mixed committee procedures (Article 45) to pass bills. Prime Ministers have the initiative in legislation (Article 39) and can engage their government's responsibility on a bill or on a programme or on a general declaration of the government's policies. None of these powers depend on the President.

It was evident early in 1959 that the practice of the Fifth Republic would not follow the lines mapped out in the Constitution. So great was de Gaulle's domination that it was asked of Michel Debré, the first Prime Minister: 'M. Debré, existe-t-il?' Authority flowed from President de Gaulle. Presidential leadership was confirmed when de Gaulle sacked Debré in mid-April 1962 and nominated as Prime Minister the unknown Georges Pompidou, who at that time had no political standing and no independent backing in Parliament. (Pompidou's nomination was taken by many to be a slap to the Assembly.) The dismissal of Debré was not in accordance with the Constitution but, as with the appointment of Pompidou, made clear who had the power. President Pompidou is alleged to have asked for undated resignation statements from ministers, but whether he did or not the power lay with the leader of the majority and to oppose that was political suicide.

Prime ministerial support

To enable the co-ordination of government work the Prime Ministers have at their disposal one hundred or so people in the General Secretariat of the Government. This is a little-known and discreet civil service institution which had developed since its creation in 1935 and is led by a senior career officer who 'is at the centre of everything and knows everything'. This remains through changes of government (although the Secretary General Jacques Fournier was changed in 1986) and its business is mainly technical, that of minutes, archives, ensuring legal compliance and proper procedure as well as relations with Parliament and other institutions. There is also a more political private office, which is composed of close associates who deal with the more pressing issues and react to events. There is usually a core membership of about 20 but many more unofficial collaborators who work in the team can complement that. They are in permanent liaison with the Elysée and with the ministries. Each office member has a sector and will be the Prime Minister's representative at meetings as well as reporting back to the Matignon on developments in 'their' sector and ministry. Prime Ministers rely on these advisers to make their authority felt in ministries and to promote their policies with (or against) the minister in charge.

It is the Prime Minister who is responsible for the development and implementation of policy both under 'cohabitation' and the executive presidency. Under an executive President the Prime Minister will have to manage a government which has been composed by the President. Prime Ministers will have their say in who makes up the Cabinet but the ministers will be subject to presidential authority (and may appeal past the Premier to the Elysée). Thus in 'normal times' during the development stage the Prime Minister will refer back to the presidential programme or imperatives (these can be public letters of instructions to government as was Giscard's practice). However, even in 'cohabitation' the Cabinet will be chosen to reflect the coalition and will not be as tightly disciplined as a British Cabinet. Prime Ministers have to attend to the weight and sensitivities of parties and the political balance within them.

But even where the President overshadows everybody on the political scene (as did de Gaulle) the Prime Ministers have control of the development, pace and direction of policy, which gives them great influence. Guided by the General Secretariat of the Government the Prime Minister conciliates and (ultimately) decides between different positions in the government in what can be a long and intricate process. It is true that any bill must be put on the Cabinet's agenda for formal approval but that is the end of the process and presidential refusal at that stage would signal a crisis – not an exercise of the President's authority. Under 'cohabitation' the Prime Minister has the last say in any disputes over finance, between ministries or over policy with the Matignon itself. This is normally true where there is presidential domination but the Elysée can intervene. As is said of all policy-making, 'the devil is in the detail' and that is the Prime Minister's province not the President's.

The Prime Minister is also expected to manage the Assembly majority and the government from which it emanates both under 'cohabitation' as well as presidential domination. This is not an easy task as collective responsibility is not a constitutional doctrine in France; although solidarity is necessary for the government to survive, there is no tradition of Cabinet co-ordination. In addition all French governments have been coalitions and discipline within the participating parties is not always strong. Coalitions have varied in composition from the virtually homogenous Socialist/Left Radical coalition of 1984–86 to the heterogeneous five-party 'plural left' of Communist, Socialist, Radical Socialist, Green and Citizens' Movement of 1997. Moreover, whereas some have had a dominant party like the 1962–67 governments, others have been very fragmented or even factionalised, as was the centre-gaullist coalition of 1978–81. Hence Prime Ministers have to be attentive to the sensitivities of both party and coalition partners in order to keep the government together and to pilot their (or the President's) legislation through the Assembly. Legislation has failed or been amended out of recognition by the deputies and support has to be earned and cannot be produced on demand. Prime Ministers do not issue orders or administer in a technical manner but also have to attend to the politics of the coalition.

The working of the Cabinet and ministries is different from the British tradition. Cabinets are meetings of all the ministers presided over by the President of the Republic and they have an agenda comprising bills and decrees, nominations and contributions from those attending. It is not clear whether the President has the legal right to refuse to sign a bill that the Cabinet has agreed. But both President Mitterrand and President Chirac refused their signatures and this was not contested.

The Cabinet

This institution is, in an old French convention, presided over by the President of the Republic (Article 9). It meets every Wednesday and it passes bills, decrees and nominations. It is not, in the Fifth Republic, a crucial institution and it is rigid in format and rarely the place for surprise or the *coup d'éclat*. Debates are unusual and the round tables by ministers are not meant to enlighten or provoke. Its main importance is to review current issues and to show a government front.

There is a long history of ministerial power in French government. Government instability and ministerial stability characterised the Fourth Republic. Governments came and went but the same people remained in key ministries over long stretches. In the executive presidency of the Fifth Republic the Foreign and Defence Ministers would have close relations with the Elysée and direct access to the President, more so, often, than the Prime Minister. But other areas that took the President's interest might also work closely with the Elysée (like education) and could become 'super-ministries' if the political situation warranted. Under 'cohabitation' ministers can represent a political group or party in the Assembly and, although they will not appeal to the Elysée, they will have great political weight.

The Prime Minister proposes ministers to the President. In the Fifth Republic ministers must relinquish their Assembly seat to their 'substitute' and if they wish to return the 'substitute' has to resign and a by-election has to be held.

This was to demark the Assembly from the government and to make it difficult for the deputies to overturn governments to obtain ministerial portfolios in the next reshuffle (deputies were accused of throwing out government to increase their own chances of a post). The Fifth Republic also made an attempt to bring into government ministers with technical expertise but without a political or party background. There have been a number of such appointments over the years, particularly by executive Presidents, and many have been a success but their progress has depended on their developing political arts quickly and effectively (others have been less impressive).

There is a hierarchy of ministers as well as honorific positions and titles are given to mark the minister's position in government. Thus the Ministries of Finance, Justice and Interior are 'heavyweight', as are the big spending ministries of Education and Equipment, but there are ministers without portfolio (though the Fourth Republic's title of Deputy Prime Minister has disappeared). There are junior ministers who, as in England, are usually younger politicians at the foot of the ministerial ladder; they do not attend Cabinet meetings unless invited for discussions on their sector. The title of Minister of State is not accompanied by any particular attribute, nor is that of Delegate Minister (a title recently given to associate-ministers attached to a bigger ministry): the exact authority of ministers is not fixed and is the result of a decree. Usually the title of Minister of State is given to the main politicians in the government or it can be intended to emphasise the importance of a sector. Under President Giscard this title was given to the representatives of the parties of the presidential coalition in the government and in the Socialist governments the main faction leaders or their representatives were so honoured. The title recognised a political reality but authority in the Cabinet did not follow from it. For example, in 1981 Michel Rocard (who had quarrelled with the President over the three previous years) was made Minister of State but cut out of the political decision-making. The size of governments in France is not limited: Michel Rocard's government included 48 ministers but the conservative governments have generally been smaller (around 30 at most).

Composing the government

Lionel Jospin's government of 1997 was formed with a minimum of presidential interference but with an eye to the politics of coalition management. The President may have hoped, following the precedent of his own 'cohabitation' of 1986–88, that the government if given the authority to govern would be responsible for its own policies and mistakes. It might have been assumed that the mistakes would occur sooner rather than later and that the government would discredit itself. There were many potentially fundamental disagreements, including the Euro (pro and anti), immigration and nationality policy and nuclear power stations, that could not be shelved or put off. Whatever the reason, the Premier had a free hand, but the 'plural left' coalition had won the elections by a narrow margin and needed to keep its majority in the Assembly happy with its activity. It was also a government that included few of those who had been eminent in the Mitterrand presidency and many were new faces. The intention was to put the discredited 'Mitterrand years' behind them; the Prime Minister's domination of the government was also thrown into sharp relief. Lionel Jospin was the only potential President on the left and none of the party potentates of the 1980s was present in the government.

The Prime Minister formed a small government of fifteen Cabinet colleagues plus ten junior ministers (including eight women). The balance was a delicate one and required rewarding the coalition partners without seeming to down-grade or dismiss the importance of others – the fear of Socialist Party domina-tion was also a problem. The key Finance Ministry went to the Prime Minister's associate Dominique Strauss-Kahn, who was a powerful force in the govern-ment but not a faction leader himself. The Education Minister was Claude Allègre, who had been a friend of Jospin's since their university years and who had also been his adviser when he was Education Minister in 1988. Jospin's associate Daniel Vaillant became Minister for Relations with Parliament. Also close to the Prime Minister was Jean-Pierre Chevènement, the Interior Minister and dissident Socialist who led the small Citizens' Movement. Chevènement was, after the Premier, the most experienced of the politicians in the Cabinet and had, for that reason, more weight than his small party would indicate. In addition the Greens' Dr Dominique Voynet was placed at the head of the Environment Ministry (logical enough but they wanted a different ministry) and the small Radical Socialist Party took the Ministry of Public Services and Decentralisation. The counterbalance was the Minister of Employment and Solidarity Martine Aubry, who was a rising figure in the Socialist Party but of a very determined nature and disinclined to suffer fools gladly.

The alliance of the 'plural left' revolved around the Communist and Socialist parties. There were two Communist ministers. The Communist leader Robert Hue could not enter government as he was under investigation (in a party funding affair) but his colleague Jean-Claude Gayssot became Minister of Transport, Housing and Infrastructure. The second Communist was the Minister for Youth and Sport Marie-George Buffet, who came from a hard-line tendency in the Communist Party. In addition Bernard Kouchner (Health Minister), Jacques Dondoux (Trade) and Emile Zuccarelli (Decentralisation) became Radical Socialist ministers. More fraught was the nomination of Hubert Védrine, President Mitterrand's former Elysée Secretary General (1991–95) and an expert on foreign relations, as Foreign Minister. Védrine had been Secretary General during the second 'cohabitation' and knew how to manage relations between Prime Minister and President with delicacy (what to avoid and how to avoid it). This was a signal that confrontation was to be down-played. The nomination of Alain Richard, the leader of Michel Rocard's sup-porters, as Defence Minister also suggested this. These two were not the best

The government of June 1997

Prime Minister Lionel Jospin (PS)

Ministers	Employment and Solidarity	Martine Aubry (PS)
	Minister of Justice	Elisabeth Guigou (PS)
	Education, Research and Technology	Claude Allègre (PS)
	Interior	Jean-Pierre Chevènement (MDC)
	Foreign Affairs	Hubert Védrine (PS)
	Economy, Finance and Industry	Dominique Strauss-Kahn (PS)
	Defence	Alain Richard (PS)
	Transport, Housing and Infrastructure	Jean-Claude Gayssot (PCF)
	Culture and Communication	Catherine Trautmann (PS)
	Agriculture and Fishing	Louis Le Pensec (PS)
	Environment	Dominique Voynet (Greens)
	Relations with Parliament	Daniel Vaillent (PS)
	Public Sector, Decentralisation	Emile Zuccarelli (PRS)
	Youth and Sport	Marie-George Buffet (PCF)

Delegate Ministers
(Under Foreign Minister)

	European Affairs	Pierre Moscovici (PS)
	Teaching	Ségolène Royal (PS)

Junior Ministers
(Under the Interior Ministry)

	Overseas	Jean-Jacques Queyranne (PS)

(Under Employment and Solidarity)

	Health	Bernard Kouchner (PRS)

(Under Foreign Affairs)

	Cooperation	Charles Josselin (PS)

(Under Transport, Housing and Infrastructure)

	Housing	Louis Besson (PS)

(Under Economy, Finance and Industry)

	Foreign Trade	Jacques Dondoux (PS)
	Budget	Christian Sautter (PS)
	Small and Medium Industry, Commerce and Artisans	Marylise Lebranchu (PS)
	Industry	Christian Pierret (PS)

(Under the Ministry of Defence)

	Veterans	Jean-Pierre Masseret (PS)

(Under Transport, Housing and Infrastructure)

	Tourism	Michelle Demessine (PS)

known politicians but showed the prime ministerial intention to direct the 'reserved domain' against a President Chirac severely weakened by the snap election of 1997.

As with previous governments the sensibilities of individuals as well as the relationships of the parties in the coalition had to be taken into account. Inside the 'plural left' the pull on the Prime Minister from the various components had to be carefully handled and concessions had to be made to the Greens and the Communists on occasion. They made their views plain outside the Cabinet and also indicated their willingness to leave government if they thought that policy drifted too far off course as they saw it.

Political power

Presidents, even as the leader of the majority, have to conciliate people and make allies. They therefore do not have a completely free hand in choosing their Prime Ministers and some general points can be made about the pattern of appointments. Presidents, like all politicians, owe favours and need support, and that influences appointments. Political calculation always forms a part of the seemingly technocratic Fifth Republic and politics was not banished from the executive presidency. In general the executive Presidents have appointed two Prime Ministers in their first term, during which they have built up their political base.

Although Prime Ministers have been chosen as faithful lieutenants, for their supposed devotion to the Presidents, they are politicians with their own ambitions. That tension between the need for the President to have a loyal servant and the Premier's own autonomy is an ambiguity, which has run through many of the President/Prime Minister tandems. Political life has its quota of people who only want to serve, but in France as elsewhere the spur of ambition drives politicians up the 'greasy pole' towards the top. Tensions between outlooks and temperaments as well as ambitions emerge over a Prime Minister's tenure and may not end amicably. There is a difficult management problem for Presidents in their relation with Prime Ministers and not all Presidents have succeeded with it.

Of the Fifth Republic's sixteen Prime Ministers from 1959 to 1999 two, Georges Pompidou and Jacques Chirac, have been elected President, although another seven have run in presidential elections. Of these seven, only one (Michel Rocard) undoubtedly had presidential ambitions before entering the Matignon but many others who did not run have harboured presidential hopes (certainly Pierre Messmer and Laurent Fabius). In other words, although the premiership may not be the ideal launch pad for a presidential bid it worked for two of the five Presidents. It helps any incumbent by providing a stage on which they are the central actor and they become for a period one of the principal players even if they have been plucked from obscurity (as many were). Thus the

Who do you think is currently the real head of the executive: the President or Prime Minister?

	October 1986			October 1993			October 1998		
	Mitterrand	Chirac	No opinion	Mitterrand	Balladur	No opinion	Chirac	Jospin	No opinion
All (%)	31	52	17	29	58	13	33	57	10
PS supporters (%)	40	49	11	36	54	10	31	62	7
RPR supporters (%)	23	63	14	23	70	7	44	44	12

Source: Pouvoirs 1999

premiership can give stature and a knowledge of government which in a politician can only point in one direction (to the Elysée).

The five Presidents of the Fifth Republic have all started their septennates in the same way by appointing Prime Ministers to whom they are indebted and who can help them consolidate their support. New Presidents have to have help to gain office and they will need support to bring their coalition fully behind them and their objectives. This is not accomplished immediately by the mere fact of election and it is not an automatic attribution of the presidency. Political support has to be built, consolidated and extended and in this the first Prime Minister of the term plays a crucial role. It is less public opinion than political party support that is the problem here. Parties do not swing round to the new President as fast as the general public, and party support is vital in the Assembly if the government is to get its programme through.

However, the Prime Minister's role in the executive presidency is an arduous one, often involving unpopular measures. A President will, while not shirking the difficult decisions, make sure that such credit as is going will end up in the Elysée. In the Fifth Republic 'normal' division of labour the President sets out the grand design and the 'high politics' of foreign policy and the Prime Minister deals with the details of application and administration. But the pressures on modern government almost invariably mean that the Prime Minister is dealing with daily problems not all of which can be resolved easily. Given this background it is unsurprising that the Prime Minister's ratings in the polls usually fall after two years and the President will find a replacement (sometimes unceremoniously). If the ratings fall too far the Prime Minister may bring down the President as well, and so a new appointment can provide a new fillip for the governing coalition and the President. Changing horses in mid-stream is, in political terms, usually a good idea.

Where 'cohabitation' does not intervene, the second Prime Minister is of a different order: likely to be more of an administrator than a politician, with very little or no political weight, and a political satellite of the Elysée rather than of the party or Assembly. The second appointment therefore reflects the President's own priorities more strongly than the outgoing Premier, and will not be a front-rank politician in their own right. This does not mean, however, that they are negligible personalities or second raters. On the contrary the trick, for the President, is to find somebody who is reliable, politically sensitive, unambitious and loyal. Unsurprisingly this combination is rare and mistakes are made.

Prime Ministers under the executive presidency: first choice, second choice and no choice

Turning to particular cases, the first Prime Ministers of the first seven-year terms of executive presidents have been as follows: Michel Debré, Jacques Chaban Delmas, Jacques Chirac, Pierre Mauroy and Alain Juppé.

Michel Debré, de Gaulle's first Prime Minister, was born in Paris in 1912 to a wealthy family (his father was an eminent doctor) and he obtained a law doctorate before entering the Council of State in 1935. In 1939 he was mobilised and then captured but escaped to join the gaullist internal Resistance and from that time on was a close associate of de Gaulle's. He took on a number of technical briefs (one of which was his establishment of the ENA) and was elected as senator for Indre-et-Loire in 1948. He had a considerable political weight in the Fourth Republic. He had established himself as a vigorous, polemical and somewhat over-the-top critic of the Fourth Republic as well as an outspoken partisan of retaining Algeria as part of France. He was at the heart of the plotting which brought de Gaulle back to power and was rewarded with the post of Minister of Justice, which he used to draw up the new Fifth Republic Constitution. When de Gaulle became President he appointed Debré Prime Minister. To Debré, therefore, fell the task of turning the Constitution into a presidential one and of making a U-turn on the Algerian policy, moving the country to independence. He was unpopular with the Assembly, and he made no attempt to charm either deputies or the public, and his poll ratings became a liability. Debré was not consulted closely over de Gaulle's change in direction and felt uncomfortable (he offered to resign); in April 1962, when the peace agreements had been signed, de Gaulle asked him to resign. Debré continued in the Cabinet and ended his career in the top rank as Pompidou's Defence Minister 1969–73. In 1981 he ran as an independent gaullist candidate for the presidency (polling 1.7 per cent).

Georges Pompidou was appointed to replace Debré but was also reappointed when de Gaulle was re-elected in 1965. Pompidou was a school teacher who had joined de Gaulle's staff at the Liberation when de Gaulle, according to legend, was 'looking for a graduate who knew how to write'. Pompidou soon proved an excellent organiser both of de Gaulle's private office and the gaullist party but he went into banking when the gaullist party was wound up in the mid-1950s. He came back to government in de Gaulle's office in June 1958 and then became a member of the Constitutional Council. Unlike Debré, Pompidou had no political reputation outside of the small gaullist circle. Pompidou was clearly de Gaulle's appointment and clearly a subordinate, but the 'secretary' soon developed unexpected political skills and became a force in his own right. He helped rally the gaullists in the 1965 election when it looked unexpectedly 'wobbly' for the President, and then organised and rebuilt the gaullist party in 1967.

It is interesting to speculate as to why de Gaulle reappointed Pompidou in 1965, a point at which a change of Premiers might have been expected. It was possibly because of his role in rescuing the elections for the President or possibly because Pompidou appeared not to threaten the President. After the 'events' of May 1968, in which Pompidou was the acknowledged master of government action, there was a landslide victory for the gaullists and Pompidou was dismissed. De Gaulle disliked having a rival in his own camp but Pompidou

Governments in the Fifth Republic

President de Gaulle (first septennate)

       8/1/59 Michel Debré

       14/4/62 Georges Pompidou I

       28/11/62 Georges Pompidou II

President de Gaulle (second septennate)

       8/1/66 Georges Pompidou III

       6/4/67 Georges Pompidou IV

       10/7/68 M. Couve de Murville

President Pompidou

       20/6/69 Jacques Chaban-Delmas

       5/7/72 Pierre Messmer I

       2/4/73 Pierre Messmer II

       27/2/74 Pierre Messmer III

President Giscard d'Estaing

       27/5/74 Jacques Chirac 27/5/74

       25/8/76 Raymond Barre I

       29/3/77 Raymond Barre II

       3/4/78 Raymond Barre III

President Mitterrand (first septennate)

       21/5/81 Pierre Mauroy I

       22/6/81 Pierre Mauroy II

       22/3/83 Pierre Mauroy III

       17/7/84 Laurent Fabius

       20/3/86 Jacques Chirac 'cohabitation'

President Mitterrand (second septennate)

       10/5/88 Michel Rocard I

       23/6/88 Michel Rocard II

       15/5/91 Edith Cresson

       2/4/92 Pierre Bérégovoy

       29/3/93 Edouard Balladur 'cohabitation'

President Chirac

       17/5/95 Alain Juppé I

       6/11/95 Alain Juppé II

       4/6/97 Lionel Jospin I 'cohabitation'

       27/3/00 Lionel Jospin II 'cohabititation'

felt ill-used by the President after many years of service. A certain coldness then entered relations between the two. Over the next year Pompidou did become the 'president in waiting' and his stature as a front-rank politician enabled him to win the presidency in 1969.

Jacques Chaban Delmas was Pompidou's first Prime Minister. He had joined the Resistance in 1940 and worked for the gaullist cause in occupied France to become a brigadier general at the Liberation. He played a major role in the liberation of Paris and became de Gaulle's Information Minister in the Liberation government. In 1946 he became a deputy for the Gironde and in 1947 was elected mayor of Bordeaux with Radical Party support (re-elected until he stood down in 1995). As a gaullist in the Assembly in the Fourth Republic he was president of the Social Republicans but that did not prevent him from participating in governments and he was Defence Minister in the last Fourth Republic government of November 1957. He used his position to intrigue for the return of de Gaulle to power. In the Fifth Republic he became one of the founders of the gaullist UNR party, was returned to the Assembly and was elected Speaker (1958–69).

When Pompidou was elected President in 1969 Chaban Delmas looked ideally placed to become Prime Minister. Chaban was a gaullist 'Baron', a member of the inner circle, a historic Resistance figure (which Pompidou was not) influential with the party which he knew well, and a popular Assembly Speaker. He also had good links with the centre parties at a time when Pompidou wanted to broaden the coalition and bring in centrist parties and politicians. However, that was to reckon without Chaban's very marked centre left politics which he immediately put into practice assisted by Jacques Delors and Simon Nora in the Matignon. This was too radical for the naturally conservative Pompidou and was, moreover, done in a manner that cut the ground from under the newly elected President. Chaban announced a programme for a 'New Society' and failed to consult the President, who felt that his prerogative had been usurped. In addition Chaban failed to bring the gaullist 'Barons' with him and annoyed many by pushing reforms (like the liberalising of the state media) too far and too fast. There were a number of scandals in the gaullist regime (and a revelation that Chaban, quite legally, paid no income tax) and the gaullist backbenches and party 'Barons' wanted him to quit. He obtained a vote of confidence from the Assembly and a few weeks later in July 1972 Pompidou sacked him. He ran for President in 1974 but was outperformed by Giscard as the conservatives' choice. He continued to play a prominent role in gaullist politics until he retired in the 1990s.

Jacques Chirac's nomination as Prime Minister in 1974 by the newly elected President Giscard seemed at the time to be a coup but it meant the appearance of hyper-presidential power and the effacing of the Premier. Giscard proved to be more overbearing than even de Gaulle, who (Algeria apart) kept to foreign affairs, and was liable to intervene in the most detailed matters without consulting the Premier. Jacques Chirac had organised gaullist support for the Giscard campaign and was assumed to be an admirer, if not devotee, of the new President. In addition Chirac was from the majority party in the conservative coalition and was expected to swing it behind the President.

Jacques Chirac was also younger than the President and seemingly presented no threat to the youngest of the Fifth Republic's Presidents. However, it became clear that the President's conception of the Prime Minister's office did not concur with the Premier's. Giscard saw the Premier as a secondary figure co-ordinating government action who had no role in policy-making or the major decisions of state. Chirac, naturally, viewed things differently and anticipated the role for himself of making decisions within the President's overall policy. When Jacques Chirac began to reorganise the gaullist party the President assumed it would become a 'giscardian' party but it in fact became the support for the Prime Minister. Judging the position intolerable, Jacques Chirac resigned in August 1976.

Pierre Mauroy, President Mitterrand's first Prime Minister, was a Socialist Party politician who had played a big role in bringing Mitterrand to the leadership of the party at its Epinay Congress in 1971. Of modest origins, from the industrial Nord of France, he was a teacher and union activist as well as leader of the young socialists before becoming federal secretary of the Nord in 1961 and mayor of Lille in 1971 (to the present). Mauroy, in addition to being a senior figure in the socialist movement representing the party from its most solid federation, was an advocate of the alliance with the Communist Party. Although he had been in a difficult position during the party's internal split in 1979 he was made Prime Minister in 1981 to implement the first stage of the reform programme and to bring the Communist Party into the coalition. The government was a large one of 43 ministers. The presence of Communist ministers, when the Cold War was still going, led to defence and foreign affairs work being done in the Elysée without the Communists but other matters were discussed with them in the government. The Socialist Party leader (at that time Jospin) and party archons were consulted weekly about business. Mitterrand's was a very extensive programme but three devaluations and a balance-of-payments crisis brought his popularity down from a (record) high to a low point. This was compounded when a bill integrating private education into the state system brought thousands onto the streets and the President withdrew the measure. Mauroy resigned in July 1984. He became First Secretary of the Socialist Party in 1988–92, defeating the President's choice (and was ostracised by the Elysée), and then became President of the Socialist International.

Michel Rocard (1988–91) was the first Prime Minister of President Mitterrand's second septennate. This was not a marriage made in heaven. Mitterrand and Rocard had fought a long battle for the soul of the Socialist Party in the late 1970s and many had not forgiven Rocard that act of *lèse-majesté*. Rocard had been a Socialist activist in his youth and had then led the small leftist Unified Socialist Party (Parti socialiste unifié, PSU) on the fringes of the main Socialist movement. Rocard had stood in the presidential elections of

1969 and polled a creditable (for a minor party) 3.7 per cent but had joined the revived Socialist Party only after the 1974 presidential elections when Mitterrand had it in hand. Rocard set himself up as an internal 'social democratic' or moderate opposition to the dogmatic left of the Socialist Party, implicitly casting Mitterrand in that role as 'archaic'.

The choice of Rocard in 1988 was conditioned by the need to appeal to the centre and moderate voter in the general elections after Mitterrand won the presidency for a second time. The need for that move was illustrated by the narrowness of the victory for the Socialist Party in the ensuing general elections and the constant need to bargain for votes in the Assembly to get bills through the house and past a hostile Communist Party. Rocard, however, proved remarkably effective as a tactician and made several important reforms as well as providing trustworthy administration. He was not helped by the continual in-fighting in the party or by the President's barbed comments on his government's action. In 1991 he was still popular but was dismissed. Rocard, who had always been seen as 'presidential material', became the Socialist candidate in waiting and went on to take the leadership of the party in 1993 after the election defeat of that year. He was not able to manage the transition from presidential candidate to party leader and, after election setbacks in 1994, quit the leadership.

Alain Juppé (1995–97) was nominated Prime Minister on President Chirac's victory in 1995. Juppé had been a close associate of Jacques Chirac since he became speechwriter in the private office of the Premier in 1976. He had then followed him into the RPR party and the Paris city council. He had little independent electoral success but rose with Chirac's support, winning a seat on the Paris council and a parliamentary seat in 1986. He was a junior minister in the 1986 government and then ran Chirac's presidential campaign in 1988. He remained a supporter of Jacques Chirac after the defeat of 1988 and fought off the challenge to his leadership of the RPR, and then was a Chirac supporter in the 1993–95 Balladur government.

During 1993–95 Juppé worked hard to keep Chirac's presidential campaign alive and his loyalty was rewarded with the premiership in 1995. Chirac's unclear programme began to make problems for a Prime Minister who was principally a technocrat and (despite promotion to the leadership of the RPR) he never won over the activists. As the government changed course and failed to explain itself adequately, the Prime Minister's popularity fell to a record low under the Fifth Republic; the President's ratings also fell. There was a public service strike in the autumn of 1995 followed by a series of other conflicts that further reduced the government's standing. Previous Presidents would have changed Prime Ministers and brought in a new personality but Jacques Chirac chose to retain Juppé, making clear his support for his Premier. Eventually Jacques Chirac called a snap election in 1997 to redress the situation: it was lost and with it went the President's authority.

Where the President gets the opportunity the second Prime Minister is an administrative lieutenant and in charge of the short-term measures within the

President's long-term plan. These figures have been promoted (often from the backroom) by the will of the President and, at least at first, owe the President for their elevation. The difficulty, for the President, is that novices can become formidable figures in their own right. Georges Pompidou, who started as a political novice, shortly became a political force of substance and then a rival to the President. Much the same was true of Giscard's premier Professor Barre, who developed as a political personality during his tenure of the Matignon. Prime Minister Barre's position illustrates another problem, which is the difficulty the President has with changing a second Prime Minister: the appointment is personal and meant to be long-lasting. The threat of resignation or of open disagreement becomes substantial in the second cycle of the presidential term and, if the Prime Minister develops ambitions for the Elysée, there might be tension.

Second Prime Ministers include Georges Pompidou, Couve de Murville, Pierre Messmer, Raymond Barre, Laurent Fabius, Edith Cresson and Pierre Bérégovoy (the last Mitterrand's third in five years). These Prime Ministers all had very different attributes but all of them were intended to apply the President's programme and manage the policies decided in the Elysée. Georges Pompidou, Raymond Barre and Laurent Fabius continued their political careers after their stint at the Matignon. The other four Premiers dropped back down the political scale. Of these Premiers Pompidou, Couve, Messmer and Barre could have been called administrators rather than politicians; although they chose to follow political careers it was in the capacity of organiser rather than stump orator. Mitterrand's appointees had other attributes as well as administrative capacity: Fabius, Cresson and Bérégovoy had spent a long time in the Socialist Party but they were not major figures in their own right before their appointment (Fabius became so).

Conservative Presidents have chosen second Prime Ministers to cater for the administrative needs of government. Georges Pompidou had headed de Gaulle's private office and the President knew his administrative capacities well and they had been honed during a time at Rothschild's Bank in the 1950s. In Couve de Murville de Gaulle had a high civil servant (inspecteur des finances) who had risen rapidly in pre-war France and who had been a member of the Franco-German Armistice Commission. He had joined de Gaulle in 1942 and had rejoined the diplomatic service after the war. He continued as a diplomat until 1958 when he had been promoted to the position of executant of the President's foreign policy and faithfully accomplished that role over ten years. This post attuned Foreign Minister de Murville to divining the President's intentions and then applying them with thoroughness through the Quai d'Orsay (though perhaps with greater diplomacy than the President used). It was a position that demanded the skill of running a large ministry with its own traditions and ensuring that the President's own eccentric foreign policy was applied. These virtues of soundness and uncomplaining application were appreciated after the turbulent 'events' of May 1968 and a contrast to the outgoing

Premier's (Pompidou's) own strong opinions on what could and should be done against the President's wishes.

In 1972 Pompidou himself faced the same problem of finding a Prime Minister who would not counter the President's strategy with a more liberal one of his or her own. His choice was Pierre Messmer, who had been another of de Gaulle's executants. As Defence Minister it had fallen to Messmer to put into effect de Gaulle's defence policy and his nuclear weapons strategy with an army demoralised after France left Algeria. This was accomplished by applying the President's wishes and pushing along the President's policy. Pierre Messmer had the additional advantages for Pompidou of leading the gaullist 'Barons' in the Assembly and being a conservative after Chaban's leftist radicalism.

Giscard's choice of Professor Barre after the independent gaullist Jacques Chirac was an attempt to resolve a conflict between centrists and gaullists at the heart of government with a personnel change. Jacques Chirac's demand for reflation (and an early election) to deal with the oil price recession of the mid-1970s was not accepted by the President, who maintained a policy of deflation and price stability. This was Barre's outlook as well and it was the policy applied by the government with determination from 1976. But Barre obtained from the President a bigger role and more control over the government (those Chirac had been refused). This was a deliberate decision by Giscard to step back: the President had realised that pushing the Premier into the front line was better than a persistent interventionism and monopoly of the front stage.

President Mitterrand's choices of Premier were conditioned by the same reasoning but he had less difficulty with the first choice than did the conservatives. After the collapse of the Mauroy government's popularity in 1984 and the decision of the Communists to leave the coalition, the choice of Fabius as the youngest ever Prime Minister was intended to emphasise modernisation and efficiency as the themes for the recovery of Socialist fortunes. Fabius was a graduate of the meritocratic elite education system and the President's 'dauphin'. Fabius's government did begin the fight back and almost won the 1986 elections but the Prime Minister disassociated himself from the President on more than one occasion, damaging their working relationship.

In the second septennate (1988–95) after Mitterrand had tired of jousting with Prime Minister Rocard in 1991 he appointed Edith Cresson as a combative Prime Minister of a narrower team of Mitterrand loyalists. Mitterrand was expecting, perhaps, to revivify the Socialist left and move the fight onto other ground than the consensus politics established by Rocard. Cresson proved singularly inept as a Prime Minister and could not manage the disintegrating government in which rivalries were endemic and the Finance Minister (in charge of five ministerial departments) carried too much authority. Neither the party nor the Assembly group (whom the Premier treated with contempt) were well disposed and in the end the Prime Minister only had the President's support and that had become weak as a result of her poor performance.

After a year President Mitterrand replaced Cresson with the Finance

Minister Pierre Bérégovoy, another close associate. Bérégovoy promoted Mitterrand loyalists close to the party's First Secretary Laurent Fabius but, settling old scores, demoted the supporters of Lionel Jospin. In Bérégovoy's government the (subsequently jailed) Radical Bernard Tapie became Minister for Inner Cities and the marginal centrists Gilbert Baumet and Jean-Pierre Soisson rejoined the team. Bérégovoy was an architect of the post-1984 economic policy and was the strong man of the government and might have been able to stop (though not reverse) the decline in the government's popularity in the year before the elections of 1993. But the President's attention was directed to the ratification of the Maastricht Treaty and Bérégovoy was then rivalled by Laurent Fabius, who was by then head of the Socialist Party, for leadership of the election campaign. He did not have the chance to make up lost ground because he was caught in a finance scandal (over a personal loan at low interest) which increasingly absorbed his energies and made him depressed. Shortly after the government's 1993 election defeat, for which he blamed himself, he committed suicide.

Prime Ministers under the non-executive presidency

'Cohabitation' brings the Prime Ministers back to their rightful constitutional places as heads of the executive. The three 'cohabitations' started with the Prime Minister using the opportunity of Article 49 (1) of the Constitution to get the Assembly to vote a confidence motion for the government. This was done in order to show that the government was responsible to the Assembly majority and not to the President. Thus in 1986 Jacques Chirac immediately went to the Assembly (on 28 April) and was supported by 292 votes to 285, and Edouard Balladur did likewise on 8 April 1993 to be supported by 457 votes to 81.

Further votes of confidence underlined the same point about the government's relation to the Assembly and not the Elysée. In 1986 Jacques Chirac used this procedure three times in the first 'cohabitation'; Edouard Balladur only used it once after the controversial GATT (General Agreement on Tariffs and Trade) Treaty had been negotiated (on 15 December 1993). In these cases, however, the 'pledging of the government's responsibility' was more to bring the majority coalition together than to counter the President's manoeuvres. Jacques Chirac used Article 49 (3) seven times in the first year of the first 'cohabitation' to overcome the majority's divisions and also appealed to the conservative Senate three times for a vote of confidence (Balladur only used this once). The Senate, on the other hand, was an obstruction to Jospin's left-wing government of 1997.

There have been three 'cohabitations' since the beginning of the Fifth Republic. In the first the Socialist President Mitterrand ended his first legislature with the defeat of his supporters in the Assembly in 1986 and had to accept a Prime Minister from the conservative majority. In the third it was the conservative President Chirac who had to face a majority of the left in 1997 after only two years of his tenure had run and a 'cohabitation' which could continue for five. Because the President is able to concentrate on presidential presentation and the Premier is the natural candidate of the majority, political rivalry under 'cohabitation' is almost guaranteed. Hence these 1986–88 and 1997– 'cohabitations' were extended election campaigns pitting President against Premier. In 1993–95 the second 'cohabitation' was not, however, a competition between the top leaders of the state because, although Prime Minister Balladur had presidential ambitions, President Mitterand would not stand again. (There was, in contrast, a bitter competition between Balladur and his party leader Jacques Chirac.)

Relative popularity of President and Prime Minister under 'cohabitation'

Date	Approve/ disapprove	President	Approve/ disapprove	Prime Minister	Difference between the ratings
April 1986	56/39	F. Mitterrand	57/33	J. Chirac	−1
October 1986	61/34	F. Mitterrand	58/37	J. Chirac	+3
April 1987	54/40	F. Mitterrand	44/59	J. Chirac	+10
October 1987	60/34	F. Mitterrand	43/51	J. Chirac	+17
April 1988	59/38	F. Mitterrand	43/53	J. Chirac	+16
April 1988	39/58	F. Mitterrand	73/17	E. Balladur	−34
October 1993	40/57	F. Mitterrand	67/30	E. Balladur	−27
April 1994	35/60	F. Mitterrand	45/54	E. Balladur	−10
October 1994	42/55	F. Mitterrand	58/39	E. Balladur	−16
April 1995	35/60	F. Mitterrand	45/54	E. Balladur	−10
July 1997	52/46	J. Chirac	66/31	L. Jospin	−14
January 1998	53/44	J. Chirac	54/43	L. Jospin	−1
July 1998	52/45	J. Chirac	63/35	L. Jospin	−13
January 1999	54/44	J. Chirac	63/35	L. Jospin	−9
June 1999	54/43	J. Chirac	63/34	L. Jospin	−9

Source: Pouvoirs

In 1986 the RPR and UDF opposition, in which Jacques Chirac led the main party, won the general elections with a narrow majority. President Mitterrand had no choice about who to nominate as Prime Minister. However, the President was backed by the Socialist Party intent on returning to power with a re-elected President who intended to stand for a second term. Prime Minister Chirac also intended to stand for the presidency in 1988 and the government was intended to ensure the victory for the conservative candidate. Thus the government expected to be able to force through radical reforms rapidly to make a dramatic impact. This led, as in other 'cohabitations', to a use of the 'rationalised' Parliament to force through legislation quickly using the government's majority. The 'cohabitation' was co-operative on the surface – with a few hostile outbreaks – but deeply conflictual in purpose as the two principal figures of state were rivals. Within the conservative coalition there was a difficult alliance of different elements all of whom hoped to find their position in the Cabinet: all the centrist party leaders and the main neo-gaullists but also the supporters of Jacques Chirac and the supporters of the (more popular) centrist Barre. During 1986–88 there was a 'liaison committee of the majority' which met each week to prepare the legislative action, government business and anticipate problems. This did not prevent rivalries and mistakes. The 'cohabitation' ended with Mitterrand's second victory.

The second 'cohabitation', which started in 1993 with the landslide for the conservative RPR/UDF coalition in the general elections, was the least conflictual of the three. In 1993 President Mitterrand had no intention of running a third time and was gravely ill. Outside the Elysée the Socialist Party had been shattered and its survival as a political force looked doubtful. It was in no position, as it had been in 1986, to support the President. This time President Mitterrand was constrained to nominate the RPR politician Edouard Balladur as Prime Minister and the RPR party leader Jacques Chirac declined to go to the Matignon for the third time. Balladur had experienced the first 'cohabitation' as Finance Minister; he was now careful in his dealings with the Elysée and was more co-operative than the 1986 government had been (avoiding decrees and respecting protocol).

Balladur nominated a small (30 strong) prime ministerial government which brought in new blood (half were new) chosen (even in foreign affairs) by the Premier, suffering little presidential interventionism and taking the initiative in European and African affairs. It was a government that brought most of the conservative party leaders into the team but regular 'majority dinner meetings' replaced the normal conservative 'liaison committee'. The President called the government to order over its pretensions to run foreign policy or amend the Constitution but it continued, in fact, to do so while paying lip-service to presidential dominance. But the main battle was between the Premier and his party leader for the pole position as conservative candidate. Jacques Chirac narrowly won the conservative 'primary' at the first ballot of the 1995 elections and went on to win the presidency.

The third 'cohabitation' resulted from President Chirac's unexpected dissolution in May/June 1997 that led to a victory for the opposition of the left. Lionel Jospin led this coalition of the left and the President had no alternative but to nominate him as Prime Minister. This 'cohabitation' resulted from a real disavowal of the President at the polls (which was not the case in 1986) and saw the presidency reduced to its constitutional status, although there were clashes over foreign policy. Prime Minister Jospin, who had been a presidential candidate in 1995, hoped to run for President again and the President hoped to win a second term. There therefore followed a 'cohabitation' similar to 1986–88 in that there was a front maintained of harmony while the manoeuvring for position went on behind the scenes.

The 'cohabitation' duels have taken place over domestic, foreign and defence policy. Although the Presidents had advanced warning of 'cohabitation', and could make their dispositions, they were immediately cut out of the government decision-making and information circuits. Resurrecting an old practice, the Prime Ministers held meetings of the government ministers (*conseil de cabinet*) before the Cabinets to take the decisions out of the President's presence. The proliferation of committees, government meetings and bi-lateral or multi-lateral ministerial meetings to keep policy-making under the Prime Minister and away from the President was a feature of 'cohabitation'.

However, it is foreign and defence policy, widely perceived as the presidential domain, where the struggle for authority during 'cohabitation' has been at its most intense. Presidents have felt it easier to defend 'their sector' than to effect sorties into domestic matters where the ministers have an information advantage (this has not prevented the Presidents from rebuking the governments for domestic mistakes). But the Prime Ministers have seen no reason to relinquish this territory and have counted on it to make their reputation as future presidential prospects. As a result foreign policy making during 'cohabitation' has a tendency to become conflictual. Foreign policy is 'high politics', the sovereign attribute of the state and the opportunity for a politician to make a mark on a world stage, and is the one area where an impact can be made quickly. Whether the public is easily impressed or not is perhaps a moot point but the perception of the political elite is that it is. Foreign policy is certainly one domain in which the public in the Fifth Republic, habituated by the gaullist assumptions of its first four Presidents, expects to see the President making a distinctive mark. During 'cohabitation' the foreign and defence sector came to be described as the 'shared domain' – a constitutionally inaccurate but politically accurate expression.

In 1986 there was a significant tussle over who should become Foreign Minister and the President opposed the names at first advanced by the Prime Minister on the grounds that they could not work effectively with the Elysée. Centrist leaders Jean Lecanuet and François Léotard had both hoped to be nominated for the posts. In the event the gaullist diplomat J.-B. Raimond was nominated. He was a career diplomat and so appeared a compromise candidate; although a member of the Prime Minister's RPR party, he was not an obvious imposition on the President. Prime Minister Jacques Chirac insisted on accompanying the President to international meetings and in effect ran foreign policy. It may be that in theory foreign and defence policy are separable from the ordinary business of government but in reality policies are inextricably interlinked and driven by the budget that the government controls. In addition the Elysée lacked the administrative staff to monitor let alone develop foreign policy and that naturally fell to the Prime Minister.

The result of this tussle over the 'reserved domain' was a brinkmanship between President and Prime Minister, which sometimes tipped over into the petty on matters of protocol (who sat where and with whom). But it had a more serious side. For example, in 1986, not all the diplomatic telgrammes, communications from the ambassadors to the Foreign Office, were passed on to the Elysée and the embassies were instructed to send 'messages' to the Foreign Ministry not 'telegrammes'. Thus was the President deprived of information. One of the Prime Minister's letters to Saddam Hussein found its way into the press and the Prime Minister declared himself 'scandalised' by the leak. President Mitterrand riposted that he 'was just about to complain that the Premier sent them to everybody except him'. These vicious battles were not repeated in the second 'cohabitation' or the third. A *modus vivendi* had to be based on something other than one of continual skirmishes.

But all the same there remained on the one side the Prime Minister, determined to make a reputation in international affairs and controlling the ministries, and on the other side the President, determined to keep up appearances and to push the Prime Minister out of foreign and defence affairs where possible. Public opinion would not have countenanced an open split at the head of the state on foreign or defence policy and the question became one of who would back down first. In the reserved domain it was usually the Prime Minister who was the more anxious to make 'cohabitation' succeed and whose intrusion into foreign policy looked less than legitimate. All Prime Ministers went on official visits and the presence of the Premier in foreign affairs was impossible to stop (though resented and sometimes undercut) and by the same token it was difficult to prevent decisions being made. In international summits, however, the main work is done long before the final meetings of leaders and little can be changed at that stage. Also the President can announce initiatives or policies at international meetings, but without the government's approval they can be disavowed (like President Chirac's promise to cancel Latin American debts). Overall the presidential standing in the reserved domain remained high throughout all the 'cohabitations'.

Does 'cohabitation' damage French government?

Commentators criticise 'cohabitation' for its undermining of the 'gaullist' settlement. The partisans of the executive presidency argue that 'cohabitation' leads to a paralysis at the top of the state and that the nation loses as a result of the internal institutional war. It should be noted that the 'cohabitation' government of 1986–88 was not immobile and that its faults were impetuosity rather than lack of direction. It might also be said that the problem is less the presidency as such than extreme political competition. In 1993–95 the President was not a contender for re-election but there was an internal war within the conservative camp not caused by 'cohabitation'. Prime ministerial government can be strong and capable of providing direction and strategy, as other European societies and as the government of Mendès France in the Fourth Republic testify. By the same token the internal war in President

Do you want 'cohabitation' to have an effect on institutions or do you want them to return to as they were before?

	October 1987 Interlude/continue		July 1993 Interlude/continue		October 1998 Interlude/continue	
All	56	33	46	40	36	51
PS supporters	51	42	49	37	29	60
RPR supporters	65	31	61	31	46	46

Source: Pouvoirs

Is 'cohabitation' positive or negative for France?

	All	PS sympathisers	RPR sympathisers
May 1986			
Positive	51	50	62
Negative	29	32	22
No opinion	20	18	16
September 1986			
Positive	56	55	67
Negative	28	29	19
No opinion	16	16	14
May 1993			
Positive	55	60	60
Negative	28	28	29
No opinion	17	12	11
July 1993			
Positive	55	55	67
Negative	30	29	24
No opinion	17	16	9
September 1997			
Positive	57	76	63
Negative	30	16	25
No opinion	15	8	12
October 1998			
Positive	66	83	38
Negative	23	11	54
No opinion	11	7	

Source: Pouvoirs

Giscard's coalition led to a timidity at the end of the septennate and Presidents can be hamstrung by coalition problems themselves. There is no reason to believe that either prime ministerial government during 'cohabitation' in itself, or presidential domination, determines any particular outcome.

Summary

- Prime ministerial power is derived from the Constitution.
- Real prime ministerial power depends on the skill of the Premier.
- Prime Ministers need to construct and maintain coalitions to ensure their power in the same way as do Presidents.
- Where the Prime Minister leads the majority coalition in the Assembly the President is reduced to a 'constitutional monarch' with the power to advise, to encourage and to warn.
- A Prime ministerial executive can be as decisive and authoritative as a presidential executive.
- This is to some extent disguised by the 'dignified' role the Presidents have managed to play.
- It is difficult for the Prime Minister to contest the representative role of the President and equally impossible to exclude the President from the foreign policy world stage.
- Moves by the Prime Minister into foreign policy have been less successful because of the President's legitimacy in that domain and not through lack of power.

Further reading

Elgie, R., *The French Prime Minister* (Macmillan, 1993)

Feigenbaum, H. B., 'Recent evolution of the French executive' *Governance* 3; 3, 1990, pp. 264–78

Keeler, J. T. S., 'Executive power and policy making patterns in France' *West European Politics* 6: 4, 1993, pp. 518–44

Keeler, J. T. S. and Schain, M. (eds), *Chirac's Challenge* (St Martin's, 1996).

Pierce, R., 'The executive divided against itself: cohabitation in France 1986–1988' *Governance* 4, 1991, pp. 270–94

Sulieman, E. N., 'Presidential power in France' in R. Rose and E. N. Sulieman (eds), *Presidents and Prime Ministers* (AEI, 1980)

Tuppen, J., *Chirac's France* (Macmillan, 1991)

Questions

1 Do you agree that the Prime Minister's authority in 'cohabitation' derives from the Assembly and in a presidential executive from the President?
2 What is the constitutional source of prime ministerial power?
3 Under what circumstances does the Prime Minister become the principal executive power?
4 What is the source of prime ministerial power during 'cohabitation'?
5 What would be the consequence of a public and insoluble clash between President and Prime Minister?

11

The Parliament

The Fifth Republic is a parliamentary regime: the government is constitutionally responsible to a Parliament composed of the popularly elected Assembly
and the indirectly elected upper house, the Senate. In this the Fifth Republic
does not depart from tradition and Parliament remains a key institution in the
political system. All the same the Fifth Republic was intended to end the Fourth
Republic *regime d'Assemblée* and set out to 'rationalise' it. Parliament has been
eclipsed by the President, relegated in importance and lost many of its previous
powers.

Historically, the French Parliament's role has not been the same as the
United Kingdom's. The main difference is that the focus of the political system
in France is less on Parliament than in Britain where the drama of political confrontation in the House of Commons has a long history. Newspapers and the
media in Britain generally look to the House of Commons in a way which they
do not in France and the significance of parliamentary action is correspondingly less. Thus the great set-piece clashes between government and opposition
and the Prime Minister's (and other ministers') question time are not replicated
in the French Parliament. These factors have been emphasised by the presidential nature of the Fifth Republic, which has changed the focus from 'what does
Parliament think?' to 'what does the President think'. Thus the constitutional
shift in the Fifth Republic has accentuated a general trend against the parliamentary power.

There are therefore two principal questions about the Fifth Republic
Parliament. The first concerns the way in which Parliament has been confined.
This requires a look at the constitutional provisions of the Fifth Republic and
then an estimate of the importance of these in the role of Parliament. The argument here is that, firstly, the Fourth Republic's parliamentarians anticipated
these provisions, but secondly, and more fundamentally, the Fifth Republic's
Assembly has been the site of majority coalitions which have been largely cohesive and have dominated the working of the institution. It is to the change in
the party system and the political climate wrought by de Gaulle that the lines

of the new situation can be traced. But there is also a question of to what extent this initial downgrading of Parliament has become permanent. The answer to the problem of what has happened to the power of Parliament is to be found in the new political line-up in the Fifth Republic. If the new situation has political and not constitutional sources, the function of Parliament might well be different and more determinant in the future.

It is important to guard against the idea of a 'golden age' of the Assembly when it was an all-powerful institution making the political weather, formulating policy and taking the principal decisions. However, there was for the French Parliament, if not a golden age, then an age better gilded. In the Third and Fourth Republics the idea of Parliament's place came close to English ideas of 'parliamentary sovereignty'.

All the same, the big change has been the existence of majorities in the Assembly supporting the government. This *fait majoritaire* accounts for much of the difference between Republics despite the constitutional provisions. It is not so much the constitutional provisions that have hamstrung a belligerent Assembly as the Fifth Republic confrontation of political blocs. In the event the Constitution has worked well for governments supported by absolute majorities or backed by cohesive relative majorities. These governments were able to use the Constitution to their advantage because the majority was unwilling to protest too much. None of the checks on the Assembly are irremediable but the Fifth Republic has yet to experience the lack of solid majorities and the onslaughts of determined opposition that brought down the Fourth Republic.

The Assembly

There are two houses of the French Parliament: the Senate and the Assembly. The Assembly was 482 strong in 1962 and was increased to 573 in 1986 and the Senate has 321 members. In the Fifth Republic a deputy is elected with a substitute in a two round system under which they require 50 per cent of the votes on the first ballot and if that is not attained a plurality on the second ballot. This means that the numbers of those elected on the first round are not usually large. (In 1997 there were ten deputies elected on the first round.)

In the Fifth Republic those deputies who are appointed as government ministers have to give up their seat to their 'substitutes' (Article 23). Ministers who quit Parliament cannot return without a by-election. It was believed that the deputies in previous Republics would bring down governments to increase their own chances of office, though there was not much evidence for this accusation. Ministers do, however, attend debates, speak and answer questions in the Assembly. The existence of the substitute system does cut down the number of by-elections during a Parliament and the disruption that attends them.

In France, however, there is also a tendency to combine elected offices (*cumul des mandats*) although this practice has begun to be restricted in the last two

Electoral systems for the Assembly

There have been diverse electoral systems in France and they are constantly being changed. However, the Fifth Republic general elections have all, with the exception of 1986, been held under a two-ballot system. Under this system each constituency returns one member who is elected on the first ballot if he or she has an absolute majority of the votes cast. If nobody has an absolute majority there is a run-off which all candidates polling over a threshold can contest. The threshold has changed but stood at 12.5 per cent of the registered voters in 1997. On the second ballot the candidate with the highest vote wins the seat.

For the general elections of 1986 the new one-round electoral system (changed after this one election) introduced a small element of proportional representation. The constituency was the department and closed party lists were presented with as many names as there were seats plus two 'substitutes'. There were two deputies per department, which meant that, with the many small departments, rural France was over-represented and split and preference votes were not possible.

Presidential elections

In 1958 there was an electoral college for the President composed of 80,000 or so elected mayors, councillors, deputies and senators. This college (representing France of the 'beetroot and barley') elected de Gaulle President by 78 per cent but its unrepresentative nature was unsuited to a powerful executive presidency. In the law of 1962 introducing universal suffrage it became a two-round electoral system and the first under the new rules was in 1965. There are two ballots unless a candidate wins 50 per cent on the first round. Only the top two candidates can go into the run-off. Candidates currently need the signatures of 500 elected officials before they can enter the first round (this is quite a high hurdle even for parties like the National Front with a substantial popular vote).

decades. Since the law of December 1985 it has not been permissible to combine the role of deputy with more than one major elected office, that is of department councillor, regional councillor, Paris councillor, mayor of a city of over 20,000, assistant to the mayor of a city over 100,000 or Member of the European Parliament (MEP). In the Parliament of 1997 there were 121 deputies who were mayors of cities over 20,000, 18 regional councillors, 6 regional presidents and 18 department presidents. The number of joint officeholders has, however, declined: in 1978, 1981, 1986 and 1988 nearly half the deputies were mayors.

The role of the Speaker (*président*) of the Assembly and Senate is different from the neutral British figure guarding the rights of the chamber and its ordinary members in the House of Commons. The French Speakers are elected by an absolute majority of members in the first or second ballot; if there is no majority after two ballots a third is held and a relative majority suffices. They therefore reflect the majority in the House. The Speaker of the Assembly is elected for the term of the legislature and the Senate Speaker for three years after every triennial renewal. They are often re-elected for long periods (Chaban Delmas was Speaker of the Assembly 1958–69) and they are usually first-rank politicians – on election they become the second and third figures in the state (after the President). In 1962 Chaban Delmas quit the Speaker's Chair (*pérchoir*) to become Prime Minister, and in 2000 Laurent Fabius left it to become Finance Minister. Other eminent Speakers have included the neo-gaullist Philippe Séguin and the Radical/gaullist Edgar Faure.

Speakers	
Senate	Gaston Monnerville 18/3/47–1/10/68
	Alain Poher 2/10/68–1/10/92
	René Monory 2/10/92–
Assembly	J. Chaban-Delmas 3/3/58–9/10/62
	Achille Peretti 25/6/69–1/3/73
	Edgar Faure 2/3/73–2/3/78
	J. Chaban-Delmas 3/3/78–22/5/81
	Louis Mermaz 2/7/86–1/3/86
	J. Chaban-Delmas 2/3/86–22/6/88
	Laurent Fabius 23/6/88–22/1/92
	Henri Emmanuelli 22/1/92–1/3/93
	Philippe Séguin 2/3/93–21/3/97
	Laurent Fabius 12/6/97–28/3/00
	Raymond Forni 30/3/00–

Speakers each nominate three members to the Constitutional Council and to other state committees like the Council for the Electronic Media and the Administrative Appeal Court. They can send laws, treaties or amendments to the Constitutional Council if they suspect that these violate the Constitution. The President consults the Speakers about any proposed dissolution and the use of Article 16 'emergency powers'. In main part, however, the Speaker has the political task of making the Assembly work by conciliating (or finding a balance) between opposed and fragmented groups and by finding a *modus vivendi* with the executive. This requires the same sorts of abilities as the Speaker of the House of Commons in the UK: an attention to individuals, eccentricities, convictions and tender sensibilities. It is, of course, the Speaker who presides over the important debates in the chamber (deputy Speakers preside over others).

The Constitution

The Fifth Republic Constitution changed Parliament in a number of key ways. These have had their effect, although too much stress ought not to be laid on technical factors. It was widely thought (and especially by the gaullists) that Parliament, and principally the Assembly, had been irresponsible, negative and destructive during the Fourth Republic. The Constitution of the Fifth Republic thus sets limits on Parliament's remit and this is the 'rationalised' or 'streamlined' parliamentary regime that the Fifth Republic has implemented over the last 40 years.

First in the list of fetters on Parliament is its 'domain of law' (Article 34) which it cannot go beyond. This is a constitutional limit to the sovereignty of Parliament in the Fifth Republic. Parliament can legislate in the 'domain of law' which is set out in the Constitution but it cannot interfere in 'regulations' which are the government's prerogative and which do not need parliamentary approval. Thus Parliament can legislate: 1) to pass organic laws as laid down by the Constitution (the budget, for example); 2) can legislate in detail over certain defined areas like civil liberties and nationalisation and so on; 3) and can only set out the 'fundamental principles' in areas such as education,

---

The Constitutional Council

The Constitutional Council is one of the innovations of the Fifth Republic but it is not a supreme court in the American sense, and does not hear appeals or form part of the court system, although it does have the power to declare legislation unconstitutional before it is promulgated. If a bill is referred to it then it can have the last word and simply rule it out as unconstitutional. It then publishes its written opinion of the constitutionality of the law. The President, the Speakers of Parliament, the Prime Minister and sixty members of the Assembly and Senate can refer laws to the Constitutional Council. There are nine members who are appointed for nine-year terms and the President, the Assembly Speaker and Senate Speaker appoint three each (one every three years). Members of the Constitutional Council are typically not lawyers or from a legal background and are usually former politicians and ministers. It has never established a reputation for impartiality. However, in the 1970s the Constitutional Council began to assert itself assisted by the amendment in 1974 allowing deputies and senators to refer bills and it began to be less the support of the executive than an independent court protecting rights and liberties and rejecting government legislation. It was particularly active during the first Socialist government of 1981–86 but it was also important in 1986–88. The Constitutional Council began to rise in esteem under the Giscardian and Mitterrand septennates but suffered a blow when its Chair (Roland Dumas) was investigated for corruption and stood down in 2000. He was convicted and sentenced to six months imprisonment in 2001.

defence and social security. Everything else is the government's 'domain of regulations' and the Constitutional Council can be asked to ensure that its domain is respected.

However, Parliament's 'domain of law' as set out in Article 34 was very broad and ill-defined as it distinguished between matters 'determined' by the law and fundamental principles without providing a definition. Parliament's domain has slowly but surely expanded over the Fifth Republic and there is every reason to suppose that an aggressive Assembly could enlarge it further. In addition Parliament has in fact encroached on government territory by passing laws to influence regulation. In addition the Constitutional Council has guarded Parliament's domain more than had been anticipated and often interpreted the vague distinction in Article 34 to the benefit of the Assembly.

In addition to the restriction of Parliament to the 'domain of the law', the Fifth Republic allows for legislation which does not go through Parliament. The first of these is Article 38, which enables Parliament to give government temporary legislative powers for a particular object. Under Article 38 urgent matters, even very important ones, can be dealt with, but any decrees issued lapse unless a ratifying bill is laid before Parliament. However, the procedure has been used principally for speed and to enable governments to avoid an embarrassing debate in Parliament. It became the object of controversy when, in 1986, President Mitterrand refused to sign decrees privatising 65 companies, making the point that Parliament should be able to debate them. The government used its majority to pass its privatisation legislation within three weeks. (The government can also use the referendum to legislate, if the President is willing, under Article 11, but this is infrequent.)

Referendums in the Fifth Republic

Date	Issue	% of suffrages	% of voters
28 September 1959	Fifth Republic Constitution	Yes 79.26	Abstentions 10.06
8 January 1961	Algerian self-determination	Yes 75.26	Abstentions 23.50
8 April 1962	Evian peace agreements	Yes 90.81	Abstentions 14.40
28 October 1962	Direct election of the President	Yes 61.76	Abstentions 19.40
27 April 1969	Regions and Senate reform	No 53.18	Abstentions 19.40
23 April 1972	Enlargement of EEC	Yes 67.70	Abstentions 39.76
6 November 1988	Agreements on New Caledonia	Yes 79.99	Abstentions 63.10
20 September 1992	Maastricht Treaty	Yes 51.00	Abstentions 30.31
24 September 2000	Presidential quinquennium	Yes 73.50	Abstentions 69.68

Within Parliament the Assembly's instruments of control have been limited. All bills are referred to committees but Article 43 limits the number of standing committees to six in each house. In the Assembly these are the Committees on Culture (140); Foreign Affairs (70); Defence and the Army (70); Finance and the Economy (70); Legislation and Administration (70); and Production (140). Most bills are taken by standing committees and each deputy is a member of only one committee. These six big committees are composed proportionately so that they are always dominated by the majority and subject to majority discipline. This is in part a reaction to the extremely powerful committees of the Assembly of the Fourth Republic.

There is no obligation on the government to accept the committees' amendments and the executive can veto anything it dislikes. Moreover, the government can demand that only its amendments should be considered or even that its original bill be considered (whatever the committee thinks). In reality legislation is amended. Amendments are not trivial and government texts are substantially altered. In 1984 Socialist Party deputies, in the grip of an anti-clerical spasm, amended their own government's carefully balanced text on independent (Church) schools. These amendments mobilised the government's opponents and eventually caused a retreat. Amendments could thus be forced by the deputies on the executive if they are sufficiently determined (it would entail vigorous conflict) but the majority normally declines to force the government's hand.

It was thought that the size of the committees would inhibit specialisation but in fact sub-committees have been formed which devote themselves to particular aspects of legislation. Deputies are informed and can get information as they require it. Bills are discussed in detail and amended in the sub-committees and then they return to the Assembly with the committee's report. All the same it is the majority's domination which is the real curb on committee power.

The power to raise money is restricted under Article 40. Amendments and private members' bills that would diminish public income or increase expenditure are out of order. The first gaullist governments interpreted this very narrowly (for example, to rule out a discussion abolishing the death penalty on the grounds that more prisoners would increase expenditure).

Budget procedures have also been streamlined in the Fifth Republic. It was widely bruited that the Fourth Republic's deputies were willing to vote expenditure but not the collection of tax and that they delayed the budget for fear of their popularity suffering from association with it. These were rather misleading accusations, and in response, the budget process was made, perhaps, too rapid as it (constitutionally) gives Parliament just 70 days to pass the budget. However, if it is not passed in the time allotted the government can introduce its budget by decree.

The executive has means such as the package vote (Article 44–3) to restrict parliamentary control. The 'package vote' is in fact a Fourth Republic measure which enables the government to demand a single vote on its bill (amended only if it agrees) and thus evade separate votes on contentious parts. Deputies are

Article 44 paragraph 3: the 'package vote'

'If the government so requests, the chamber concerned decides by a single vote on all or part of the Bill or motion under discussion, together with only those amendments proposed or accepted by the government.'

Article 49 paragraph 3: bills passed on a confidence vote

'The Prime Minister may, after deliberation by the Cabinet, pledge the responsibility of the Government before the National Assembly on the vote of a bill or motion. In this case, the bill or part of a Bill is considered adopted unless a motion of censure, introduced within the following 24 hours, is passed in the conditions set out . . . [in the preceding paragraph].'

Article 43 also stipulates that in a motion of censure only the votes for the motion are counted and that for the motion to be carried these must be a majority of the whole Assembly's membership. Those absent are implicitly counted for the motion. The provision does place an obstacle on censure motions but in the Fourth Republic governments rarely fell at a censure motion – they recognised that their time was up and departed before that stage was reached.

thus obliged to state their opinions on the bill as a whole and not on particularly difficult issues within it. This 'package vote' avoids the confidence question and thus keeps the majority together. It was used frequently in the first years of the Fifth Republic (about six times per session), but since the Algerian crisis in the early 1960s it has in fact been used to settle problems for the government's majority rather than to rout the opposition. It was used, for example, 37 times between 1988 and 1993 when the government had no overall majority. Governments used to pass controversial bills on a motion of confidence and the Fifth Republic package vote enables them to avoid that credit-sapping process.

Confidence motions are now subject to restrictions and the government can even use the Constitution to ask deputies to vote a bill on a motion of confidence. It is then discussed in the context of the government's overall record. When the government pledges its responsibility on the passage of a bill under Article 49–3 it is adopted unless the opposition carries a successful censure motion within 48 hours. This weapon can be used at any time in the passage of a bill and it is often employed at successive readings. It began to appear normal at some times and the opposition often does not respond with a censure motion.

Reliance on Article 49–3 can discredit a government and the uses of it against the government's own supporters can be undermining. A good case is the last three years of Giscard's septennate when the gaullists disputed the direction and leadership of the President's coalition. In 1978–81 the Barre government used the article to enact its budgets and to push the neo-gaullist

RPR into either bringing the government down or supporting its legislation. In the Fourth Republic censure motions were rarely the cause of a government's fall and absolute majorities were needed before they were carried. In the 1950s governments usually realised that their coalition had disintegrated and departed before the vote. Once again it is difficult to disentangle the effect of solid majorities from the impact of the Constitution.

Article 49 stipulates that a censure motion must be passed by an absolute majority of the whole Assembly (289) and in effect this means that abstentions and absent votes are counted for the government. Government supporters, given these rules, sometimes leave the Assembly without taking part in the vote. But by the same token oppositions table censure motions without any hope of success simply to mark their disagreement and to bring their attitude on certain issues to public attention. It is, however, the presence of government majorities, rather than this article's restriction, which has meant that only one motion has been carried in the Fifth Republic (in 1962). Interpellations, which were the scourge of ministers in the past, were ended. These were motions calling for an explanation from a minister and ended with a vote of approval of the government's conduct. These snap interpellations were used to destroy governments in previous Republics even though majorities, where they were solid, could easily reject them.

Fifth Republic censure motions and confidence motions

		Censure motions	Confidence motions
First legislature	9/12/58–9/10/62	4	3
Second legislature	6/12/62–2/3/67	2	1
Third legislature	3/3/67–30/5/68	3	—
Fourth legislature	11/7/68–1/3/73	2	3
Fifth legislature	2/3/73–2/3/78	4	3
Sixth legislature	3/3/78–22/5/81	7	1
Seventh legislature	2/7/81–1/3/86	8	6
Eighth legislature	2/3/86–14/5/88	1	3
Ninth legislature	23/6/88–1/3/93	10	2
Tenth legislature	2/3/93–21/3/97	3	5
Eleventh legislature	12/6/97–	2	1

Motions of censure and confidence questions are subject to strict limitations. Only deputies can censure the government and a censure motion must be signed by at least 10 per cent of the deputies (58 of 577); there is then a cooling-off period imposed by the Constitution of 48 hours before it can be voted and then a majority of the whole Assembly is needed for it to pass. Deputies who sign a censure motion cannot propose another for that session. A government can make a bill a matter of confidence and a censure motion must then be proposed within 24 hours and passed by a majority of the Assembly to defeat the measure or the law is passed.

The government plans and pilots its legislation through Parliament and under Article 48 government business has priority. The 1995 constitutional amendment gave one day a month to the Assembly to control its own agenda. This provision is limited not by the time available but the opposition's ability to organise itself to exploit it. Were there a determined objection to the government's agenda there would be ways round the Constitution, and if there was a more dramatic confrontation, deputies could refuse to release bills from committees. But the government's control of the agenda and timetable of debates and government business prevents the use of the chamber to ambush the government or draw attention to its failings in a snap debate.

Furthermore, private members are not like the senators or representatives of the United States: they have very little role in drafting and promoting legislation and there are also strict constitutional restrictions on what they can propose (no increases or reductions in state expenditure). Parliamentarians have correspondingly less impact on the legislative timetable than in the Fourth Republic. Private members' bills are rare and the restrictions on the deputies' rights mean that they account for only about 10 per cent of Parliament's business and about half of these proposals will be government-sponsored (and most come from the government's side of the house). That figure is, however, one well in line with other European countries. Moreover, deputies can and do change the distribution of taxes and benefits (moving the burden from one group to another) and can amend a bill by stating how revenue is to be raised. The governments frequently accept these amendments and spending is accordingly changed.

Parliament in politics

Parliament in France is also a less significant rung in the promotion ladder than it is in the United Kingdom. Very few politicians in the UK make their way to top ministerial positions without having progressed from the backbenches and then up the junior ministerial ranks. There is less structure in France. Politicians can make their name in Parliament leading attacks on the opposition. In 1981 the Young Turks of the conservative right made the passage of the nationalisation bills (and other legislation) particularly difficult and senators also proved their worth in opposition. However, this is less the means of ascent than it is in the UK.

Presidents since de Gaulle (who went out of his way to sideline the Assembly) have felt able to promote non-parliamentarians to vital ministries. Presidents have shown a particular penchant for Foreign Ministers who are experts and not parliamentarians, but this choice of technocrats has extended to other ministries like Economics and Finance. Even the Prime Ministers have not been chosen for their abilities in Parliament (although many grew into it) and some came from outside Parliament itself. Of Georges Pompidou the deputies remarked that 'de Gaulle had sent his secretary to govern us', and neither

Couve de Murville (1968) nor Raymond Barre (1976) had been in Parliament before being appointed Premier. These were, however, signs of the presidential drift, but then Prime Ministers Messmer (1972), Chirac (1974), Fabius (1984), Cresson (1991), Bérégovoy (1992), Balladur (1993) and Juppé (1995) also did not rise through the Assembly's ranks. Although Pierre Mauroy, Lionel Jospin and Michel Rocard were distinguished parliamentarians, they did not progress, as they would have done in the United Kingdom, mainly as a result of their parliamentary stature. These Prime Ministers were with the exception of Balladur presidential choices and reflected the President's priorities not the Assembly's.

Furthermore politicians can make their names and their careers as mayors of cities, as party leaders or even as interest group leaders, and their work outside Parliament is as important as their parliamentary activity (or more so). Thus the Greens' leader Dominique Voynet was a prominent figure in the party, a presidential candidate and a well-known environmental activist before being elected to Parliament in 1997 and then being immediately replaced by a substitute to become Environment Minister. This pattern is not unusual and is not an effect of presidentialism – though that has accentuated it.

However, the main difficulty in the reassertion of the Assembly's authority has been its lack of determination to do so. When the majority in the Assembly and the government are from the same team there is little incentive for 'backbenchers' to exercise power. This is similar to elsewhere in western Europe where the government is a 'committee' of the majority in the lower house and the interests of the coalition and of the Cabinet are the same. Parliamentarians want to be returned at the next elections and will not help reduce their chances of re-election by attacking the government. In Fifth Republic France the Assembly majorities, whether prime ministerial or presidential, have been in the same position and have not asserted themselves against the government. This majority effect runs through the relationship between the Parliament and executive in the Fifth Republic and is the effective barrier to Assembly influence. What would happen if the Fifth Republic Parliament became fragmented like the Third Republic's or without a stable majority like the Fourth's is a moot question.

As a result of this common interest and joint fate, the majority of the Assembly is unlikely to be severely critical of the government of the day. It is this western European system in which the government comes from the legislature which inhibits the development of an opposition or committee system as in the United States. This lack of critical spirit has been deplored (usually by the opposition) and has been contrasted with the Assemblies of the Fourth and Third Republics, but little has been done to remedy it and it is a feature of the Fifth Republic. French majorities are in this way no different from the majorities in the United Kingdom House of Commons where their respective backbenchers support Labour or Conservative governments. French governments have been able to rely on the discipline of their parliamentary supporters in much the same way in the Fifth Republic. By the same token the opposition can rely on its backbenchers and there has been an adversarial confrontation between the two (as in the UK) with restrictions on the play of give and take.

This is a political situation, however, and not a constitutional one. Parliament in the Fifth Republic has not been a rubber stamp. Backbenchers can become critical where they think the government is leading them on the wrong path and concessions do have to be made. Governments have to be attentive to their supporters and have to listen to what they say about how their constituents will vote, but they also have to dragoon members into the votes to pass laws they think will be of benefit but which their supporters may not all like. Broadly speaking the Fifth Republic has been characterised by solid majorities and not by the fragmentation of political coalitions – as was the Fourth Republic.

The social composition of the Assembly is not unlike those of other western countries. The massively over-represented groups are the teachers (in secondary and higher education) on the left and the lawyers on the right. Also over-represented are finance (not business), civil servants, doctors, engineers and high-level managers. The under-represented groups are also similar and include farmers, manual workers and women. Under-representation of women in the French Parliament has drawn recent attention and steps have been taken to change this situation. After the 1997 elections, the Assembly with 10.9 per cent women was the second most masculine in the European Union, above Greece with 6.3 per cent but far behind Sweden with 42.7 per cent. There had been an increase mainly due to the Socialist Party's drive to put women in winnable constituencies. Their 42 women were 17 per cent of their parliamentary group (they were only 4.5 per cent in 1993), but the most balanced group was the ecologists whose 8 deputies included 3 women. (In the Socialist government of 1997 8 of 26 Cabinet ministers were women.)

Women in European Parliaments

	Election	Number of seats	Women	% women
Sweden	1998	349	149	42.7
Denmark	1998	179	67	37.4
Finland	1999	200	74	37.0
Netherlands	1998	150	54	36.0
Germany	1998	669	207	30.9
Austria	1995	183	49	26.8
Spain	1996	350	86	24.6
Luxembourg	1999	60	12	20.0
Belgium	1999	150	29	19.3
United Kingdom	1997	651	120	18.4
Portugal	1995	230	30	13.0
Eire	1997	166	20	12.0
Italy	1996	630	70	11.1
France	1997	577	63	10.9
Greece	1996	300	19	6.3

The Senate

In 1958 the Senate, thought likely to be a government ally, was the beneficiary of the suspicion of the 'irresponsible' Assembly. It was given legislative and financial powers and recovered some of its former status. Although its approval is not required for a bill, the Senate can slow down legislation and in parliamentary politics, where time is of the essence, this is a significant power. If the government assists it the Senate can stop bills dead and in a dispute between the two houses the government can use the upper house against the lower.

The 321 senators are elected indirectly by departments for nine-year terms. The Senate is, under the Constitution, the representative of the communes of the Republic (an old idea). Under the Fifth Republic it is a functioning part of the Parliament and has authority and power which has been used to obstruct measures which governments have thought important. In the 1960s it was one the centres of opposition to de Gaulle. Its Speaker Gaston Monnerville denounced the 1962 referendum as unconstitutional and in 1963 declared that France was 'no longer a Republic'. In 1969 de Gaulle determined to reduce the status of the Senate and proposed to reform it through a referendum. His proposal was not successful. The current Speaker of the Senate, elected in 1998, is the neo-gaullist Christian Ponclelet.

Senators represent the rural and stable local governments and the low turnover of senators means that they lag behind changes in the Assembly. Prime Minister Jospin, frustrated by the Senate's obstruction of the Socialist government, called it the most absurd of upper houses (though, it must be assumed, without considering the House of Lords). But the Senate has a built-in conservative majority and the left is in an almost permanent minority. Hence it can be counted on to slow down reform and to obstruct the left in any confrontation, which it did in the 1980s and the 1990s, although when the conservatives returned to power in 1986–88 it was an equally vigorous government supporter. The reason for its bias is the electoral system.

The Senate's electoral college of about 150,000 is composed of the elected regional, departmental and town or city councillors. Some 304 senators are returned for the departments, 3 for the TOM, 1 for Mayotte, 1 for Saint-Pierre-et-Miquelon and 12 for overseas French people. Every department has at least two senators; the smaller departments operate a two ballot system and the bigger departments operate a list system (the more populous use a highest average). Small communes of under 1,000 people (17 per cent of the French population) are over-represented and the big cities of over 20,000 (40 per cent) are under-represented, and that means that about 85 per cent of departments have a skewed representation. There is a 1:3.5 disparity between the most over-represented and the most under-represented. Senators have a high average age of over 62 and only 5 per cent are women.

As might be imagined, the Senate is effective and perceptive on rural, agricultural, local and departmental matters where its voters' interests are closely involved. It has also been an efficient and critical revising chamber with a particular interest in budget and civil liberties matters. However, this is vitiated by its closeness to the conservative majorities and its willingness to act as a further arm to the politics of the centre right. A serious prospect of reform is not in view.

Parliamentary malaise?

Presidential politics moved the focus of attention from the Assembly to the Elysée. Majorities elected in the Fifth Republic were 'normally' returned to support the President. Thus the voter's power became the President's because the elections returned the President's supporters to the Assembly. Deputies therefore looked to the President to take the lead and to decide on strategy and tactics. This moved the spotlight off the National Assembly and on to the presidency.

Legislatures are the site for majority politics. Deputies are elected to support the government or the 'opposition'. Given that background the observer should not look for governments falling to their legislative critics, or to deputies' policy-making or law-making. Law and policy-making belong to the executive and their critics are in the minority playing to the court of public opinion. If these points are kept in mind the French Fifth Republic legislature does not suffer badly in comparisons. On the contrary its members are active, have a say in legislation, amend bills and criticise measures, bills and the budget. The main failure was pointed out at the beginning of the Fifth Republic: a lack of presence on the political scene. As Williams (1971), comparing the Fourth and Fifth Republics, says, 'while the bull-fight attractions of the Assembly have fortunately disappeared, no alternative spectacle has taken their place'.

The Assembly majorities were, until 1986, always returned to support the President and the decisions of the Elysée were what mattered. The Assembly did have some influence and governments had to take care of the sensibilities of its majority but in main part the President decided the composition of government and the programme of bills. The government was in reality – if not in constitutional terms – responsible to the President, as was repeatedly demonstrated by the five Presidents. One of the functions of Parliament, of selecting the executive, had been (willingly) passed to the President.

Since the left's victory in the general elections of 1997 the government and the Prime Minister (in particular) have appeared frequently before the National Assembly to make important announcements and to respond to questions. This has been done to make it clear that the government is responsible to the Assembly not the Elysée. Politically the effect has been the intended one: to sideline the President, who has no similarly privileged platform. But it does mean that the 'cohabitation' of 1997 has revived the function of the Assembly as the place of debate.

There is a tendency to look back to previous Republics when, unlike the Fifth Republic, Parliament was sovereign and when the deputies were free of party control. There are reasons to doubt the veracity of this picture and party control is a fact of contemporary political life in western Europe. However, the Fourth Republic suffered not from the lack of party control but the absence of majorities. This had unintended but debilitating consequences. When a general election was held there might be a swing in one direction which was not reflected in the government which then took office.

In the Fifth Republic the voters are presented with a choice of government and opposition coalitions and they vote for or against. There is no ambiguity: voters know whom they voted for and which side won the elections. In other words the bewildering shifts of governments (to all but initiates) during legislative terms, and sometimes rapidly in sequence, characteristic of the 1950s have been ended in the Fifth Republic – so far.

Summary

- Laments about the decline of Parliament in the Fifth Republic are common.
- Parliament has been constitutionally downgraded in the Fifth Republic but has suffered more from its own lack of assertiveness than from its constriction.
- Because, as elsewhere in Europe, executive emerges from Parliament, the interests of the majority and the government are the same. The Assembly majority does not undermine its own government.
- The French Assembly is as assertive and as good at controlling the executive as most of its counterparts in western Europe.
- Parliament has emerged from its eclipse under 'cohabitation' as the government (and the Prime Minister in particular) has used it as a platform from which the President is excluded.
- Acquiring and keeping the majority in the Assembly at general elections is the key to power in the Fifth Republic. A President or Prime Minister must be supported in the Assembly in order to exercise power.

Further reading

Andrews, W. G., 'The constitutional prescription of parliamentary procedures in gaullist France' *Legislative Studies Quarterly* 3, 1978, pp. 465–506

Frears, J., 'Parliament in the Fifth Republic' in W. Andrews and S. Hofmann (eds), *The Impact of the Fifth Republic on France* (SUNY, 1981)

Frears, J., 'The French parliament: loyal workhorse, poor watchdog' *West European Politics* 14: 1, 1991, pp. 32–51

King, A., 'Modes of executive–legislative relations' *Legislative Studies Quarterly* 1, 1976, pp. 11–34

MacRae, D., *Parliament, Parties and Society in France: 1946–58* (University of Chicago Press, 1967).

Mény, Y., *The French Political System* (IIAP, 1998)

Rizzuto, J., 'France: Something of a rehabilitation' *Parliamentary Affairs* 50: 3, 1997, pp. 373–9

Smith, P., 'A quoi sert le Sénat? Reflections on French bicameralism' *Modern and Contemporary France* 4: 1, 1996, pp. 51–60

Williams, P. M., *The French Parliament, 1958–1967* (Allen and Unwin, 1968)

Williams, P. M., 'Parliament under the Fifth Republic' in G. Loewenberg (ed.), *Modern Parliaments* (Aldine-Atherton, 1971)

Questions

1 In what circumstances could the French Assembly increase its control over the government?
2 What justification is there for the current composition and role of the Senate?
3 Should the Fifth Republic Parliament be more representative?
4 In what ways is the Assembly prevented from increasing its remit and authority?

12

Foreign policy

Although an active foreign policy conducted through the presidency is distinctive of the Fifth Republic, the second half of the twentieth century was, for France, one of relative peace and security. From the Franco-Prussian War of 1870 until 1945 French foreign policy makers had, in one way or another, to grapple with the actual or potential German domination of the continent. After 1945 this remained a problem but became increasingly a diplomatic one as long as the Cold War maintained the division of Europe and of Germany. France was protected from the main threat – as it was perceived – from Russia by the presence of the United States on the front line against the Soviet Union. France had relative safety behind the lines and away from the main European confrontation. This was the position of the Fifth Republic: lacking an external threat but also giving a sense of direction to and control over foreign policy. De Gaulle, for the most part, set the new tone for the Fifth Republic.

In the Fifth Republic, in particular, the idea of France having a special vocation in world affairs has remained strong (although the content of the message differs in different parts of the political spectrum) and Presidents, from de Gaulle, have tried to give it effect. One aspect of this is the importance given to culture in France's diplomacy. This is itself unusual amongst states and the French network of exchanges, cultural assistance and associations is by far the largest. Moreover, the French language is the object of special attention and the network of French-speakers in 'la francophonie' is carefully maintained through a variety of institutions.

However, France is not a superpower and has not the capacity of the USA to be an effective presence in every part of the world. France's real impact is therefore somewhat more limited than (perhaps) its own politicians have recognised. There has been, in the Fifth Republic, an ambition that has gone beyond the means of contemporary France, and that imparts dynamism to French foreign policy but detracts from its effectiveness.

French language

France's language is a political issue. The French Academy guards linguistic purity and is constantly on the alert for the threat from English. It is an issue that crosses party and left/right boundaries. It also affects regions which have their own languages and is a particular issue in Corsica where the Corsican language is defended by separatists and has become a part of Corsican identity. In 1999 the French Constitutional Court handed down the decision that minority language rights would infringe the principle of the indivisibility of the Republic. There was insufficient support to change the Constitution to allow recognition of regional languages (in conformity with the 1992 Charter of the Council of Europe).

Francophonie

French-speaking populations have always formed an interest of the French state but it was Mitterrand's presidency that gave this organisational form in 1986 with a meeting of interested states to develop the French language. It was an ambitious initiative (but has not yet borne full fruit) and divisions appeared between members over many issues, although there continue to be regular summits of about 40 states with big French-speaking populations.

French armed forces

The active strength of the French Army was 203,000, the Navy 63,000 and the Air Force 78,100. About 37 per cent of these numbers are conscripts but this is being phased out and the numbers are being reduced in what will be a fully professional force.

Decision-making

French foreign and defence policy were defined at the beginning of the Fifth Republic as the 'presidential reserved domain' and were run under supervision from the Elysée from 1959 to 1986. With the first 'cohabitation' the control of foreign policy became an area of dispute (though rarely in public) between the President and Prime Minister. Under 'cohabitation' France maintained a façade of unity behind the scenes although the struggle for control was intense.

However, in 'normal' times the decision-making authority in foreign affairs resided in the Elysée with the President's entourage. The key controller of the presidential staff is the Secretary General, whose interest in foreign affairs varies (Chirac's Monsieur de Villepin is a seasoned diplomat). Each week the main figures from the Foreign Ministry, the Matignon and the Chiefs of Staff involved in foreign policy making met in the Elysée. The Elysée Secretary General has a much wider remit than foreign policy and is a generalist, but there is also a group which prepares papers for the President as well as speeches and acts as a go-between with the ministers. There is a separate group that looks after African policy which, in the Fifth Republic, has been run from the Elysée.

Presidential domination of policy has also led to intervention in foreign affairs where a topic or crisis caught the President's interest. This was a feature of all the presidencies but reached a pitch under President Mitterrand, who used a variety of envoys for secret missions – some successful and others less so. For the presidency the use of unusual personnel had the advantage of freeing the President from depending on the ministerial staff (sometimes suspected of lack of empathy with the President's initiatives) and establishing a personal link with other heads of state or reinforcing the presidential source of authority in policy. It could also, however, lead to incoherence in policy as well as to some egregious bungling and bad errors of judgement.

The foreign policy establishment is the Foreign Ministry (known from its location as the 'Quai d'Orsay'), which is similar in prestige and reputation to the Foreign Office in Whitehall. It is a substantial bureaucracy divided into geographical and functional departments and overseen by a secretary general and two deputies who report to the political office of the Minister of Foreign Affairs. In keeping with the normal presidential domination of foreign policy, the Foreign Ministers work very closely with the Elysée, travel with the President, and are typically presidential confidants: they are their master's voice. They do not have their own political backing and are often from a professional background rather than politics itself. The Ministers of Defence and, at one time, of Co-operation (the latter once dealt with francophone Africa) are also close associates of the Presidents in 'normal' – non-cohabitation – times.

'Cohabitation' proved to be a struggle over the so-called 'presidential sector' of foreign policy making. Foreign policy became both a symbol of the presidency as well as the way to carve a presidential role as an international figure. Pre-eminence in foreign policy was disputed during the coexistence of opposition politicians at the head of the state. President Mitterrand negotiated the appointment of a career diplomat, Jean-Bernard Raimond, as Foreign Minister, whose close links with the Prime Minister, were not widely known. At the start of the first 'cohabitation' in 1986 President Mitterrand, who was steadily undercut, parried an impetuous lunge for the control of foreign policy by Prime Minister Chirac. In 1986, although President Mitterrand maintained public appearances and gave the impression of full control, the Matignon slowly cut the Elysée out of the decision-making loop and co-ordinated policy away from the President. All the same President Mitterrand had some notable public successes and prevented the impression arising that policy had escaped presidential control.

In the second 'cohabitation' of 1993–95 between President Mitterrand and Prime Minister Balladur, the illness of the President and the collapse of the Socialist Party led to increasing Matignon control, although again appearances were maintained. For example, Minister of the Interior Charles Pasqua seemed at one point to develop his own policy for dealing with the terrorist groups in the Middle East.

With the 'cohabitation' of 1997– between President Chirac and the Socialist Prime Minister Lionel Jospin, the repudiation of the President at the polls did not prevent an immediate backstairs clash over foreign policy. The incoming Prime Minister climbed down on his election to avoid a crisis but the wrestle for the control of policy continued even as public appearances of both harmony and presidential control were maintained.

However, the experience of 'cohabitation' appears to be that foreign policy has to be seen to be coherent but that its making slips from presidential control. This is because the bulk of foreign policy is a matter of detail and the daily interaction between ministries (not just the Foreign Ministry but also Agriculture, Trade, etc.) is determinant. The presidential staff is not big enough (nor does it have the expertise) to maintain control over this spread-eagled domain. On the other hand the Prime Minister and the Matignon staff do have the expertise and they have the authority which comes with the backing of the majority in the Assembly. Yet the President cannot be publicly repudiated or rebuked and an appearance of business as usual is vital to the public standing of both President and Prime Minister. In addition the Prime Minister, if not the President's nominee, will normally aspire to the presidency and will want to reassert presidential prerogatives over foreign policy if he or she is elected to the Elysée.

France retains a permanent seat on the United Nations (UN) Security Council (along with China, the USA, Russia and the UK), has an independent nuclear capability and maintains the third largest world-wide diplomatic presence. These are not negligible attributes and the presence of France in world politics with an individualistic policy has been marked. French foreign policy has four distinctive features: European policy, African interests, a diplomatic presence in the Middle East and nuclear deterrence.

Europe

France, as President Mitterrand said, 'is a part of the continent, not just a balcony overlooking the Atlantic'. French European policy is based on reconciliation with Germany. In the course of one hundred years, France went to war three times with Germany (1870, 1914 and 1939) and the departments of Alsace and Lorraine were occupied between 1870 and 1918. For France the rise of Germany as the major state on the European continent posed a threat, but now the new institutions of Europe are a new way to work out a *modus vivendi*. France was the dominant state on the European continent until the rise of Bismarck's Germany but it remained thereafter the second political force on the mainland.

After 1945 the situation was transformed. Germany was divided into East and West and the European continent fell into two spheres: the west and the Soviet eastern bloc. Germany abruptly ceased to be a threat and the Cold War started. When the United States took up leadership of the non-Communist free world, the destiny of Germany was determined in Washington and it was decided to rebuild Western Germany. This step was necessary because Europe, under threat from a rising Communist movement, needed to be industrially resuscitated and that necessitated a revived Western Germany. For all too evident and recent reasons, French opinion was divided about this development and many regarded a new German state, as the first step towards a Third World War. French plans for an agricultural Germany did not find support in other western capitals and France had to accept the recreation of the German state, albeit a smaller one anchored to the west.

It was at this time that one of the most creative acts of statesmanship took place and the direction of French foreign policy swung round to the building of a special relationship with the new Western Germany. Coming, as it did, shortly after the murderous Second World War, it took considerable courage, but the Fourth Republic established a Franco-German axis and constructed institutions to enable problems to be solved consensually. For France these were the problems of German power and competition from German industry (then the most efficient and dynamic in Europe), but co-operation gave France as the principal continental power the preponderant say in European institutions and the main political role. Germany, on the other hand, could not take the lead for fear of destabilising the new Europe but was able to work within the European state system without arousing fears of domination.

The institutional expression of Franco-German understanding was the European Coal and Steel Community (ECSC), whose founding treaty was signed in May 1950. This treaty, based on the ideas of Jean Monnet, established a European market for coal and steel under the control of a High Authority. Again it was seen by many as a threat to France's weak coal and steel industry. France, however, gained a degree of power in the new industrial market (along

---

European Coal and Steel Community (ECSC)

On 9 May 1950 the French Foreign Minister proposed the creation of a common coal and steel market by eliminating tariff and transport barriers between Germany and France and the other participants (Benelux and Italy). The National Assembly approved it in December 1951. This institution was to be run by a High Authority with expensive powers and its first President was Jean Monnet. It was so successful that it encouraged the six states to create the European Economic Community and Erratum, the basis for today's European Union.

with Italy and Benelux) and Germany's industry could expand and develop without military implications. This institution was a success, contrary to widespread fears, and French industry was not destroyed by competition.

When the Korean War broke out in June 1950 the rearmament of Germany became pressing and that led to further worries in France. An attempt to extend the ECSC format to the creation of a European army were not successful but Germany joined the Western Alliance (NATO). However, the setback to integration led to a determination to extend European co-operation and to the 1957 Rome Treaties creating the Common Market and Euratom. The creation of a European agricultural policy was of direct benefit to France, which was an exporter of food, but it also deepened the difficulties with the United Kingdom, which had a different agricultural system and lower-cost food. A European union based on Franco-German understanding and restricted in membership, was at the beginning politically advantageous to France.

De Gaulle's return to power in 1958 did not stop the development of European integration but set it on a new course: the sovereignty of the states and the inter-governmental nature of the institutions was to be emphasised. France gained substantially in markets and in subsidies from the Common Agricultural Policy as well as from its political advantages. De Gaulle maintained the Franco-German rapprochement, which was formalised in a treaty with Germany in 1963, but henceforth the interests of the participant states were to be protected from 'federal' encroachments. De Gaulle pushed the institutions of the new Europe to the verge of crisis of June 1965, in which France boycotted the Council of Ministers and blocked further development of the power of the Commission or Assembly.

In the Fifth Republic the election of a new government has sometimes led to a brief attempt to reanimate the Franco-British relationship and this happened in 1981, 1986 and 1993. These diplomatic efforts usually foundered on the UK's Atlantic ties and on its excessive (from a French viewpoint) free market economic policies. In 1969 President Pompidou was elected and the way to the enlargement of the European Economic Community (EEC) to the UK, Norway, Eire and Denmark was open. One impetus to the entry of the UK was President Pompidou's doubts about the direction of German policy and his fear that it might move eastward (under Chancellor Brandt); the understanding with Prime Minister Heath enabled the UK to negotiate to join the EEC.

By contrast Presidents Giscard, Mitterrand and Chirac reinforced the Franco-German relationship. In 1974 the regular European Councils of Heads of State and governments were started, direct elections for the European Parliament were instituted in 1979 and the decision to establish a European monetary system (EMS) was taken in 1978. EMS was one in a series of attempts to create a zone of stability during the disruption in the world financial markets in the 1970s and controlled the limits on fluctuations. It was one step towards a common currency and it used a European currency unit (ecu) within its own organisation.

The election of President Mitterrand and a Socialist government in 1981 led to an initial difference of direction between France (reflating to deal with unemployment) and the European Community (deflating to control inflation). This was solved in 1983 by France's decision to join the European mainstream after its solitary experiment in growth had led to severe balance-of-payment problems and devaluations of the franc. There were a number of developments promoted by the renewed Franco-German alliance after 1983. These included the enlargement of the EEC to include Spain and Portugal and the nomination of former Finance Minister Jacques Delors to the presidency of the European Commission. The single market that came into force on 1 January 1993 followed the 1987 Single Act. In 1992 the Maastricht Treaty was signed and the first steps were taken to monetary union. In 1990 the Schengen agreement on the free circulation of people in the European Community was signed (without the UK).

The steady consolidation of the European Union was a result of the French decision to tie the West German government to the west as German unification came back on the agenda. The reforms of the eastern bloc and its eventual collapse in 1989 led to the prospect of reuniting East (Communist) and West (Federal) Germany and the creation of a massive power on the continent. This in the late 1980s was regarded as theoretical but events moved with astonishing rapidity and the landscape of the Cold War, which had seemed fixed, vanished. From 1989 to 1990 French policy seemed to hesitate between accepting the inevitable and looking to the Communist USSR (still under Gorbachev) to balance the new Germany on the east. If there was a real intention to slow down or halt reunification it was brief. On the other hand the institutions established in Europe proved as valuable for Germany as they had done in the past as a way of establishing consensus first and foremost and with France.

France, however, still has doubts about the direction in which Europe is moving. Until the late 1980s the main parties and politicians were pro-European but doubts surfaced in 1992 during the referendum campaign on the Maastricht Treaty. The expected opposition of the Communist Party and the National Front turned out to be only part of a general Euroscepticism and the referendum was only narrowly approved (by 51 per cent of voters). Many on the right and the left saw the new Europe and the single currency as restricting rather than providing opportunities. The most vigorous opposition to Maastricht Europe comes from the extreme left (Trotskyists polled over 5 per cent in the 1995 elections) and the extreme right (from a divided National Front) but Euroscepticism is also strong in the Communist Party and in the (small but influential) Citizens' Movement. There is an extremely effective opposition to Maastricht located, as might be expected, within gaullist ranks. Jacques Chirac (as candidate, not as President) has expressed it at times, as has the maverick Philippe Séguin and former Interior Minister Charles Pasqua (who founded a Eurosceptical RPF party).

French-speaking Africa

France has expressed its concern for the Third World and has supported demands from the developing countries for a North–South dialogue. It also concentrates its arms sales there. Although the gaullist regime hoped to give a lead to the emerging decolonised states it was unable to do so despite some attention-grabbing gestures. But in de Gaulle's presidency alliances were made with the People's Republic of China and US intervention was condemned in Santo Domingo in 1965 and in Vietnam in the 1960s. France maintained a rhetorical distance from the USA by criticising intervention in Nicaragua in the 1980s. However, the country has lacked the means to be more than a token presence in the Third World – Africa and the Middle East excepted. Most attention was devoted to francophone Africa and to threats to order there.

Arms sales

France is one of the big arms exporters and for most of the Fifth Republic ranked third after the United States and the former Soviet Union in its share of the market. Its share of the market has fluctuated but did reach about 13 per cent in the mid-1980s. France is deeply involved in sales to the Third World where its low-cost and relatively unsophisticated weapons sell, but it is less of a presence in industrial countries than the other big two. It has been particularly important in French-speaking Africa, India and the Middle East. With the end of the Cold War, and the diminishing market in the Third World, the French arms exporters face keener competition from other industrial countries.

Africa was regarded as falling within the 'presidential sector' in normal times outside of 'cohabitation'. There was a Ministry of Co-operation devoted to relations with the former French Africa (although its remit expanded over the years beyond the continent to other less-developed countries). It is a measure of the presidentialisation of this area of policy that there was also a presidential network extending directly from the Elysée to deal with these matters. The main part of the old Empire was in Africa, constituting, it was said, a France which extended from 'Dunkirk to Yaoundé'. It consisted of 100 million people and covered 12 million square miles (or so it was reckoned in 1931). For French colonialists this was a civilising mission in which the European powers brought the benefits of law, order, administration, science and religion. At the end of the Third Republic the objective was for a long-term integration of the colonies into France and French political life. In 1932 Gratien Candace (from Guadeloupe) became Secretary of State for the Colonies and during the Second World War the (African) governor of Central Africa (Félix Eboué) rallied Central Africa to the gaullist cause. In the Fourth Republic there were representatives of the African colonies in the Assembly

French military intervention in Africa

1962	Support for President of Senegal
1964	Support for the government of Gabon
1968–72	Support for the government of Chad
1977	Jaguar fighter aircraft sent after hostages were taken in the western Sahara
1978	Parachute regiment in Kolwezi (Zaire) and in Chad
1979	Troops sent to the Central African Republic on the deposition of the Emperor Bokassa
1983	Operation 'Manta' to prevent the take-over of Chad by Libyan-backed rebels
1986	Intensification of war in Chad and intervention in Togo after an abortive coup
1989	Small contingent sent after the assassination of the President of the Comoros
1990	Troop reinforcements after riots in Gabon
1990–93	Detachment of 300 troops sent after a rebellion started in Rwanda
1991	Troops sent after a rebellion started in the north of Djibouti
1994	Operation to evacuate foreigners from Rwanda, then 2,500 soldiers sent
1995	Support for the Prime Minister of the Comoros after an attempted coup
1997	French military contingent in Africa reduced from eleven to five bases (Senegal, Gabon, Chad, Ivory Coast, Djibouti) with a small contingent in Bangui

French aid through the Caisse française de dévelopement (French Development Fund) contributes to the following countries: Angola, Benin, Burkina Faso, Burundi, Cambodia, Cameroon, Cape Verdi, Central African Republic, Chad, Comoros, Congo, Democratic Republic of the Congo, Djibouti, Gabon, Gambia, Guinea, Guinea-Bissau, Haiti, Ivory Coast, Lesser Antilles, Madagascar, Mali, Mauritius, Mauritania, Mozambique, Namibia, Niger, Rwanda, São Tomé, Senegal, Seychelles, Togo, Zaire.

and there were distinguished ministers (like Houpouët-Boigny) from the Ivory Coast in West Africa.

Effectively, however, this 'integration', although real for a few, was an elite affair and the main part of the populations of the colonies were excluded from political life. In Algeria, where the settler population was predominant, Europeans dominated. During the Fourth Republic the ties were loosened and in 1956 the framework for independence (the Defferre law) was put in place and the protectorates of Tunisia and Morocco were given independence. French disengagement from the colonies was remarkably messy and deeply disturbing to French political life, as well as violent.

Decolonisation started under the Fourth Republic and was completed under the Fifth in de Gaulle's time when twelve African states entered the United Nations. However, these were small, impoverished and weak states and French links with sub-Saharan Africa remained remarkably strong and led to accusations of 'neo-colonialism', a system which, in the ability of the French government to intervene, it did resemble. To a small but significant extent French soldiers have been deployed in French-speaking Africa and a variety of pressures including training, education, aid and weapons have been used to maintain a status quo favourable to French interests. These interests are strategic: maintaining a French sphere of influence, cultural and educational, and the retention of resources of crucial importance (like uranium and oil) in friendly hands. In the former colonies in Africa there is a Central African franc tied to the French franc. Thus France maintains a 'franc zone' in central Africa which protects the former colonies from the vagaries of the world market and helps political stability, but this also isolates the states from involvement with the world economy. It would be too simple to say that the French economy gains from the zone and the value of the connection has been doubted, especially since Prime Minister Balladur devalued the Central African franc by 50 per cent in 1994.

De Gaulle and subsequent leaders saw the continuation of French influence as a necessary part of French status in the world. Cultural and language ties were emphasised in the new relationship with the metropolitan authorities. However, the use, by French policy-makers, of the mineral (principally oil) resources of the former colonies was a part of the gaullist strategy of remaining free of the ties which bound France to the 'Anglo-Saxon' world and giving France some independence. For many French leaders the former French Africa was their 'sphere of influence' in much the same way as Latin America was for the USA. They supported a status quo which was mainly favourable to France and intervened to stabilise it (usually by supporting one or other of the factions). Mainly, however, the military intervention was low key and at an elite level. It involved training police and an officer corps in the new armies and providing weapons and technical backing, but it could mean aid, commercial credit and the detachment of small contingents of troops.

Under Georges Pompidou the largely gaullist inspiration of policy was maintained even if the sales of arms (to Libya, Portugal and the South African regime) were contradictory. Pompidou might have been about to change the relationship with Africa and had amalgamated the Ministry of Co-operation with the Foreign Ministry when he died. President Giscard had a special interest in Africa, which he visited regularly ('Giscard the African' was a great hunter of endangered wildlife). Giscard re-established the Ministry of Co-operation after a five-year hiatus in 1979 and appointed his own adviser (René Journac in succession to the gaullist Foccart). It was during Giscard's septennate that the Mobutu regime in Zaire was propped up, Libyan intervention started in Chad, and the 'Emperor' Bokassa of the Central African Republic was deposed in 1979. (Bokassa had his revenge, claiming that gifts of diamonds had been given to the President.)

Because of the Socialist Party's anti-colonial sentiment, President Mitterrand's septennate was expected to usher in a new form of Franco-African relationship. However, this was one of the areas where the radical outlook of opposition did not translate into government, although aid had increased by the time Mitterrand left office. The Elysée remained as dominant as ever and Jean-Christophe Mitterrand became the presidential adviser (nicknamed 'papamadit', 'dad says') in an Elysée unit which continued the presidential emphasis. In broad policy the thrust of maintaining the status quo continued but the diplomatic action moved to support countries in the front line against South Africa. In 1986–88, in 'cohabitation', Jacques Foccart returned to take charge of African policy for Jacques Chirac, which marked a 'gaullist' renewal. In 1993, when the second 'cohabitation' took place, the Minister of the Interior (Charles Pasqua) moved the control of African networks to the Interior. Much the same was true in 1995 when Jacques Chirac became President and the old relationships (including the return of the 82-year-old Foccart) appeared to be re-established, with close associates running policy and African heads of state treated in a privileged manner. President Bongo of Gabon stated that 'France without Africa was like a car without petrol and Africa without France was like a car without a driver'.

The largest recent commitment (though varying in intensity over the period) was in Chad, where, between 1978 and 1987, the French backed the opponents to the Northern Libyan supported rebels (who took the capital in 1980). Libya threatened France's special relationship with francophone Africa and moved into northern Chad claiming a disputed strip along the frontier. At the same time negotiated solutions were sought and the Franco-Arab relationship was preserved. In 1983 operation 'Manta' was mounted when pro-Libyan forces appeared to have the upper hand and 3,000 French troops were deployed to help defend the fifteenth parallel. In 1986, when there was a further Libyan advance, the 'Epervier' operation brought air force and 1,200 troops, and ended with the eviction of the Libyans and an end to 20 years of Chad's civil war. There had been no direct French engagement with the Libyan forces but French backing with men and materièl was crucial in forcing the Libyans back to their frontier.

For many years French African policy was run through the very personal links of the Elysée, highly solicitous of the African heads of state, and by the clandestine and shadowy figure of Jacques Foccart. There was therefore both a conventional diplomacy and a parallel presidential system of influence. Jacques Foccart had both an entrée to the Elysée under successive Presidents of the conservative right (de Gaulle, Pompidou, Giscard, and Chirac) and a network of contacts and agents. How these worked, and what they did, is not known for sure but there were secret funds and both official counter-espionage (Direction générale de la sécurité extérieur – then under a different name) and unofficial gaullist (Service d'action civique) institutions. Payments under the table and laundering of funds threatened to become public in the late 1990s as French investigating authorities got more active.

The populations of the former colonies have not uncritically accepted French neo-colonialism in Africa, and France has become increasingly unpopular because tottering and corrupt dictatorships appear to have been supported by France. France has been criticised for giving aid to 'bullies in uniform' around the former French Africa and has been held responsible for 'its' sphere of influence. This became an international matter when the French were criticised for slow action during the massacres of Tutsis by the Rwandan regime. In this history of the slaughter of perhaps as many as 500,000 people in about three weeks no government emerges blameless, although France had a bigger presence than most in the region. However, French support keeping the corrupt and incompetent General Mobutu in power in Zaire was deeply resented. France was also blamed for supporting the murderous Hutu regime in Rwanda.

French power is increasingly difficult to maintain for moral and resource reasons and French involvement might be wound down over the next ten years as the military bases already have been. In 1999 the government abolished the Ministry of Co-operation (and replaced it with a Ministry for Francophone Relations) in a shift away from the former very close 'neo-colonial' association with Africa. Economic and social reform are now at the top of the agenda and the stability provided by outside support is not an adequate response to local needs. When Africa was a stake in the east–west rivalry France's role had some rationale and the support of dictatorships seemed to be *realpolitik*; with the collapse of the eastern bloc the international stakes have changed. France is adjusting to the new era.

The Middle East

France, as a Mediterranean power, has always had an engagement with the Arab countries and the Middle East. De Gaulle sought to develop a special relationship with the Arab world and took up an old theme in French policy of encouraging the development of nascent nation-states. Under the Fourth Republic France had a close relationship with the new state of Israel, with which it shared worries about the rise of Arab nationalism, and this closeness was manifest at a number of levels until the Fifth Republic. It was changed by de Gaulle's stance, critical of Israel in 1967 and imposing an arms embargo on the region, which (because Israel bought French arms in quantity) was one-sided. Shortly after this there was a massive push to sell arms to Arab states. This policy was rewarded with the sale of 200 Mirage fighters to Libya in 1973, a deal which launched the French air arms industry as a major international force. Israel ceased to be the main market for French weapons. Oil exporters also treated France more favourably than other western states during the oil embargo in 1973.

This unpopular, pro-Arab policy condemning Israeli aggression (in de Gaulle's words) became a mark of the Fifth Republic policy and was followed through subsequent septennates. President Mitterrand moved away from the bias against the Israelis which characterised gaullism but had little impact. In Mitterrand's time France had to recognise its marginal position in its old colony of the Lebanon which had descended into civil war after 1975. De Gaulle's policy also had the pay-off of disrupting the main relation these countries had with the US and the UK, and France moved into the area as a supplier, a purchaser and a political support.

Both Pompidou and Giscard d'Estaing developed Fifth Republic policy. Pompidou also faced the problem that France was almost totally dependent on imported oil and after the oil price rises of 1973 turned to Iraq and Saudi Arabia in particular (but also courted Iran). Shortly before Pompidou's death, Michel Jobert, who was briefly Foreign Minister, pugnaciously established a pro-Arab and anti-American position. France became a host to the Palestinian Liberation Organisation (PLO) in 1975 and has called for a recognition of the rights of Palestinians. President Giscard visited Algeria, the first step to normalising relations with former enemies, followed by a further pro-Arab move. During President Giscard's septennate there was a determined wooing of Iraq accompanied by arms sales and the building of a nuclear reactor (destroyed by Israel in 1981).

France, in the Middle East, played on Cold War divisions and exerted pressure where they created an opening, but at the end of the century it had little to show for its independence and had only a small influence. In the 1970s France began to suffer the effects of closeness to the shaky regimes of the Middle East. Despite having been hospitable to the Ayatollah Khomeini, France was seen as one of the western supporters of the Shah and suffered accordingly, and its pro-Iraqi policy of supplying weapons to Saddam Hussein during the wars of 1980–88 was resented.

France was not, despite its independent policy, a power in the Middle East, where policy was determined by the local states and outside pressure was exerted by the United States. This was recognised to some extent in the Gulf War. French opponents of the war argued a gaullist line – that it was not in France's interest to reinforce the American sphere of influence – but France was a full participant in the alliance. There were attempts to mediate, to play on France's special relation with Iraq and to go the 'last mile' to find a peaceful solution, but this proved ineffectual and France joined the UN forces. President Chirac did not, however, relinquish the hope of a distinctive French policy in the area and both defended the rights of the Palestinians to their own state and extended a hand to the regimes of the region in the expectation of countering American influence. This distinctiveness was continued by the Socialist government of 1997, which indicated its preparedness to listen to the national aspirations of Arab countries like Iraq. When Iraq moved into Kurdistan and the USA replied with bombings, France refused to back the action. Chirac's France also started a 'critical dialogue' with the Iranians.

France's relations with its former North African territories were colder than with its sub-Saharan ones. De Gaulle's idea of a clean break which would allow France to forget the past and move on, proved beside the mark. France had supported the regimes in place in former French North Africa. This became an acute problem in 1990. Sheikh Abbas Madani's Islamic Salvation Front won the Algerian elections with 54 per cent of the vote, whereupon President Chadli Ben-Jedid declared a state of siege. In 1992 the ruling party was again defeated at the polls but the elections were declared invalid by the military. There were some hopes that President Bouteflika, who took over in April 1999, would find some solution through negotiation. However, France had protested feebly and was caught up in the rise of Islamic fundamentalism opposed to the tenants of power in Algeria as well as in Tunisia and Morocco and was condemned both for supporting the regime and for implicitly condoning the suppression of oppositions.

France spends 0.6 per cent of its GDP on Third World aid, which is about twice the European Union average and (proportionately) about five times what the United States spends, and that, in some views, is unsustainable. France has indicated that perhaps three of its six remaining African bases might be closed (not done by 2001). France, even here, needs European backing to maintain its level of influence in sub-Saharan and northern Africa.

Nuclear diplomacy

De Gaulle gave France nuclear forces, creating a consensus around an independent and autonomous nuclear defence force which was not part of the western alliance and was completely under French control. It is comparable in size and capacity to the United Kingdom's, although it is independent of US technology or decision-making. De Gaulle, in a series of spectacular actions, established France's sovereignty in this domain and there is no going back even though the conditions of its creation (the Cold War and the division of Europe) are no longer relevant.

France chafed at its subordinate position in the western alliance and sought parity with the United States and the United Kingdom within NATO and the Atlantic Alliance. However, this was not forthcoming and actions took place (like the rearming of Germany) which French governments regarded as having been taken without their consultation. This was the background to the Fifth Republic and de Gaulle expected that his France, as a stable and determined ally, would be recognised as a partner in a tripartite directorate. When this was not forthcoming de Gaulle stepped up the nuclear testing programme (exploding a bomb in 1960) and then developed Mirage IV bomber, submarine and land-based intermediate range missile delivery systems. Under de Gaulle, these were

puny but independent of US and NATO technology and targeting. In 1966 de
Gaulle withdrew from the NATO military command and evicted US and NATO
personnel from French soil.

There then developed a series of justifications for the new policy (though de
Gaulle was never quite clear), for example, the 'doctrine' (as strategists say) that
the French nuclear force was based on 'proportional deterrence'. It was a 'dis-
suasive' force which would prevent any larger enemy from attacking because
the possession of nuclear weapons would ensure France's safety. A 'national
sanctuary' would be formed. In this doctrine France might be small but nuclear
weapons meant the enemy would suffer a retaliation far beyond what the prize
was worth. Nobody attacks a scorpion because the reward is meagre. In this
view France did not have to have a weapons system comparable with the superpowers but did have to have an independent national nuclear force. This was
constructed in de Gaulle's time and expanded and modernised under subsequent Presidents.

However, while maintaining the commitment to independence, the edge of
de Gaulle's policy was taken off. From Pompidou to Mitterrand the drift back
into the Atlantic Alliance started and under President Chirac a re-entry into
NATO became thinkable. America was even urged to play a more active role.
Close co-operation in the Gulf War gave the French army a taste for multinational forces and showed how their organisational costs could be shared –
though not, of course, the nuclear force.

In the late 1990s President Chirac accepted that French defence was better
conceived within NATO than without, a position which budget cuts were
pushing. In the early 1990s France was spending 3.3 per cent of its GDP on
defence compared to the NATO average of 2.5 per cent. President Giscard had

Defence spending

Country	$bn 1999	Rank
Greece	5.2	1
USA	267.8	2
France	37.8	3
United Kingdom	36.3	4
Sweden	5.4	5
Portugal	2.3	6
Italy	22.6	7
Netherlands	6.7	8
Germany	31.2	9
Denmark	2.6	10
Belgium	3.4	11
Finland	1.6	12
Spain	7.2	13
Austria	1.7	14

Source: International Institute of Strategic Studies

France's defence statistics (1999)

Budget	243,500 million francs
Strength of the armed forces	
Nuclear:	8,700
Army:	203,200
Navy:	63,300
Air Force:	78,100
Total:	353,300 (including 129,250 conscripts)

Western European Union

This institution was, reportedly, thought of by British Foreign Secretary Eden while in the bath as a way of bringing a rearmed Federal (West) Germany into the discussion of European defence. It first met in May 1955 and consists of a Secretariat, a Council of Foreign Ministers and an Assembly in Strasbourg. It was not an important body until it was reanimated in 1984 by President Mitterrand in the persistent French desire to develop a distinctive European view of regional security. Although the organisation expanded and co-ordinated military matters it did not move to full military co-operation.

---

doubted the rationale of the French deterrent, varied some of the 'doctrine' and began to control the resources going to the nuclear forces (cancelling a sixth submarine). President Mitterrand was more ambiguous but supported the western campaign against the USSR's deployment of SS20 missiles, even going as far as to urge the German government to accept American missiles (in a speech in 1983 to the Bundestag). Mitterrand also stepped up co-operation with allies through the West European Union (which excluded the USA) and with Western Germany.

A French propensity to act unilaterally (for example, deciding to professionalise the army without consultation) has not helped the relations between the allies. Mitterrand, however, retained the gaullist all-or-nothing French 'doctrine' of dissuasion. Although President Chirac started the septennate with tests in the south Pacific (causing world protest) and shuttle diplomacy in the Middle East, the attitude was one of closer co-operation and involvement in crisis operations. After a 30-year boycott, France rejoined the NATO Military Committee in December 1995. President Chirac accepted a discussion of nuclear deterrence within NATO, although France demanded a clear European defence 'pillar' within the alliance. France, however, maintains that there is a need for a European command structure within the Atlantic Alliance, while other NATO countries are apprehensive that America might become isolated within NATO. Most Europeans also believe that the disposition for a separable European force in NATO (should it be needed) is already adequate and will not

go much further. Certainly some French demands, like a European comman-
der-in-chief, are out of the question at present.

Conclusion

France aspires to a world presence and, amongst contemporary Europeans, this
has parallels only in the diplomacy of the United Kingdom. France invests
heavily in foreign policy and in diplomatic effort and is recognised as a great
power. However, France has an impact only in three areas: the Middle East,
former African colonies and Europe. It is present, but only secondary, in the
Middle East and it ensures a modicum of stability in its former sub-Saharan territories. It is, however, a real political force and a determinant of the direction
of Europe, where it has more power than its physical resources might
command.

Yet France, like every other state, has had to adjust to the post-Cold War
world after the collapse of the Communist bloc and the unification of Germany.
France's go-it-alone policy and its anti-Americanism has been reduced (though
it still asserts its individuality in opposition to the USA) as it has sought to maintain some influence by making judicious alliances and poised interventions.
There is the problem of spending on defence and foreign policy, which is high,
but also the need to work through Europe. This implies a greater effort at negotiation and co-operation in the key area of foreign relations where France has
traditionally been prickly about its independence.

Whether France's effort to play a world role is worth the price it costs is a
matter for its politicians and people. It can be judged on a number of criteria
and the result will be different according to the values used to weigh the pros
and cons. However, France has had the ambition to rival the superpowers but
has not carved itself its own sphere of influence. In nuclear policy a vain
attempt to match the superpowers took resources from other purposes and,
even in defence, prevented the modernisation of the army. Where events have
impinged on France it has been absent from decision-making and has therefore
not been taken into account. Sometimes it has come in late to support western
policies, a backhanded recognition of its position in the western alliance.

Only in Europe has France been the force it would like to have been. Decision-
makers have had to come to terms with the end of the Cold War and have had
difficulties (as have other powers), but the European arena remains significant
and France's position in it has been enhanced. France remains a European
power and the building of European institutions offers France a role and a significance which it has recognised. Europe is not without its problems, but the
development of its institutions can give French diplomacy opportunities. If the
domestic settlement holds, allowing further integration, the integration
process might be used for French foreign policy purposes, allowing France to
speak for Europe on many issues. Europe is, in this way, France's future. France

may appear idiosyncratic but it can only keep up its world presence in the long term if it has Europe's backing and therein lies the paradox. France must either work to create a consensus (which would inevitably mean compromises) or go it alone without adequate resources.

Summary

- The Fifth Republic has been characterised by a forceful foreign policy.
- French foreign policy is seen as a presidential responsibility and the President is present at major international negotiations or gatherings.
- In 'cohabitation' foreign policy is made by the ministries under the supervision of the Prime Minister and presented by the President.
- When the President heads the executive the President determines foreign policy often with the Foreign Minister and Defence Minister. The Prime Minister and other ministers may or may not be involved.
- France is one of the major world powers and its foreign policy is distinctive.
- France's key position in Europe is its foreign policy strength.
- The Franco-German relationship is key to European developments and the future of the European Union.
- In Africa France has begun to disengage in its former colonies, but not without difficulties.
- France's nuclear force is sizeable but has no major diplomatic role.
- In the Middle East France is a distinct presence but not a force.

Further reading

Cole, A., 'Looking on: France and the new Germany' *German Politics* 2: 3, 1993, pp. 358–76

Grant, R. P., 'France's new relationship with Nato' *Survival* 38; 1, 1996, pp. 58–80

Gregory, S., *French Defence Policy into the Twenty-First Century* (Palgrave, 2000)

Guyomarch, A., Machin, H. and Ritchie, E., *France in the European Union* (Macmillan, 1998)

Howorth, J., 'French defence reforms: national tactics for a European strategy?' in *Brassay's Defence Yearbook 1998* (Brassay's, 1998)

Imbert, C., 'The end of French exceptionalism' *Foreign Affairs* 68: 4, 1989, pp. 48–60

Kassim, H., 'French autonomy and the European Union' *Modern and Contemporary France* 5: 2, 1997, pp. 167–80

Menon, A., 'Defence policy in the Fifth Republic: politics by any other means' *West European Politics* 17: 4, 1994, pp. 74–96

Menon, A., *France, NATO and the Limits of Independence, 1981–97* (Palgrave, 2000)

Tiersky, R., *France in the New Europe* (Westview, 1994)

Tiersky, R., 'Mitterrand's legacies' *Foreign Affairs* 74: 1, 1995, pp. 112–21

Woodhouse, R., 'France's relations with Nato 1966–96' *Modern and Contemporary France* 4: 4, 1996, pp. 483–95

Questions

1 Is it accurate to depict French foreign policy as having 'ambition without means'?
2 Why does France have a strong position in European Union politics?
3 In what ways is French foreign policy distinctive?

Appendix 1

General elections, 25 May and 1 June 1997

First ballot

Registered   39,200,461
Voters   26,639,236
Abstentions %   32.04
Spoilt %   4.94
Valid votes   25,324,536

Political families	Votes	% of vote	% of registered	Seats on first ballot
Total conservative right	9,155,732	36.15	23.36	11
RPR	4,255,671	16.80	10.86	7
UDF	3,723,616	14.70	9.50	3
LDI	709,764	2.80	1.81	—
Other right	466,681	1.84	1.19	1
Total left	10,664,489	42.11	27.21	1
PS and PRG	6,469,766	25.55	16.50	—
PCF	2,509,357	9.91	6.40	1
Greens	912,921	3.60	2.33	—
MDC	265,921	1.05	0.68	—
Other left	506,524	2.00	1.29	—
Extreme left	552,024	2.18	1.41	—
Extreme right	3,822,519	15.09	9.75	—
FN	3,783,623	14.94	9.65	—
Other ecologists	675,338	2.67	1.72	—
GE	4,323,198	1.71	1.10	—
Others	454,434	1.79	1.16	—

Second ballot

Registered   38,440,714
Voters   27,343,902
Abstentions %   28.87
Spoilt %   6.32
Valid votes   25,614,720

Political families	Votes	% of vote	% of registered	Seats on first ballot
Total conservative right	11,792,433	46.04	30.68	245
RPR	6,057,623	23.65	15.76	132
UDF	5,374,563	20.98	13.98	106
Other conservative	360,247	1.41	0.94	7
Total left	12,387,403	48.63	32.22	319
PS and PRG	9,950,280	38.85	25.88	246
PCF	963,915	3.76	2.51	36
Ecologists	437,735	1.71	1.41	8
Other left	1,035,573	4.04	2.69	29
FN	1,434,884	5.60	3.73	1

Source: Le Monde Dossiers and Documents 1997

Appendix 2

The French government of October 2001

Prime Minister   Lionel Jospin

Ministers

Economy, Finance and Industry	Laurent Fabius
Employment and Solidarity	Elizabeth Guigou
Justice	Marylise Lebranchu
Interior	Daniel Vaillant
Education	Jack Lang
Foreign Affairs	Hubert Védrine
Defence	Alain Richard
Transport, Housing and Equipment	Jean-Claude Gayssot (PCF)
Culture and Communication	Catherine Tasca
Agriculture	Jean Galvany
Environment	Yves Cochet (Greens)
Relations with Parliament	Jean-Jacques Queyranne
Public Services and Reform of the State	Michel Sapin
Youth and Sports	Marie-George Buffet (PCF)
Research Roger	Gérard Schwartzenberg (PRG)

Junior Ministers

Europe	Pierre Moscovici
Francophone World	Charles Josselin
Handicapped, Family and Children	Ségolène Royal
Health	Bernard Kouchner (PRG)
Cities	Claude Bartelone
Old People	Paulette Guinchard-Kunstler
Women	Nicole Pery
Solidarity	Guy Hascoët (Greens)
Professional Training	Jean-Luc Melenchon
Housing	Marie-Noëlle Lienemann
Tourism	Jacques Brunhes
Budget	Florence Parly

Small and Medium Businesses	François Patriat
Industry	Christian Pierret
Trade	François Huwart
Veterans	Jacques Floch
Heritage	Michel Duffour (PCF)

(All Socialist Party except where noted)

Appendix 3

The 1999 European parliamentary elections

Party	% votes	Seats	% change since 1994
UDF	9.28	9	−3.5
RPR and DL	12.82	12	—
PS and PRG	21.95	22	+7.45
RPF	13.05	13	—
FN	5.69	5	−4.81
National movement	3.28	0	—
PCF	6.78	6	−0.12
CPNT	6.77	6	—
Energie radicale	—	—	−12.0
Greens	9.72	9	—
LO/LCR	5.18	5	—
Others	5.48	0	—
Total	100	87	—

Note: In 1994 the UDF and RPR stood on a joint ticket and Energie radicale was part of the PS/PRG list in 1999.

Appendix 4

Five Presidents of the Fifth Republic

General Charles de Gaulle (b. 1890 d. 1970)
President 1959–69

By any reckoning General de Gaulle is one of the most remarkable political personalities and it is apposite that the Fifth Republic was known as 'de Gaulle's Republic'. Before the Second World War he was a career army officer, although his advancement was slow (no doubt because of his unbending disposition). He was made Under-Secretary for Defence briefly (for ten days) before the fall of France and he then refused to accept the capitulation of the new Pétain government. He arrived in London and established the Free French forces to continue the fight. It was in this capacity that he made his famous broadcast of 18 June calling for Resistance to the invader. De Gaulle's relations with other allies were stormy (leading Churchill to remark that the cross he had to bear was de Gaulle's Cross of Lorraine) but he established both his independence and his position at the head of the united French Resistance. De Gaulle was therefore the leader of the provisional government when France was liberated in 1944. De Gaulle's government re-established the Republic and the authority of the state after the war.

However, de Gaulle had a number of disputes with the Assembly and resigned in January 1946 and proposed a new Republic. De Gaulle's ideas were rejected and the Fourth Republic came into being. He then formed the RPF party, which had an immediate and startling success but won only 120 of the 627 seats in 1951. The Fourth Republic proved resilient and de Gaulle's breakthrough never came. The RPF was disbanded in 1953 and he devoted himself to writing his memoirs. De Gaulle's supporters made only a token gesture at the 1956 elections.

It was the Algerian crisis that brought de Gaulle back to manage affairs. In May 1958 an army uprising in Algeria threatened civil war and the only figure with the authority to prevent it was de Gaulle. He was called back by the politicians he disdained but the price de Gaulle demanded was the creation of a new Republic and this was conceded. De Gaulle took power on 1 June and a new constitution was drafted and approved by referendum on 28 September. He again re-established the authority of the Republic but this time he did not quit and became the first President of the Fifth Republic, nominating his close associate Michel Debré as Prime Minister.

De Gaulle's immediate task was to establish Algerian independence and this was achieved in 1962. After that time his principal efforts were devoted to foreign affairs. He decided to keep the EEC confined to a modest role and rejected the UK's applications. He withdrew France from NATO and developed a special relationship with the Soviet Union. Although he was re-elected President in 1965, there were signs that his authority was slipping and it was fatally undermined by the 'events' of May 1968. In April 1969 he held an ill-advised referendum and was defeated. He resigned immediately and went into a silent retirement to write further volumes of memoirs.

Georges Pompidou (b. 1911 d. 1974)
President 1969–74

Georges Pompidou is sometimes called the 'forgotten president', but his impact on the Fifth Republic was far from negligible. He was born in the Auvergne and his family were teachers, a profession he also entered before the war and which he continued after demobilisation. He joined de Gaulle in 1944 and headed the General's private office in government and then in the RPF. He left de Gaulle to join the Rothschild Bank in 1955 but returned to de Gaulle's staff in 1958.

In 1962 he was made Prime Minister, not a post for which he had had any training, but he rapidly developed a mastery of politics and was left to deal with domestic politics. As Prime Minister Pompidou chose to promote industrialisation and modernisation, and also built up the gaullist party organisation and extended its alliances. In the 1967 election he won a seat in the Cantal. The crisis of May 1968 was the making of Pompidou as a presidential hopeful. During the month of May he gave the impression that he knew what to do (which de Gaulle did not) and guided ministers with indefatigable energy towards a successful outcome for the government. After the gaullist landslide in the June elections de Gaulle sacked him. Relations between the two worsened, but in 1969, when de Gaulle resigned, Pompidou was the natural gaullist candidate and won the presidency.

As President, Pompidou continued his domestic economic policy but changed the emphasis of foreign policy. It was Pompidou who encouraged the UK's application to join the European Common Market and began a rapprochement with the United States (not as far as rejoining NATO). He was the architect of the right's general election victory in 1973 but fell ill and his health deteriorated rapidly. As a result his grip on politics weakened in the year to his death in April 1974. He was a patron of modern art and one of his legacies is the Pompidou centre in Paris.

Valéry Giscard d'Estaing (b. 1926)
President 1974–81

In the 1960s there were many aspirants for the title of the 'French Kennedy' and one of these was Giscard d'Estaing. He was young, ambitious, modern in outlook (and rich) and of a centre right persuasion. He had had a blue riband career and belonged to the Fifth Republic meritocracy, although his family was one of provincial Catholic notables active in conservative politics. He had inherited his grandfather's parliamentary constituency in the Auvergne.

Giscard led a small group of conservative parliamentarians who rallied to de Gaulle and he began to climb the ministerial ladder, starting as a junior minister in 1959 and becoming Minister of Finance in 1962. He began to be seen as 'presidential timber' but, in what is the nearest thing to a setback he experienced in his climb to the top, he was left out of the government in 1966 because the slower growth he had engineered were blamed for de Gaulle's poor election result. He used his freedom to good advantage and became critical of the President and urged his supporters to vote against de Gaulle in the 1969 referendum. When Pompidou won the presidency he was returned to the Ministry of Finance and used the post to continue to build a presidential image. When Pompidou died he was the best-placed candidate of the right and won the presidency by the narrowest of margins (50.7 per cent) against the left's François Mitterrand. There then followed a '110 day' flurry of liberal social reforms and new non-gaullist politicians were promoted to prominence. However, Giscard had to wrestle with the problems of rising inflation and unemployment and the discontented gaullist party. This quarrel grew and came to dominate the politics of the conservative right. Although the conservative right won the 1978 elections, he was unable to pursue a more pro-European policy or more Atlanticist pro-American stance. In fact his indulgence to the USSR contributed to his defeat in 1981, as did the quarrel with the gaullists which consumed energies after 1978. His defeat in 1981 came as a personal blow. He returned to the Assembly in 1984 but was unable to find a role (and expected to return to the presidency), although he remained as a minatory presence on the backbenches.

François Mitterrand (b. 1916 d. 1996)
President 1981–95

There is only one President of the Republic who has completed two terms and that is François Mitterrand. Although his supporters lost the general elections in 1986 and 1988 that must alone stand as a record for the books. All paths to the top are winding, but Mitterrand's is a ziggurat. He was born into a middle-class Catholic family in Jarnac and attended the Sciences Po in Paris to take a law degree. On the outbreak of war he was mobilised, captured (won the Croix de Guerre) and then escaped to the Vichy zone. He worked for prisoners of war for the Vichy regime and was awarded the *Francisque* medal but also joined the Resistance. He emerged from the war with a Resistance record and joined a small centre party. He was elected for the Nièvre in 1946 and in January 1947 became Minister for Veterans. This was the beginning of a Cabinet career which saw him in eleven ministerial posts before the return to power of de Gaulle ended the Fourth Republic.

He opposed de Gaulle's return to power and did not win a seat in the 1958 general elections. His career was almost ended by a scandal in 1959, but by 1962 he was back in the Assembly. He had begun his move to the left which resulted in a bid for the presidency in 1965 against de Gaulle and with Communist backing. His success in forcing de Gaulle into a run-off made him the principal presidential aspirant of the left and gave him an authority which he used to federate the fragmented non-Communist left and forge an alliance with the Communist Party. Although the 'events' and the invasion of Czechoslovakia in 1968 broke this fragile structure, the poor showing of the Socialists in the 1969 presidential elections apparently vindicated his strategy of alliance with the Communists. Mitterrand did not suffer through the left's discredit in 1969 but was able to enter and take over the new Socialist Party a year after its formation. He used the party to conclude a governmental programme with the Communists (the 'Common

Programme') and began to rebuild the moribund Socialist Party. His second presidential campaign in 1974 was even more impressive and again, although he lost, it was the launch for a modern and bigger Socialist Party.

The growth of the Socialist Party was not to the liking of the Communists, who started a quarrel which lost the left the 1978 elections. Mitterrand, despite the Communists and internal party opposition, was able to campaign for the 1981 presidential elections and win. He dissolved the Assembly and the Socialist Party won an absolute majority; despite having no need of the Communist Party there were four Communist ministers in the government. This first government of the septennate introduced a raft of reforms and extended rights and social protection. It did not, however, solve the main problem of unemployment and in the face of a burgeoning trade gap the government dropped its expansionist economic policy. This 'U-turn' was regarded as a set-back and the Socialist Party never really recovered from it or explained it convincingly to its supporters. Nevertheless, although the Socialist Party was defeated in 1986 it was not humiliated.

In 1986 began the Fifth Republic's first experiment with 'cohabitation' between a President of one persuasion and a Prime Minister of another. Mitterrand, by distancing himself from the government's errors, emerged in a winning position very quickly and had no difficulty in securing a second term in 1988, defeating his Prime Minister Jacques Chirac in the run-off. The Assembly was dissolved but the Socialists failed to gain an absolute majority. There then began a more centrist administration under Prime Minister Michel Rocard, who had to contend with Communist hostility. In the second septennate Mitterrand's ambitions were more restrained but the President took a number of initiatives, including French participation in the Gulf War under US command and the signing of the Maastricht Treaty. However, like many other leaders, he did not realise the significance of Gorbachev's leadership of the USSR or the implications of the reforms. But when Rocard was dismissed in 1991, the appointment of Edith Cresson as Prime Minister turned out to be a disaster. The Socialist Party, involved in factionalism and hamstrung by scandals, saw its popularity plummet and Cresson was replaced by Bérégovoy as Prime Minister in 1992. Bérégovoy was soon embroiled in a scandal and the Socialist Party went down to a bad defeat in 1993. A second 'cohabitation' started but this time the President was seriously ill and his opposition to the Prime Minister was fitful and, unlike 1986–88, not sustained or determined. Mitterrand's second septennate ended with the 'normal' passage of power to the elected successor, Jacques Chirac.

Jacques Chirac (b. 1932)
President 1995–

From a provincial family of middle-class origins, Jacques Chirac was educated at the Institut d'études politiques in Paris and then at the ENA. His national service was in the cavalry in Algeria and he might have become a professional officer but elected instead to work in the Court of Accounts from where he moved to the government Secretariat under Pompidou. He was rapidly promoted by the Prime Minister and, having won the constituency of Corrèze from the left in 1967, was made Secretary of State for Employment and was promoted rapidly so that in 1971 he was Budget Minister and in 1974 Minister of the Interior. As Minister of the Interior he organised a revolt of gaullist deputies in the

1974 presidential elections to support Giscard d'Estaing in preference to his own party's candidate (Chaban Delmas) and was rewarded with the Premier's job. He soon disagreed with the new President and resigned in 1976 to found and lead the neo-gaullist RPR party. In 1977 he was elected mayor of Paris and stepped down only when he became President. It was as mayor of Paris that he built up a team of collaborators and gave himself a place on the national and international stage. He was the first 'cohabitation' Prime Minister in 1986–88 and was for most of Mitterrand's septennate the *de facto* leader of the conservative opposition. Jacques Chirac ran for president twice (in 1981 and 1988) before winning in 1995. He called a snap election in 1997 which he lost but he remained popular as a figurehead President with a popular touch and genuine warmth, and by 1999 looked a likely winner in the next presidential elections.

Index